We Are Not Starving

AFRICAN HISTORY AND CULTURE

SERIES EDITOR
Peter Alegi, *Michigan State University*

African History and Culture is a book series that builds upon and expands Michigan State University's commitment to the study of Africa. The series features books in African history, anthropology, sociology, and political science, as well as interdisciplinary studies, works on the African diaspora, and digital scholarship.

INTERNATIONAL EDITORIAL BOARD
Nwando Achebe, *Michigan State University*
Walter Hawthorne, *Michigan State University*
Yusufu Lawi, *University of Dar es Salaam*
Peter Limb, *Michigan State University*
Ghislaine Lydon, *University of California, Los Angeles*
Gregory Mann, *Columbia University*
Enocent Msindo, *Rhodes University*
David Newbury, *Smith College*
David Robinson, *Michigan State University*
Abdi Samatar, *University of Minnesota*
Robert Trent Vinson, *University of Virginia*

We Are Not Starving

The Struggle for Food Sovereignty in Ghana

Joeva Sean Rock

MICHIGAN STATE UNIVERSITY PRESS | *East Lansing*

Copyright © 2022 by Joeva Sean Rock

Michigan State University Press
East Lansing, Michigan 48823-5245

Library of Congress Cataloging-in-Publication Data
Names: Rock, Joeva Sean, author.
Title: We are not starving : the struggle for food sovereignty in Ghana / Joeva Sean Rock.
Other titles: African history and culture.
Description: East Lansing : Michigan State University Press, 2022. |
Series: African history and culture | Includes bibliographical references and index.
Identifiers: LCCN 2021052758 | ISBN 9781611864328 (paperback) | ISBN 9781609177010 (PDF) |
ISBN 9781628954692 (ePub) | ISBN 9781628964639 (Kindle)
Subjects: LCSH: Food sovereignty—Ghana. | Transgenic plants—Ghana.
Classification: LCC HD9017.G4 .R63 2022 | DDC 338.19667—dc23/eng/20211027
LC record available at https://lccn.loc.gov/2021052758

Cover design by Shaun Allshouse
Cover art is Independence Arch, by guppyimages, Adobe Stock

Visit Michigan State University Press at www.msupress.org

Contents

vii List of Abbreviations
ix Acknowledgments
xiii Introduction

1 CHAPTER 1. Agricultural Development and So-Called NGOs
35 CHAPTER 2. From Peasantry to Prosperity
63 CHAPTER 3. Our Stomachs Are Being Colonized
93 CHAPTER 4. The Patents Are Out There
117 CHAPTER 5. (Im)Possibilities

147 Epilogue
153 Notes
159 Bibliography
179 Index

List of Abbreviations

AATF	African Agricultural Technology Foundation
ABNE	African Biosafety Network of Expertise
ABSP	Agricultural Biotechnology Support Program
AfDB	African Development Bank
AFSA	Alliance for Food Sovereignty in Africa
AGRA	Alliance for a Green Revolution in Africa
BMGF	Bill & Melinda Gates Foundation
BNARI	Biotechnology and Nuclear Agriculture Research Institute
Bt	*Bacillus thuringiensis*
CAS	Cornell Alliance for Science
CGIAR	Consultative Group on International Agricultural Research
CIAT	International Center for Tropical Agriculture
CIKOD	Centre for Indigenous Knowledge and Organizational Development
CSIR	Council for Scientific and Industrial Research (Ghana)
DFID	Department for International Development (United Kingdom)
ECOWAS	The Economic Community of West African States
FBO	Farmer-based organization
FSG	Food Sovereignty Ghana
GAAS	Ghana Academy of Arts and Sciences
GAFP	Ghana Association of Food Producers

GAWU	General Agricultural Workers' Union of Ghana
GM	Genetically modified
GMO	Genetically modified organism
GNAFF	Ghana National Association of Farmers and Fishermen
IFPRI	International Food Policy Research Institute
IMF	International Monetary Fund
IPR	Intellectual property right
ISAAA	International Service for the Acquisition of Agri-biotech Applications
LVC	La Via Campesina
MESTI	Ministry of Environment, Science, Technology and Innovation
MOFA	Ministry of Food and Agriculture
MP	Member of Parliament
NDC	National Democratic Congress
NERICA	New Rice for Africa
NEWEST	Nitrogen efficient, water efficient, salt tolerant (rice)
NGO	Non-governmental organization
NPP	New Patriotic Party
NUE	Nitrogen use efficient (rice)
OFAB	Open Forum on Agricultural Biotechnology in Africa
OPV	Open-pollinated variety
PBB	Plant Breeders Bill
PBS	Program for Biosafety Systems
PFAG	Peasant Farmers Association of Ghana
PI	Principal investigator
PPP	Public-private partnership
ROPPA	Réseau des Organisations Paysannes et de Producteurs de l'Afrique de l'Ouest (Network of Peasants and Farmers in West Africa)
SG 2000	Sasakawa Global 2000
UPOV	International Union for the Protection of New Varieties of Plants
USAID	US Agency for International Development
USDA	US Department of Agriculture
WACCI	West Africa Centre for Crop Improvement

Acknowledgments

This book exists thanks to those whose who opened their homes, offices, and workshops to me. The Food Sovereignty Platform—and especially the Ghana Association of Food Producers—allowed me to join meetings, ask a lot of questions, and hang around. Without their hospitality, none of this would have been possible. I am forever grateful. Thank you to the farmers of Bono East, Upper East, and the Northern Region who took time out of their busy schedules to share talk about food and farming. I especially want to thank Matthias, who shared his experiences unabashedly with Francis and me and made us feel welcome far away from home. Additionally, I owe thanks to officers at the National Biosafety Authority, who graciously invited me to workshops which allowed me to develop greater insight into biosafety and regulatory processes.

Traveling to and from Ghana for over a decade has resulted in incredible friendships, and I am grateful for friends who have shared meals, challenged my interpretations, and welcomed me into their lives along the way. First, Francis Adi Sabara, a friend through and through since we met at Legon in 2008, and the best research assistant anyone could ask for. Gidi, Gladys, Eli, Loveth, Janet, Victoria, Joseph, Lucky, George, and Hannah welcomed me into their family and home, for which I feel immensely lucky. Thanks also to Nii Ayertey-Aryeh, Aunty Tina, Simon Tsike-Sossah, Yvette Tetteh, and Kobina Amoako-Attah Hudson.

My research was made possible by the American University Graduate Studies Office, the Explorers Club of Washington Group, the Fulbright-Hays Program, New York University, and the Wenner-Gren Foundation.

This project was conceived first at American University, where William Leap, Adrienne Pine, Dolores Koenig, Brett Williams, David Vine, and Sue Taylor were steadfast guides into the world of anthropological thinking and inquiry. My time in DC was made exponentially better by my brilliant colleagues Jeanne Hanna, Laura Gilchrest, Beth Geglia, Matthew Thomann, Siobhán McGuirk, Justin Uehlein, and Nikki Lane.

A postdoctoral fellowship at the Department of Nutrition and Food Studies at New York University provided me with the extraordinary gift of a year to reflect and write. Special thanks to Marion Nestle, Fabio Parasecoli, Jennifer Shutek, and Krishnendu Ray who helped make this time memorable.

Other institutions and individuals have been instrumental in this book's development along the way. At Berkeley, Khalid Kadir, Clare Talwalker, Alice Agogino, Chetan Chowdhry, and James Church made Zoom rooms feel like community. Many thanks to Matthew Schnurr for inviting me to join the GEAP3 team for a year of research and colleagueship. At Dalhousie, I also have to thank Alanna Taylor for answering my endless questions about all things Canadian!

I feel very lucky to be able to collaborate with folks who are not only incredible scholars, but are also just really kind people. Thanks to Rachel Schurman, for offering to write together and for allowing our work to line these pages. Many thanks as well to Brian Dowd-Uribe, who is both a fantastic neighbor (Oakland!) and a fantastic research collaborator. Moreover, over the years, I've been immensely fortunate to float ideas around, and engage in long conversations with Amanda Logan, Hanson Nyantakyi-Frimpong, Siera Vercillo, and Alex Park.

Writing can be quite a lonesome endeavor, and throughout it all I was buoyed by some amazing friends who made sure I came up for air every now and again. I owe Rachel and Koji Kizuka, Abbie Engelstad, Kaye Cain-Nielsen, Matthew Hesse, Jake Blanc, Cody Griffin, Jonathan Dillon, and Sarah Brierly a great debt of gratitude for continually asking about the book and always staying patient when they received the same answer year after year ("It's ... fine.").

The book itself benefited greatly from the reading, insight, and expertise of many colleagues; thanks to Youjin Chung, Jessie Luna, William Leap, and Brooke

Pearson for your gracious time and feedback. Participating in the Anthropology and Environment Society's 2019 Junior Scholar Workshop was immensely helpful; thank you, Mascha Gugganig and Liron Shani, for helping reorient my discussion of Kofi the Good Farmer. Many thanks also to Cristina Villegas, who designed the map, and to Eric Kesse who assisted with manuscript editing. At Michigan State University (MSU) Press, Catherine Cocks believed in this project very early on. Many thanks to her and Peter Alegi for being the best editors I could hope for; to the two anonymous peer reviewers for their thoughtful feedback and direction; and to the entire MSU Press production team for turning this manuscript into a reality. Any errors are of course mine and mine alone.

My family—Eden, Pat, Terri, and Richelle Rock—have supported this journey from day one, and for that I am most grateful. Last, but certainly not least, there aren't enough words in the world to thank Brooke and Theon Pearson for their unwavering love and grace throughout these past years. Thank you for the endless hype, the patient ear, and the many hikes.

Portions of chapters 2, 3, 5, and 6 are adapted from my previously published work:

> Joeva Rock, "'We Are Not Starving': Challenging Genetically Modified Seeds and Development in Ghana," *Culture, Agriculture, Food and Environment* 41(1): 15–23.

> Joeva Rock and Rachel Schurman, "The Complex Choreography of Agricultural Biotechnology in Africa," *African Affairs* 119(477): 499–525.

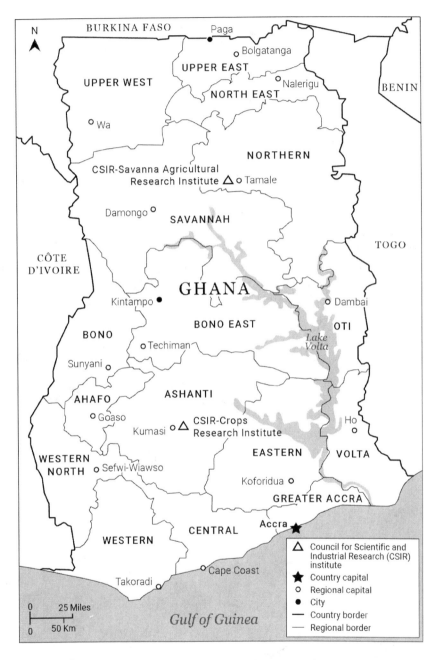

Ghana's administrative regions, showing towns and research institutes referenced in the book.
CREDIT: CRISTINA VILLEGAS

Introduction

People in America, who have no idea of how Africa is, think that, 'Eh! So this Africa is [a] jungle.' You know, that kind of thing. And these people are not helping by depicting Africa [as] starving with disease, you know? Disease, starving, we are so poor... and they have the solution!" Constance was on a roll. As the head of the Ghana Association of Food Producers (GAFP), one of the Ghana's largest networks of smallholder farmers, Constance could not risk mincing her words; there was too much on the line.

Sitting at GAFP's headquarters in Accra, Constance and I had been discussing genetically modified (GM) crops, several of which were being tested across Ghana's public research institutions. Supported by global donors and industry, proponents had high hopes that GM crops, once commercialized, would help Ghanaian farmers produce more. Constance, and the farmers she represented, weren't so sure. "*No, what do we know? We don't have any solutions for our problems,*" she continued, sarcastically. "Why do they think that we cannot find solutions? *If* they left us alone, maybe we would have found solutions to our answers. *If* they wanted to work with us on equal fields, we would have found solutions. But to exploit us, make money out of us, after all the money you took away!"

For years, Constance, GAFP, and allied groups had mounted a strong opposition to GM crops, a technology they had not asked for, nor one they thought was appropriate for the challenges Ghanaian farmers faced. They were suspect, too, of the narrative proponents used to frame the technology: as a humanitarian gift for a burdened continent. Such narratives circulated both locally and globally. "The peculiarities of Africa, and therefore Ghana," Dr. Ahmed Alhassan Yakubu, a former deputy minister of food and agriculture, told reporters, "should let us have a re-think about the negative dirt that we throw at biotechnology as a science. It is extremely important we do so" (Gakpo 2017c).

To pronounce something as peculiar is to denote exception and, at times, urgency. Agriculture in Africa ("and therefore Ghana," as Yakubu suggested) is certainly considered as such, described by observers as under- and even non-productive, and lagging behind the rest of the world. To counter this, international development agencies, private foundations, and major corporations have tasked themselves with sparking a "new" Green Revolution for Africa. The project is underscored by major investment to transform African foodways, markets, and farms so that African farmers purchase high-yielding seeds and chemical inputs, and in turn, ideally increase yields and "feed the future." Of the various interventions being prescribed, perhaps none are as controversial as GM crops, a technology that is fiercely opposed in some circles and widely endorsed in others. These crops, advocates argue, are necessary to tackle challenges on a so-called peculiar continent. "The Europeans have decided they don't want to use it . . . which is fine, they're not facing malnutrition and starvation," said Bill Gates, whose foundation has placed significant backing into the research and design of GM crops for Africa. "[But] the Africans, I think, will choose to let their people have enough to eat" (Wall Street Journal 2016).

Over a decade ago, a global consortium of donors and industry came together to develop GM crops for African farmers. Early on, consortium officials identified Ghana as a potential partner. With a strong public research institution and a population heavily employed in smallholder agriculture, Ghana seemed to be the perfect location to conduct field trials of GM rice and cowpea.[1] But unlike conventionally bred seeds, GM crops are governed globally and cannot simply be imported into a country or placed on the market without special oversight. The Cartagena Protocol on Biosafety decrees that signatories, of which Ghana is one, must establish regulations regarding genetically modified organisms (GMOs) and regulatory bodies to enforce said regulations.[2] And so, in order to participate in the donor-driven GM crop projects, Ghana had to set up complex infrastructure to support the technology, including the development of new laws, regulatory policies, and a regulatory agency. In other words, before GM seeds were commercialized, before farmers could access them, the state had to transform.

This book focuses on this transformation, the controversy it garnered, and those who sought to shape it. In the chapters that follow, I focus on the actors—Ghanaian and otherwise—who were a part of early planning and continue to drive the push for GM commercialization. I posit these narratives against discourse and activism of the Food Sovereignty Platform, a nation-wide social movement that Constance and GAFP belong to that seeks to halt GM commercialization. Lastly, I consider smallholder farmers, whose lives and livelihoods are debated daily in boardrooms across Accra, Seattle, and Washington, DC.

In Ghana, as Constance alluded to, GMOs have become a vehicle to explore larger contentions—of sovereignty, of "development," of food and agriculture, of a nascent country. Thus, in the chapters that follow, GM crops are not the singular object of inquiry; there are no agronomic surveys or detailed tables of farmer yields in this book. Rather, this book explores how at the core of contests over GMOs in Ghana is something much deeper. GMOs have become an avenue to air grievances centuries in the making; the systematic de-valuing and exploitation of African land, labor, and knowledge. As such, the book is an ethnography of how global powers, local resistance, and capital flows are shaping contemporary African foodways.

The manuscript contributes to a small but growing literature on the daily contours of "new" Green Revolution efforts on the African continent (Boafo and Lyons 2021; Moseley et al. 2016; Schnurr 2019; Shilomboleni 2018). Central to my inquiry are global financial flows, tensions of the nation-state as they relate to governance and sovereignty, and the agency of African actors—government officials, farmers, activists, and development practitioners—who work on and against global forces to shape development outcomes. Urgency, which so often underscores discourses on food and agriculture in development spaces, is not central to my discussion. By approaching GMOs neither as an urgently needed nor as an exceptional intervention, I discovered a particular tension across actors in Ghana, that of recipient fatigue, a collective feeling of distress and disappointment after decades of donor-driven development plans. It is because of this collective failure of development that Ghanaian scientists and bureaucrats take an explicitly *political* stance on supposedly "anti-political" science, and that farmers and activists, and sometimes even scientists, challenge the development industry backing GMOs. This is a story about Ghanaians exerting agency, refusing to be written by history as passive or dominated, and seeking food sovereignty as an integral aspect of political freedom.

GMOs, Food Sovereignty, and Science in Ghana

On May 12, 2017, breaking news hit Ghana: research trials of Bt cotton, a cotton genetically modified for pest resistance, had been suspended indefinitely. The news was abrupt: there had been no prior indications that the project was in trouble, at least not any that were made public. But as the story unfolded, a complicated picture began to appear. Though the project's suspension was first reported in 2017, work on Bt cotton had actually stopped an entire year prior. The reason? The project's sponsor, US agribusiness company Monsanto, had decided to terminate their role in the project, leaving the state scientific council hosting the research trials without funds to move forward.[3]

That evening, Joy News, one of the nation's largest media outlets, hosted a four-person panel to discuss what Monsanto's exit meant for the country's cotton sector. The host of the show, Gifty Andoh Appiah, sat in front of a photo of a field of cotton and introduced viewers to her guests: Edwin Kweku Andoh Baffour, communications director for Food Sovereignty Ghana; Joseph Opoku Gakpo, a reporter at Joy News who had recently returned from a two-month communications fellowship at Cornell University; and Patrick Apullah, the vice chairman of the (Ghana) Cotton Farmers Association, who joined by phone.

A few minutes into the program, the host addressed Apullah, the sole farmer among the group: "You are calling for government to step in now that Monsanto has withdrawn their funds. But what is the basis upon which you are calling for government to step in?"

In his reply, Apullah cited Burkina Faso, Ghana's northern neighbor, a large cotton exporter and a former producer of Bt cotton. Apullah stated that both Burkinabè farmers and government had reaped hefty profits thanks to Bt cotton, and that he hoped Ghanaian farmers could equally benefit. But there was just one problem: "Okay, so you just mentioned Burkina Faso," Appiah cut in, "and Burkina Faso is the very reason why Monsanto has withdrawn the funding, and not just to Burkina Faso, but to Ghana as well. Are you aware of that fact?"

"No, I am not aware of that because GMO cotton is still produced in Burkina Faso—"

"Burkina Faso farmers are no longer using GMO," Appiah interrupted.

"It's not true!" Apullah retorted, "last year I led . . . Ghanaian farmers to Bobo-Dioulasso, and we inspected GMO cotton farms."[4]

The camera remained on Appiah, who grew increasingly annoyed: "Hold on, sir. You said you are not aware of the developments on that case in Burkina Faso. Is that correct?"

"Yes. I'm not aware of that."

"Are you also aware that some of the [Burkinabè] farmers are taking the company to court and that they are seeking compensation because the quality of the cotton that they harvested was not the same as the conventional seed? Are you aware of that as well?"

"I'm not aware of that."

Exasperated, Appiah turned to her other guests to continue the discussion.

Burkina Faso's cotton industry is largely orchestrated by cotton companies who supply contracted farmers with seed and chemical inputs, a top-down model that ensures company needs drive cotton operations (Dowd-Uribe 2016: 5). In the early 2000s, Burkinabè cotton companies partnered with Monsanto to determine if genetic modification—in this case, introgressing the *Bacillus thuringiensis* (Bt) gene into cotton—could help control bollworm infestation. After five years of research, Burkinabè cotton companies distributed Bt cotton to farmers in 2008 (Dowd-Uribe 2016: 2).

In the initial years of production, output increased, and producers were happy (Dowd-Uribe and Schnurr 2016: 164–65). However, excitement began to fade in 2015. That year, officials announced that cotton lint from Bt varieties was smaller and of inferior quality compared to previously grown conventional varieties (Dowd-Uribe 2016: 2). It turned out the issues were not recent: lint irregularities had been identified as early as 2006, long before Bt cotton had even reached Burkinabè farms (Luna and Dowd-Uribe 2020). While Monsanto and Burkinabè researchers attempted to determine the cause of the problem and find a solution, Burkinabè cotton companies were losing millions on the global market. Impatient with profit loss, Burkinabè industry heads decided to stop using Bt cotton and return to conventional varieties. They sued Monsanto for damages and the parties settled in

March 2017 (Bavier 2017). Soon thereafter, Ghanaian media announced Monsanto's exit from Ghana. But Ghana too had troubles that went undisclosed; interviews I conducted with Ghanaian officials revealed that Monsanto had abruptly left the project an entire year before the project's closure was made public.

Before Monsanto and Burkina Faso's relationship disintegrated, Ghanaian and Monsanto officials had hoped that Ghana could replicate Burkina Faso's success with Bt cotton. With full knowledge of the issues unfolding in Burkina Faso, Monsanto decided to import the same variety used in Burkina Faso—Monsanto's Bollgard II (MON15985)—to Ghana. In their research application submitted to state regulators in 2013, Ghanaian officials cited Burkina Faso as evidence that Monsanto's Bt cotton was safe and productive, writing, "in 2011, MON15985 and stacks[5] were grown on more than 11 million hectares, including in Burkina Faso and *no adverse effects have been reported*" ("Application for Confined Field Trial"; emphasis added). If Ghanaian officials knew of the issues their Burkinabè colleagues were having with lint quality, they did not disclose it in their application.

Ghanaian regulators who reviewed the application raised red flags around apparent "inadequate preparation to handle" an accidental environmental release of Bt cotton or the herbicide used to treat it, but approved the application all the same. Additionally, Ghana's regulatory officials made another concession: they allowed Ghanaian scientists—and their Monsanto counterparts—to forgo the standard first step of this sort of research process: confined field trials (CFT; Schnurr 2019: 95–96). Instead, officials "accept[ed] data from CFTs conducted previously in Burkina Faso . . . [and] decided to grant an exemption for local CFTs and move to [multilocational field trials] right away" (Komen et al. 2020: 5). And so, in 2013, multilocational field trials of Bt cotton began. From there, the Burkinabè and Ghanaian projects regularly overlapped; Bt cotton from Ghanaian field trials were sent to Burkina Faso for testing. Monsanto's Burkinabè office handled any business in Ghana and offered resources and support for "show-and-tell" events, much like the trip to Bobo-Dioulasso Mr. Apullah mentioned (Sam 2015).

However, Burkina Faso and Ghana could not be more unalike in their cotton production. Cotton from Burkina Faso is renowned for its high-quality lint, and the country's cotton industry is regimented and "vertically integrated" (Dowd-Uribe and Schnurr 2016: 163); Ghana's is not. In fact, some say there is *no* cotton industry. And so, when their Burkina business folded, Monsanto decided to withdraw financial and technical support from the Ghanaian project (Gakpo 2017b). Jesus Madrazo, then vice president of commercial and global supply chain at Monsanto, was quoted in Ghanaian media as saying, "in Ghana, or in any other African country, if we see respect for intellectual property[,] a functional regulatory system, respect for private contracts, and ability for us to bring value and be rewarded for the value we create, if we have those four principles, we will always be there to participate" (Ibrahim 2018). Madrazo's reference to "respect for intellectual property" was a nod to the Plant Breeders Bill (PBB), an intellectual property rights law that has been under consideration by Ghanaian Parliament—and fiercely contested by activists—since 2013. The beleaguered bill is an essential aspect of the Ghanaian GMO story and will be discussed thoroughly throughout the book.

With Monsanto out of the picture, Dr. Emmanuel Chamba, the principal investigator (PI) on the Ghanaian Bt cotton project, said his team was looking for "money from any other place to finish the [trial]" (Gakpo 2017b). Back in the Joy News studio, Apullah told Appiah that he had appealed to his regional minister for government funds to continue the trials. Unfortunately for Ghanaian Bt cotton proponents, missing from the statements from Dr. Chamba, Apullah, and the other guests were details about the agreement between Monsanto and the state research council overseeing the project, the Council for Scientific and Industrial Research (CSIR). Though CSIR's name lined bureaucratic paperwork, Monsanto owned the product and was funding the field trials, testing, and oversight. Thus, when Monsanto pulled out, the whole project folded. In other words, it would not be possible for the project to continue if new funds were somehow generated; Monsanto would need to release their proprietary technology to CSIR, an unlikely scenario. "I don't think they will come to us again," a defeated-sounding scientist close to the project told me in reference to Monsanto.

Ghana has been embroiled in public contestation over GM crops since 2013. These crops—cotton, cowpea, sweet potato, and rice—have been lauded as "a science" ripe for countering the supposed "peculiarities of Africa, and therefore Ghana" (Gakpo 2017c), and essential to the country's national trajectory. "Biotechnology is so important," Kwabena Frimpong-Boateng, Ghana's minister of environment, science, technology and innovation, said at a public event in 2017, "and we can't develop without it" (Gakpo 2017a).

Efforts to introduce GM crops to Ghana are part and parcel of the "new" Green Revolution for Africa, which is premised on techno-scientific interventions to increase productivity throughout the continent, with the goal to "not only feed itself but . . . contribute to feeding the world" (Bacchi 2017; Juma 2011). Funding and technical impetus for GM projects stem from the United States, but American and African officials alike package these projects as "homegrown" initiatives. They are housed in African research institutions; African researchers serve as PIs on the projects; development partners establish in-country organizations (which I will refer to as "brokers" and "boosters") to lobby for biosafety and plant patent laws, and fund farmers to travel to other African countries and the United States on "show-and-tell" visits in hopes that they return home and lobby their governments to support GM crops.

The corporate partners of the projects—those that lease patented genetic material for modification—are rarely mentioned, except to applaud their efforts to make technology available to African farmers. The planners and promoters of these projects—the Bill & Melinda Gates Foundation (BMGF), the US Agency for International Development (USAID), the Rockefeller Foundation, African governments, and state research councils—rarely make mention the unequal balance of these so-called public-private partnerships (PPPs). They do not mention that the base of the entire project, patented genetic material, is owned and temporarily leased by multinational agribusiness "partners"; they do not mention that if the corporate partner or funder exits, the project may very well collapse.

Back in the Joy News studio, the host asked Edwin Baffour, an activist and member of a national food sovereignty movement, for his final word: "I think it's very interesting that we have been saying that this GMO agenda has been a foreign initiative, and now Monsanto pulls out of funding, we see that we have issues with going forward. It is not a Ghanaian initiative. Ghanaians have not even been included in the debate."

A "New" Green Revolution?

In 2004, former UN secretary general Kofi Annan called for a "uniquely African Green Revolution," arguing that the first Green Revolution of Asia and Latin America had missed the African continent (Annan 2004). Annan's call resonated within international development circles (and in his homeland, Ghana), where the first Green Revolution is often perceived as an apolitical triumph of the use of improved inputs and technology to increase agricultural production. In particular, two of the largest private foundations in the United States—the Rockefeller Foundation and the BMGF—heeded this call. In 2007 they launched the Alliance for a Green Revolution in Africa (AGRA), signaling to donor organizations, government agencies, and African governments that a new style of funding was underway.[6]

What was the first Green Revolution that Annan spoke of, and (how) did it miss the African continent? And further, what global events were occurring at the turn of the twenty-first century that converged to create a consensus around the need for a "new" Green Revolution, and how did biotechnology become part of it? In this section, I detail the African Green Revolution's predecessor—now dubbed the "first" Green Revolution—and the long political-economic arc, or what Raj Patel (2013) refers to as the "longue durée," that led to the creation of the "new" Green Revolution.

In the mid-twentieth century, the world was profoundly changed after back-to-back world wars. Citizens of colonized countries, many of whom fought for the Allied powers and supported war efforts in various ways, demanded independence from colonial occupiers. A weakened Europe—both from the wars and from growing unrest in the colonies—left room for the United States to emerge as a new global superpower. In light of their new position, American lawmakers, policy analysts, and private foundations saw it as their duty to maintain a particular world order, and worried about newly independent nations across continental Asia and Africa. Organizations such as the Rockefeller Foundation, influenced by Malthusian thinking, were concerned that growing populations in the Global South would place an undue strain on resources, resulting in unrest and, the ultimate fear of the time, "communist insurrection" (Perkins 1997: 119). Academics in international relations held similar concerns, and contemplated in conferences and journals whether newly independent countries posed a significant threat to the "white world order" (Vitalis 2015).

These fears were central to the development of the (first) Green Revolution, whose architects, including its "father," Norman Borlaug, believed that "the achievement of higher yields ... [was] a way to buy time while other efforts sought a reduction in the population growth rate" (Perkins 1997: 224; Eddens 2019). Furthermore, US officials considered food aid as an essential component in winning global allies in their fight against the Soviet Union (Patel 2013: 14). Thus, "American plant-breeding science ... became part of the cold war's defense of capitalist political economies," and the Green Revolution served as both a "biopolitical [and] geopolitical process" (Perkins 1997: 139; Patel 2013: 4).

Efforts were originally concentrated around the development and distribution of high-yielding wheat, rice, and maize across Mexico and India. These new varieties required "highly resource-intensive method[s] of production," including irrigation and timed application of corresponding non-organic fertilizers and agro-chemicals (Gupta 1998: 14; González 2001: 102). Encouraged by yield outputs—in India, large-scale adoption of high-yielding wheat varieties "resulted in a fourfold increase in ... wheat output" (Gupta 1998: 2)—international agricultural consortia distributed Green Revolution technologies to other parts of Latin America and Asia. Overall, Gordon R. Conway and Edward B. Barbier write, Green Revolution technologies helped spur an increase in "food production in developing countries ... by 7%" and "27% in Asia" (1990: 20).

But with increased production came environmental and social setbacks; commercial farmers generally benefited more than smaller farmers, and intensive mono-cropping resulted in decreased biodiversity and "increase[ed] incidence of pest, disease and weed problems" (Conway and Barbier 1990: 11, 21–22; González 2001: 125). And then there were experiences unable to be captured in strict quantitative statistics, stories that are often under-shared in development narratives. In northern India, for instance, Akhil Gupta found that farmers preferred using manure as a fertilizer, citing that it resulted in tastier food and healthier soils, but that their Green Revolution high-yielding wheat variety required chemical fertilizer to grow (1998: 2).

Despite stories like this and other narratives of uneven development, environmental destruction, and biodiversity loss, the legacy of the Green Revolution has become almost mythicized (Patel 2013: 24). Decades later, at the dawn of a new century, world development agencies and private foundations again found themselves discussing agricultural transformation. In 2007, the prices of basic foodstuffs—like wheat, rice, and maize—skyrocketed. This sudden price surge—what would become known as the Food Price Crisis and would last into 2008—was devastating; the number of hungry rose from 830 million in 2007 to 1 billion by 2011 (McMichael and Schneider 2011: 134).

The Food Price Crisis revealed a number of weaknesses in the global food system. Importantly, it showed what to many was already obvious; that a legacy of structural adjustment reforms throughout the Global South, enacted by the International Monetary Fund (IMF) and World Bank, had negatively transformed agricultural markets. Under structural adjustment, nations were driven to turn their focus toward exportable cash-crops at the expense of growing basic foodstuffs, like rice. This meant that when the price of staples such as rice and maize suddenly spiked as they did in 2007, many countries did not have domestic reserves to fall back on, leaving the world's poorest in a lurch. Unable to feed their households, from Egypt to Indonesia people took to the streets to protest the inequitable price of food.

The uprisings that followed the Food Price Crisis were worrying for global leaders, for whom popular dissent is always a threat to their grasp on power. Similar to the racialized anxieties that underwrote the first Green Revolution, the Food Price Crisis built upon existing fears of a "youth bulge," the idea that an increasingly young population in the Global South was ripe for political and religious extremism (Urdal 2006). This narrative only intensified as an increasing number of African migrants traveled through the Sahara Desert to seek refuge and opportunity in Europe. While accepting the 2017 World Food Prize, Dr. Akinwumi Adesina, president of the African Development Bank, told reporters that he was determined to "make agriculture cool for young people" in part to ensure that "the future of African youth [does not lie] at the bottom of the Mediterranean Sea," a reference to the thousands of migrants who drowned making the perilous journey to Europe (Bacchi 2017). Food again was seen as a way to pacify a supposedly restless Global South.

Though many understood the Food Price Crisis to be borne out of globalized, industrial agriculture, others saw it as an opportunity to further integrate farmers into global markets and value chains (McMichael and Schneider 2011). Global financiers had already shifted focus—and capital—toward the African continent, mainly through the form of private equity. Slowly, development practitioners caught on and began writing about Africa as the "final frontier" for capital. Soon, there was growing consensus, noted in government reports, leaked cables, and articles in the *Economist*, that what the African continent needed was not necessarily strong infrastructure and capable states, but rather liberalized, business-friendly markets. The "new" Green Revolution was born.

Greening the "Dark Continent"

"The year was 2006. The place was ripe with possibilities," an excited voice narrates as a camera flies over green fields, lush rivers, and little sign of human life. "That place was Africa, a land waiting for transformation that could bring astonishing change" (AGRA 2017a). This quote comes from a video produced by AGRA, the organization initiated by donors to actualize Kofi Annan's call for a "uniquely African Green Revolution." Videos like this set the tone for the African Green Revolution: supposedly vast, untouched lands "waiting for transformation." No farmers, no labor: just passive re-rendering of environment. "It is not rocket science," said Joe DeVries, vice president for program development and innovation at AGRA, describing AGRA's goal to render eleven countries food secure in ten years, "you grow a new variety of grain, put it in a bag, and sell it" (Gebre 2016).

Soon after AGRA was established in 2007, other initiatives that sought to link African farmers with private investors popped onto the scene: Feed the Future, President Barack Obama's flagship food security program, was launched in 2010, and the New Alliance for Food Security and Nutrition was formed by the G8 in 2012. Combined, the formation of these initiatives signaled to the international community—as well as private investors and industry—that food and agriculture were on the table, and that Africa was indeed "ripe with possibilities" for investment (AGRA 2017a).

As donors came together to construct and finance a "new" Green Revolution, proponents drew on long-standing constructions of the African continent and its peoples as remote and on the fringes of global culture, finance, and modernity. Speaking on the supposed necessity of an African Green Revolution, Dr. Adesina described the continent as apart from the world: "After languishing for decades on the fringes of the global markets, Africa is now being increasingly integrated into the globalization process" (Adesina 2014).

Smallholder farmers make up about 60 percent of the total population of the African continent. And globally, the Food and Agricultural Organization (FAO) of the United Nations estimates that small-scale farmers produce around 70 percent of the world's food supply (Wolfenson 2013). Despite this, dominant discourse surrounding the "new" Green Revolution for Africa suggests smallholder producers are on the margins (fringes) of production. Jack Halberstam argues that the "fringe" is a powerful discursive rendering, used by those interested in maintaining the status quo to designate so-called fringe actors as out of time and place, and thus, threatening (2005: 10). Therefore, by positing African farmers as on the margins of global capitalism, hegemonic actors—in this case, those who control development agendas and funds and partner with private industry to expand their market reach—are able to justify large-scale interventions by which African farming, and with it, the African farmer, is pulled into productivity. One discursive strategy used was by proponents is to call on the narrative of the "Dark Continent."

"Africa is no longer in the dark," David Ameyaw, an AGRA official, told a reporter in 2016. "It has done a lot towards agricultural transformation in the past decade" (Esipisu 2016). In another example, a video uploaded to YouTube by ISSAfricaTV (2012) titled "An African Green Revolution" begins with a darkened outline of the African continent. "Here's Africa," says the narrator, "[and] here's land." The outline begins to lighten to a gradient brown. Over the next two minutes, as the narrator describes the idea of the African Green Revolution, the continental outline shifts in color from black to brown, and finally, to green. Finally, the narrator compares two futures: one that follows the Green Revolution paradigm, and one that does not. To compare, two continental outlines are posed next to each other. The image depicting the African Green Revolution quickly greens and stacks of cash grow on top of it. The continental outline of the non-Green Revolution remains brown with only a small stack of bills.

In videos like this—as well as reports, interviews, and marketing materials—proponents highlighted financial models that posited African markets to be the "last great frontier" for capital, the agricultural sector alone thought to be worth between 1 trillion to 2.3 trillion dollars (AGRA News 2015; Polman and Verghese 2016; World Bank 2013). Articles in the *Economist* described this final frontier as a "scramble" (2015b) and encouraged its readers to hurry up and "[climb] aboard the African train" (2015a). Invoking the term "scramble" to refer to frontier lands is reminiscent of the 1884 Berlin Conference—which catalyzed the "scramble for Africa"—in which European imperialists partitioned Africa for their own taking. Similarly, a C-level executive of a South African agricultural investment firm told *Bloomberg* that "there are 54 countries in Africa, so you are spoiled for choice" (Cohen and Ombok 2016).

It was not only financial magazines and professionals who wrote about African agriculture as a frontier for the taking. In multiple publications Dr. Agnes Kalibata, president of AGRA, urged investors to "come for the food security, but stay for the economic opportunity" (2017). In another instance, she wrote, "The vast potential of Africa's agriculture remains largely untapped... The reality is that agriculture in Africa today represents both an incredible development and a lucrative business opportunity ... [It] is both an economic and moral imperative, to include millions more of Africa's smallholder farmers in agriculture's lucrative markets" (AGRA News 2015: 4, 5).

Discourse used by supporters of the "new" Green Revolution was framed by both possibility and urgency: that of the "moral imperative" to feed a continent, and an economic urgency to be among the first to access "agriculture's lucrative markets." Thus, a particular discourse emerged from those eager to build an African Green Revolution: one which regarded the African continent as the "final frontier" for capital expansion, a project grounded in racialized discourses of greening a so-called "Dark Continent." Importantly, describing the African continent as one "waiting for transformation" not only obscured those who already live, work, and labor on the land, but also obfuscated past efforts to enact widescale agricultural change.

Development Discourses

Why do I focus so much on discourse? Discourse refers to the ideas, understandings, and supposed truths that circulate across photos, texts, and videos and is an essential aspect of international development. Discourses can travel with institutions, actors, and materials, and can be embodied and challenged (Escobar 1995; Pierre 2012). As critical discourse scholars like Norman Fairclough (2012) argue, discourse is laden with ideology. Hegemonic discourses, such as those emanating from the state and its development partners, often contain markers of the "right" and "wrong" way to do things, as well as ideas about certain people, ideas, and places. Thus, interrogating discourse helps us understand how development projects are framed and understood, and the different ways in which people interact with them.

In dominant discourse—whether emanating from colonial rule or development agendas—outside observers have long described Africans as poor stewards of the land, and African foodways as "scarce" (Logan 2020).[7] Anthropologist Christine Walley writes that during the colonial era, European administrators in Tanzania assumed "Africans lacked or possessed faulty knowledge" and thus could not comprehend science (2002: 277). In South Africa, in an effort to maintain romanticized naturescapes and "conserve" desired wildlife, white South Africans created game reserves, enclosing land and criminalizing hunting (by declaring the hunt of certain species "poaching"), which black Africans relied upon (Carruthers 1989). In Guinea, "early colonial administrations first became concerned with the perceived destructiveness of African environmental management" because it threatened their capital gain (Fairhead and Leach 2005: 285). Across these cases, the management of wildlife, land, and communities were racialized projects.

Important here is the concept of *racialization*: "the construction, constitution, and maintenance of racial categories and meanings" and "the various processes—historical, economic, political and cultural—that have worked to create and structure [such] racial meanings" (Pierre 2012: 4). Critical scholars have long called for investigations into the ways that development aid is racialized (Benton 2015; Kothari 2006; Pierre 2020; Wilson 2012), how racialized development schemes reflect US structural racism (Harrison 2002), and how such aid and discourse circulate and are reproduced and embodied throughout the African continent (Daley 2013; Fanon [1952]; Pierre 2012; Thomas and Clarke 2013). For instance, Kalpana Wilson argues that the commonly held binary of "developed" and "un/der developed" is a legacy of colonial rule, and an inherently racial one (2012: 4, 46). Similarly, Pierre contends that "the terminology of development thrives on the construction of a notion of fundamental African racial difference (and white Western normativity) while rendering the unequal institutional and material relations . . . through terms that sediment cultural narratives of this presumed African inferiority" (2020: 87). An example of this might be one I considered earlier, that of describing African farmers as "languishing . . . on the fringe of global markets" (Adesina 2014) rather than describing the global historical, economic, and political phenomena that have marginalized African markets and producers.

Another example can be found in *Starved for Science: How Biotechnology Is Being Kept Out of Africa*, a book by political scientist Robert Paarlberg with forewords from Norman Borlaug and Jimmy Carter. In it, Paarlberg describes African farming as exceptional in the world: "Even compared to other developing regions, African farming stands out as *dramatically nonproductive*" (2008: 83; emphasis added). To explain this supposed nonproductivity, Paarlberg draws explicit links between agricultural modernity (the opposite, he argues, of nonproductivity) and whiteness: "When the states of Africa gained formal independence in the 1960s, the expatriate European community departed and took much of Africa's modern farming knowledge with them" (2008: 87).

It is troubling to suggest that Europeans possessed and also "took" African farming knowledge, and that, as a result, African farmers are so unproductive they are "nonproductive." Such a claim erases the fact that African smallholders feed the continent and that agricultural knowledge, practice, and experimentation existed long before European contact (as if this even needs to be said!).[8] Analyzing these troubling claims shows how, as Pierre argues, development discourses obscure "unequal institutions" and instead present material inequities as naturalized and normal (Pierre 2020: 87). But Paarlberg is not alone in this.

As described earlier, the frames of "modern" and "traditional" have long been used stand-ins for "European" and "African," respectively (Decker and McMahon 2021). Such a framing has become naturalized in the world of agricultural development. For example, writing on GMOs in Africa, author Mark Lynas refers to the stance of anti-GMO activists as a "rejection of modern farming" and therefore a "deference to traditionalism" (2018: 139).[9] In a 2017 interview, Lynas explained why he believed some Africans oppose GMOs:

> Kevin Folta: You've talked about a number of different innovations that could really change the lives of small farmers. And I guess something like 80% of people in Africa are small, subsistence farmers. But when you talk about the pushback, you mentioned that the West and Western NGOs, they talk about this idea of health effects.... Do they really worry about things like appealing to colonial control? Or maybe multinationals controlling the crops? Or what are some of the other things they use to kind of poison the well, for lack of a better term, regarding genetic engineered crops?
>
> Mark Lynas:... There were some of the Anti's[10] who were going out into the villages in Uganda and saying, "They'll take a gene from a snake, and they'll put it into a banana to make a banana long like a snake." So that's the level of the debate we're talking about... You know, these are not people with degrees in molecular biology and I'm talking about the villages here, nor do they know Photoshop, by the way. And so, some of the Anti's show these ghastly, mocked up pictures of like, babies' heads emerging from ears of corn and you know, dark skies overhead and stuff like that. And say, "These are GMOs. So when these plant scientists come around to tell you, you could use GMOs, you must say no, because this is what this means."
>
> You know, these are places where they still have witchdoctors, they still believe in witchcraft, and there's all sorts of superstitious stuff going on underneath the surface. So, and of course, that's the same everywhere, it's not unique to Africa. And so, people are quite susceptible to this kind of really, this kind of extreme levels of scaremongering. And it is very damaging, because then you try to have a rational debate, but it's not really a rational concern that's being had. (Folta 2017)[11]

The suggestion that Ugandans living in the countryside ("villages") are unable to discern whether an image is altered or not—especially one that shows a child's head emerging from corn—is preposterous. Lynas's description of Africans—as village-dwelling, uneducated ("these are not people with degrees in molecular biology"), superstitious, irrational, and believing in "witchcraft"—relies on age-old tropes of Africans (and their knowledge and practice) as unscientific and inferior (Decker and McMahon 2021; Walley 2002). Between the examples noted here and earlier that directly call on the construct of Africa as the "Dark Continent," it becomes apparent why the conception of racialization and the work of Jemima Pierre (2020), Kalpana Wilson (2012), and others are not only instructive but essential for analyzing agricultural development schemes (Eddens 2019; Luna 2017).

Moreover, these discourses and images are pervasive and powerful. Powerful in that at the very least they result in resources for the authors: fellowships at Cornell (Lynas), professorships at Harvard (Paarlberg), and invitations to speak as "experts" on panels. Importantly, they set the tone for conversations in public as well as policy spaces, drawing on well-versed humanitarian discourse of African as sufferer (Daley 2013). This discourse—as Patricia Daley (2013) and others have argued—is profitable. For instance, before spinning off into Corteva Agriscience, American agri-giant DuPont Pioneer advertised their hybrid maize seeds with the claim that it can "overcome the elements" in Africa, where, they posited, "farming . . . can often be traumatic" (DuPont 2013).[12] What is not captured in this dark statement are the partnerships that DuPont—and now Corteva Agriscience—held with USAID, whose various programs have paved the way—diplomatically and legally—for DuPont to operate in a number of African countries. In Ethiopia, USAID lobbied the Ethiopian government on behalf of DuPont to allow them to sell hybrid maize seeds (USAID 2017). Similarly, in Ghana, a USAID-funded project, facilitated by Iowa State University, sponsored new national legislation that allowed private sector breeders to operate in the country for the first time. Speaking to reporters in 2018, USAID administrator Mark Green described why the agency pursued these types of partnerships:

> What we do for them is we did de-risk some of the investments. What we get from our side is those farmers get access to the technology that our farmers have had for a long time. Corteva [DuPont Pioneer] will make a buck; we actually think that's a good thing that they make a dollar from this process. (quoted in Rock and Grumbach 2019)

Further integrating African farmers into global markets and "making a buck" for global agribusiness is at the core of how global planners envision sparking a Green Revolution in Africa.

Thus, to date most donor efforts have focused on increasing the ease of business for the private sector—both African and foreign—to supplement states as the main source of agricultural services (McMichael and Schneider 2011: 122). The private sector, donors believe, can build and integrate African farmers into regional and global value chains (Amanor 2019a; Moseley 2016). An emphasis on value chains and the private sector is one of the main ways the "new" Green Revolution differs from the first (Moseley 2016). But hidden from this discussion is the idea of the "agricultural exit," a theory of change that posits positive agricultural change as the growth of a concentrated commercial farming sector, a relationship that requires smallholder farmers to relinquish their farms and livelihoods (Ignatova 2015: 153–54). The agricultural exit underscores policy documents of the World Bank, Rockefeller Foundation, USAID, and AGRA, who described the model in a 2017 publication:

> Over time, African nations will follow the pattern of economic transformations elsewhere: a more productive, more profitable agricultural sector that diversifies and, eventually, shrinks. As fewer farmers grow more food, others will leave their farms to create a thriving rural economy that moves beyond primary production to add value to harvests. Eventually, *some people will leave the rural sector altogether* and contribute to growth and innovation in other sectors. (AGRA 2017b: 14; emphasis added)

The agricultural exit is one way in which proponents of the "new" Green Revolution for Africa seek to re-arrange African landscapes. Following Raj Patel (2013: 4), rather than new or novel, this latest African articulation might be considered a chapter in the longue durée of the Green Revolution, a massive project in opening markets, enclosing land, and making peasants legible to late capitalism (Scott 1998). To support this project, proponents utilize racialized language, which functions in part as coded language, to invoke images of African inferiority and vast wastelands. In turn, the same proponents suggest that relief is available through the form of private financial investment. In other words, proponents use affect "[as] a marketing tool and the circulating site for value" (Adams 2012: 211). Similar to how, as Walter Rodney argued (1972: 215), it was "fashionable to speak of how Europe brought Africa into the twentieth century," the "new" Green Revolution for Africa is premised on the Global North—mainly the United States—supposedly bringing Africa into the twenty-first century of agricultural tools and technologies. One such technology is GM seeds.

GM Crops for Africa

In June 2003, thousands of protestors took to the streets of Sacramento, California, to protest the Ministerial Conference on Agricultural Science and Technology, a three-day biotechnology-focused conference held by the US Department of Agriculture (USDA; Chicago Tribune 2003). Under President George W. Bush, the USDA was leading the charge to increase the use of agricultural biotechnology, an industry dominated at the time mainly by American companies. While the USDA sought to persuade the world leaders who had gathered in Sacramento on the technology's promises, in Washington, DC, President Bush pressured European countries to end their ban on GMOs. Though biotech companies were eager to enter European markets (which the Bush administration attempted to facilitate through filing a complaint at the World Trade Organization [Democracy Now 2003]), the potential of bringing biotechnology to developing countries offered a humanitarian, rather than competitive, lens through which to build their campaign. Speaking at the annual conference of the Biotechnology Industry Organization, President Bush used essentialized images of Africa as a hungry place to make his case: "For the sake of a continent threatened by famine, I urge the European governments to end their opposition to biotechnology. We should encourage the spread of safe, effective biotechnology to win the fight against global hunger" (Chicago Tribune 2003). The following year, the USDA held another ministerial conference on biotechnology, this time in Burkina Faso, presumably to be closer to the sites they wished to intervene and perhaps further away from seasoned Californian activists. American and African officials would continue to meet in 2005 in Mali and in 2007 in Ghana for high-level meetings related to biotechnology.

Efforts to bring GM crops to Africa had begun in the United States almost a decade prior. By the time the first GM food, the Flavr Savr tomato, hit American grocery stores in 1994 (Stone 2021), USAID, Monsanto, and the Kenyan Agricultural Research Institute (KARI) were already three years into developing a virus-resistant sweet potato. These efforts were housed in a larger USAID project, the Agricultural Biotechnology Support Program (ABSP), carried out in Kenya, Egypt, and Indonesia.

Though officials had high hopes that the collaboration would be fruitful, the results of the project were less than satisfactory. An official evaluation of the project found that after "almost 12 years and investment in the order of $13 million, no technology developed under ABSP [had] completed the product development phase" (Brenner 2014: iv). However, evaluators noted two important accomplishments and lessons from the project. First, GMOs were brought into global conversations surrounding food security and agricultural development. Second, evaluators argued that future projects regarding GMOs for the African continent needed an African front leading the way, rather than an American lead. The Rockefeller Foundation heeded this call.

By the early 2000s, the Rockefeller Foundation was on the front lines advocating for GMOs for the world's smallholder farmers (Schurman 2016). The foundation believed genetic modification was a more precise and faster way to develop improved crops than conventional breeding methods, and thus saw them as an important tool in the fight against hunger. However, officials within the foundation knew they had a problem; for years the foundation had funded research into GM technologies, but, as a result of new patenting laws, these projects were becoming increasingly privatized and no longer available for public use (Boyd 2003; Cleveland and Murray 1997; Kloppenburg 2004; Schurman 2016: 4–5). And so, the issue was this: how to get technology that was patented and held by some of the world's largest agribusiness companies to smallholder farmers on the African continent.

Sociologist Rachel Schurman (2016) describes how the Rockefeller Foundation navigated this challenge. To help bring agribusiness executives to the table, the foundation hired the consulting firm the Meridian Institute who helped arrange a 2001 meeting between the Rockefeller Foundation and five major agribusiness and biotech players: "DuPont/Pioneer, Monsanto, DowAgro, Syngenta and Aventis" (Schurman 2016: 7). Officials from the Rockefeller Foundation presented their position—that GM crops could help the fight against hunger—and industry officials presented theirs: African markets were risky from a foreign-direct investment perspective and presented little profit incentives. No decisions were made at that meeting, but industry heads eventually came back to the Rockefeller Foundation with a proposal; they would lease proprietary technology—traits such as pest and drought resistance—to be genetically modified into African crops so long as the Rockefeller Foundation built biosafety and intellectual property rights laws in African countries, provided funding for the projects, and established legal protection for the companies involved. To facilitate this, the group decided to create a third-party broker: the African Agricultural Technology Foundation (AATF; Schurman 2016).

AATF was created in part to establish African oversight of GMOs to avoid accusations, like those made by protestors in Sacramento, that US officials and industry were pushing GMOs onto Africa (Schurman 2016: 12). By the time AATF came on the scene, the world was largely divided between countries that allowed and those that banned GMOs (Schurman and Munro 2010). Only one continent remained in question, that which proponents described (again) as the "final frontier" for GM crops (Karembu et al. 2009).

However, officials soon learned that AATF would be a harder sell than anticipated. In 2002, Peter Matlon, the Rockefeller Foundation's deputy director for food security, traveled to Rome to present the development of the AATF at a workshop sponsored by the FAO of the United Nations titled "Public Agricultural Research: The Impact on Intellectual Property Rights on Biotechnology in Developing Countries." According to a US diplomatic cable describing the event, African delegates conveyed interest in the use of biotechnology, but "expressed concern about the sustainability of donor-funded biotech initiatives" (WikiLeaks 2002). This was especially true of AATF. After hearing Matlon's presentation on AATF, "African delegates, while applauding the program, again raised concerns about the AATF's sustainability" (WikiLeaks 2002).

It's difficult to know whether Rockefeller officials took these concerns into consideration. Nevertheless, the Rockefeller Foundation launched AATF in 2003, with the BMGF and USAID later joining as principal funders. Today, AATF is housed in Nairobi, Kenya, has 501(c)(3) tax-exempt status in the United States, and acts as a broker, facilitating the lease of patented genetic material from private industry to African research councils. To encourage some of the world's largest multinational companies to temporarily license their genetic material—and name—to projects, AATF offers indemnification clauses, provides private funding of projects, and lobbies for industry-friendly laws across the continent. In other words, AATF essentially subsidizes the biotechnology industry's entry into African markets.

With AATF in place, the next step was to build regulatory and political infrastructure in select African countries. In early meetings between the Rockefeller Foundation and biotech giants, industry leaders were wary of entering African markets, as few countries had biosafety regulations—required for signatories of the Cartagena Protocol—in place (Schurman 2016). (Few countries had domestic capacity for GMO research in place either, though this might have been more of an advantage to large companies wary of potential competition.) To remedy this, donors pumped millions of dollars into broker organizations they created—mainly the Program for Biosafety Systems (PBS, created and funded by the US Department of State), the Open Forum for Agricultural Biotechnology (created and funded by the AATF), and the African Biosafety Network of Expertise (ABNE, created and funded by the BMGF)—to work across Ethiopia, Ghana, Kenya, Nigeria, Tanzania, and Uganda to build support for biotechnology. As one may glean from the donors listed earlier, the same core set of donors who fund biotech research and development are those who fund and advise biotech regulation. This overlap not only creates a conflict of interest but also weakens attempts by biosafety officials to claim the role of a neutral arbitrator (Schnurr 2019: 41). The ABNE is a prime example of this.

From 2007 to 2014, the BMGF awarded a series of grants totaling nearly $12 million to Michigan State University (MSU) to establish a biosafety organization within the African Union (AU). ABNE was the resulting product, whose mission was to assist African countries develop national biosafety regulations and authorities.[13] In 2018, my colleague Alex Park and I requested documents from MSU through Michigan's public record law to learn more about the creation of ABNE. Hundreds of pages of documents reveal a rocky start to the organization, who struggled to maintain a happy, mainly English-speaking international staff at the organization's original headquarters in landlocked, francophone Burkina Faso.

Though staff were unhappy, the program met their programmatic goals. First and foremost, they created an organization within the AU, Africa's top governing agency, signaling a green light on biotechnology from the continental agency. Second, ABNE offered technical support to numerous countries, helping country officials develop biosafety laws, gain expertise in biosafety, and review applications for importation and field trials as they came in. In 2014, for instance, ABNE sent officials to Ghana to review applications for confined field trials of GM rice, cowpea, and cotton, including a week alone to review an application from Monsanto and Ghanaian researchers requesting permission to conduct confined field trials of Bt cotton in country.[14] And third, ABNE helped bring organizational and regulatory legitimacy to a technology many worried was coming from the "outside." Though country-level and continental biosafety officials often say that their job is to regulate, not to promote, biotechnology, documents obtained from MSU reveal that university officials envisioned "the ABNE network [to] play *a key role* in advocacy focusing on biosafety and safe applications of biotechnology" (emphasis added).[15] In other words, MSU officials intended that ABNE would help build biosafety regimes *and* promote the technology. "Biosafety regulations across

Africa," as Matthew A. Schnurr argues, "have served a dual function: to mitigate against any negative health or environmental risk that might result (its stated purpose) and simultaneously, to accelerate the expansion of GM crops across the continent" (2019: 41). As subsequent chapters will show, this blurred line between promoter and regulator creates not only potential conflicts of interest but also skepticism and distrust of biotechnology in Ghana.

Skepticism over GMOs as a supposed humanitarian technology has also been fueled by a long history of lobbying efforts by US government officials (including known white nationalist and Iowan congressional representative Steve King). In numerous African countries, US delegates have lobbied both for biotechnology projects in general, as well as on behalf of the biotechnology industry itself. For instance, "in 2005, the [US] embassy in South Africa informed Monsanto and Pioneer about two recently vacated positions in the government's biotech regulatory agency, suggesting that the companies could advance 'qualified applicants' to fill the position" (Food and Water Watch 2013: 9). "We informed both Pioneer and Monsanto the following day about the two new positions," a US diplomatic cable outlining the interaction revealed, "and they immediately saw the benefits from encouraging qualified applicants to apply" (WikiLeaks 2005c). And in Nigeria, US officials established two in-country pro-biotech groups, the West African Biotechnology Network and Nigeria Agricultural Biotechnology Project; encouraged the Nigerian government to forgo mandatory labeling of GM products; and funded the drafting of the National Biosafety Framework (USDA FAS 2009a: 10; USDA FAS 2011a: 7). US officials worked similarly elsewhere on the continent, using taxpayer dollars to set up biotech-friendly organizations, fund African scientific research councils, and hold high-level events for African policymakers.

Over the past decade and a half, AATF and other donor-created initiatives have made some progress across the African continent. When AATF was first launched, only South Africa (and then a few years later, Burkina Faso) was growing GM crops on the continent. Today, twenty-one countries have biosafety laws in place or in consideration (Otunge et al. 2017: iii) and thirteen countries have either approved and/or are undertaking field testing of GM crops (Ojanji and Otunge 2018: 4–5). On paper, these statistics may look appealing. However, the track record of GM crops in Africa has been mostly underwhelming (Schnurr 2019). Overall, it is mainly industrial crops—namely, GM maize, soy, and cotton—that are grown on the continent, and most are grown in South Africa.[16] Though AATF and other donors offer considerable financial and technical support for breeding GM food crops, at the time of writing, only one GM crop developed under AATF has been commercialized: Bt cowpea was made available for commercial sale in Nigeria in June 2021.

The network of broker organizations I have described here is essential to understanding the story of biotechnology in Africa. Though these groups seek to appear as homegrown civil society or non-governmental organizations (Harsh 2014), they are funded and organized from afar by groups and individuals with clear objectives: establishing political and public acceptance of GMOs and moving GMOs from labs to markets (Muraguri 2010; Rock and Schurman 2020; Schnurr and Gore 2015). Thus, centering brokers as multinational actors reveal how these groups act as an important site to facilitate the circulation of capital through lobbying, project design, and more. Moreover, applying an analytical lens to these actors begins to chip away at the strategic attempts to "render [GMOs] technical" and as simply "seeds of science" (Li 2007: 7; Lynas 2018). Instead, as this chapter and subsequent ones will show, the question of GMOs *has always been political*, from lobbying efforts by US representatives, to AATF first meeting with politicians, not scientists, at the 2002 FAO workshop, to the PPP between public institutions and private entities, to donors assisting African governments to re-write seed laws and beyond. Science is political, farming is political, development is political. And as US officials and other development donors worked to build consensus around biotech, African civil society groups were beginning to raise alarms.

Seeking Food Sovereignty

In 2007, hundreds of representatives from various civil society organizations gathered in Nyéléni, Mali, for the International Forum for Food Sovereignty. The forum, organized by representatives from nine global groups, including the Network of Peasants and Farmers in West Africa (ROPPA), Coordination Nationale des Organisations Paysannes (CNOP; Mali), and La Via Campesina (LVC),[17] was held nearly a decade after LVC had declared a global movement for food sovereignty at the 1996 United Nations World Food Summit.[18] At Nyéléni, delegates spent six days strategizing how to strengthen a global commitment and platform for food sovereignty. Organizers described the meeting as a "People's Forum[;] there were no power point presentations, no white draped tables, nobody in suits and ties" (Nyéléni Steering Committee 2008: 14). What resulted was the Declaration of Nyéléni, a manifesto that outlined the participants' intentions to "strengthen a global movement for food sovereignty" (Forum for Food Sovereignty, Nyéléni 2007). In it, delegates laid out a collective vision food sovereignty and a call for its urgent adoption:

> Food sovereignty is the right of peoples to healthy and culturally appropriate food produced through ecologically sound and sustainable methods, and their right to define their own food and agriculture systems. It puts those who produce, distribute and consume food at the heart of food systems and policies rather than the demands of markets and corporations. It defends the interests and inclusion of the next generation. It offers a strategy to resist and dismantle the current corporate trade and food regime, and directions for food, farming, pastoral and fisheries systems determined by local producers. Food sovereignty prioritises local and national economies and markets and empowers peasant and family farmer-driven agriculture, artisanal fishing, pastoralist-led grazing, and food production, distribution and consumption based on environmental, social and economic sustainability. Food sovereignty promotes transparent trade that guarantees just income to all peoples and the rights of consumers to control their food and nutrition. It ensures that the rights to use and manage our lands, territories, waters, seeds, livestock and biodiversity are in the hands of those of us who produce food. Food sovereignty implies new social relations free of oppression and inequality between men and women, peoples, racial groups, social classes and generations. (Nyéléni Steering Committee 2008: 9)

The declaration continued, laying out what the collective was "fighting for," "fighting against," and what they were going to "do about it." Some of the items included under the "fighting against subheading" included, "the so-called 'old' and 'new' Green Revolutions, ... food aid that disguises dumping, introduces GMOs into local environments and food systems and creates new colonialism patterns" (Nyéléni Steering Committee 2008: 10).

Just a year after the Nyéléni Forum, the Food Price Crisis would unfold, plunging many of the world's poorest into crisis. While some world leaders responded to the crisis by doubling down on commercial agriculture and further building global value chains—like the architects of the "new" Green Revolution for Africa—others interpreted the crisis as a "crisis *of* industrial agriculture" (McMichael and Schneider 2011: 120; emphasis added). For those who interpreted the Food Price Crisis as one of industrial agriculture, it offered an opportunity to advocate for urgent and radical reform. And coming off the momentum of the Nyéléni Forum, global food sovereignty activists were ready to respond (Holt-Giménez 2009).

In June 2008, Nyéléni organizers co-published and circulated a statement titled "No More 'Failures-as-Usual'!" The statement, which garnered hundreds of signatories (Nyéléni Steering Committee 2008: 6), argued that the roots of the Food Price Crisis could be found in global institutions, neoliberal reforms (such as Structural Adjustment policies), and the industrial consolidation and financialization of global food systems (IPC 2008: 1; Clapp and Isakson 2018). The letter also contained several demands, including "a local and global paradigm-shift towards Food Sovereignty," and an explicit "rejection" of the "new" Green Revolution for Africa (IPC 2008: 3, 5). Pressure ramped up in 2011, when, "Africa's food sovereignty groups consolidated to establish the Alliance for Food Sovereignty in Africa (AFSA)" (Shilomboleni 2017: 48).[19] Today, AFSA is "a network of networks . . . with 30 active members," administered by a secretariat and a member-elected board of directors (AFSA 2019).

Between the Declaration of Nyéléni, the "No More 'Failures-as-Usual'!" statement, and active, on-the-ground organizing by AFSA and others, the global food sovereignty movement has long had the "new" Green Revolution for Africa in their sights. But how individual organizers and groups actually thought about the "new" Green Revolution, and whether they actually saw it as oppositional to food sovereignty, is a question worth asking.

Studying Food Sovereignty

Following the 1996 World Food Summit, interest in food sovereignty across civil society, academia, and even policy arenas boomed (Bini 2018; Pimbert 2009). Subsequently, "food sovereignty" has turned into an all-encompassing term; "it is at once a slogan, a paradigm, a mix of practical policies, a movement and a utopian aspiration" (Edelman 2014: 2). Since its beginnings, academic studies of food sovereignty have been interdisciplinary and largely theoretically based rather than ethnographically based inquiries. Many have argued that the food sovereignty framework is marked by a "lack of conceptual clarity" (Dekeyser et al. 2018: 223), and others have debated questions of scale (Iles and Montenegro de Wit 2015).

Some scholars have questioned the framework's ability to create meaningful policy change (Borras 2008: 282), and whether and how the international movement is "aligned with the understandings of peasants at the ground level" (Burnett and Murphy 2014: 10; Boyer 2010). For example, drawing from research with Ecuadorian peasants engaged in industrial export markets, Rachel Soper (2020) argues that food sovereignty advocates utilize "problematic discourse that essentializes indigenous and peasant people as inherently ecological and opposed to capitalism" (2020: 265).

Writing from a more optimistic view, some food sovereignty scholars have focused on the ways in which food sovereignty promotes agroecological methods of farming and biological and food diversity (Holt-Giménez and Altieri 2013). Such diversity, studies have shown, enhances food security; if one crop fails, the farmer has backup(s) (Altieri 2009; Nyantakyi-Frimpong and Bezner Kerr 2015; Welthungerhilfe, IFPRI, and Concern Worldwide 2012: 47). In terms of food sovereignty in practice, "researchers have identified approximately 15 countries . . . where food sovereignty-inspired legislation has been adopted" (Schiavoni 2017: 2). Other scholars have studied food sovereignty groups on the ground to ask how these groups operationalize the food sovereignty framework in practice. In rural Mexico, Devon Sampson and Chelsea Wills (2013) have studied how food sovereignty advocates determine, define, and pursue "culturally appropriate" food (a key tenet of food sovereignty). In the Philippines, Sarah Wright has shown how the adoption of a food sovereignty framework helped increase yield, "soil fertility," income, and diet diversity within one farmers' collective (2014: 201–2).

Elsewhere, Rachel Bezner Kerr's (2013) study of Malawi demonstrates how the struggle to maintain indigenous seeds is an integral part of food sovereignty efforts. And Helena Shilomboleni's (2017) ethnographic exploration of a Mozambican peasant farmers union highlights the complexities food sovereignty organizers face in trying to operationalize a food sovereignty framework while working with a heterogeneous member-base and limited funding. Such studies revealed that food sovereignty—as an idea and as a practice—differs greatly across contexts, and that more long-term, on-the-ground scholarship is needed to understand how food sovereignty is actually operationalized.

That's where this book comes into play. Despite the existence of over 150 food sovereignty groups globally (La Via Campesina 2014), there is still relatively little literature on the ways that food sovereignty organizations work on the ground and in specific settings (Ayres and Bosia 2011; see Bezner Kerr 2013; Massicotte 2014;

Richardson 2013; Sampson and Wills 2013; Shilomboleni 2017; and Wright 2014 for exceptions). Thus, this book responds to growing calls for more context-specific case studies of food sovereignty (Bezner Kerr 2013: 868) and the ways in which food sovereignty is constructed. By *constructed*, I draw on Christina M. Schiavoni (2017: 3), who asks "what food sovereignty means and what it might look like, conceptually and in practice, [as] ongoing processes of contestation and negotiation." By examining how Ghanaian food sovereignty advocates take an international framework and shape it to meet local contexts and practices, my research approaches food sovereignty as "a living process" (Iles and Montenegro de Wit 2015: 482; Hansen and Stepputat 2006: 297), something that is constantly being shaped and contested. Finally, this book contributes a case study of food sovereignty (in action, in construction, in contestation) specifically from the African continent. Despite the prominent role African organizers have played in building the global food sovereignty movement, from organizing the Nyéléni Forum to the rise of AFSA, the literature remains mainly based in examples from Latin America and North America. This book centers the African continent as a crucial site for understanding food sovereignty.

Methodology

I conducted research for this book between 2013 and 2021, during which time I traveled to Ghana four times and spent a total of fifteen months conducting ethnographic fieldwork.[20] Ethnography, research that happens "at the site" and "in the moment" (Leap 1999: 13), allowed me to obtain a deep understanding about a particular place and time (Flachs 2019). As part of this work, I interviewed seventy-eight individuals, including farmers (thirty-five), Food Sovereignty Platform members (fifteen), biotechnology boosters (nine), and actors within Ghana's agricultural development spaces (nineteen).[21] Some of these interviews were formal—with a list of questions and a recorder—and others were more informal, on the sidelines of events, on the phone, and over meals. The real meat of ethnography, however, lies in the broad category of *participant observation*. As I moved through space and time, at events, on farms, or simply in the office of GAFP, I took copious notes on the conversations I had, the scenes I witnessed, the questions that were asked. It was the everyday conversations, the WhatsApp threads, the radio shows, the long road trips, and stories told where I learned the most poignant of lessons.

In designing my methodology, I followed Roberto J. González and Rachael Stryker's (2014) call for anthropologists to re-engage with Laura Nader's idea of "studying up, down, and sideways" (González and Stryker 2014: 7). Doing so requires cutting a "vertical slice" through a phenomenon of study to analyze "dynamics of power by examining the links between various strata of society" (González and Stryker 2014: 11). The vertical slice I ultimately cut contained four main groups of actors: the Ghanaian Food Sovereignty Platform, farmers, GMO boosters, and donors. Studying across this range of actors allowed me to approach development as a "social process," something that is alive and contested, debated, and reconfigured on a regular basis (Benton 2015: 10; Hodžić 2017; Yarrow 2011). To draw from Chaia Heller, by researching across numerous actors and geographies, I was able to see the "new" Green Revolution for Africa and "GMOs as an uneven and heterogeneous network of . . . people, organisms, tools, and policies" (2013: 34). Later, I introduce each group I conducted research with, explain the various methods I used, and describe the research sites I frequented to further illustrate my approach to "studying up, down, and sideways" (González and Stryker 2014: 7).

I came to this research having already spent several years living and working in Ghana, first as a student at the University of Ghana (2008–2009), and later as an employee of an NGO in Cape Coast (2010–2011). It was my experience working in the Ghanaian development sphere, as well as being raised by a parent working in the development industry, that piqued my interest in studying development as an object of inquiry. As a white American woman, I was granted entry to spaces and access to materials that were difficult for my Ghanaian peers to obtain. In a few cases, I encountered folks who wondered if I was an agent for Monsanto, a spy for USAID, or an activist masquerading as a researcher. These interactions revealed larger anxieties about the topics of inquiry at hand—development, sovereignty, food, and agriculture—and, as I discuss in chapter 1, were moments of profound learning.

Finally, a quick note about naming: despite a population of five million (GSS 2020), Accra's development circles, where many have spent the entirety of their career and know one another intimately, are quite small (Yarrow 2011). To protect the identities of my interlocutors, I have used pseudonyms for people, places, and organizations throughout, except for texts I've cited from public sources and people speaking at public forms.

Farmers and the Food Sovereignty Platform

The Ghanaian Food Sovereignty Platform is a network of activist, environmental, and civil society groups in Ghana, bound by their collective opposition to GM crops and the Plant Breeders Bill. Given the size of the platform, I devised a methodology that would embed me within a single platform member, which would serve as a gatekeeper into the larger movement. Luckily for me, Constance and GAFP agreed to host me during my larger research stint (2015–2016). I was based at GAFP's headquarters in Accra, which is run by a small and passionate team of program officers, volunteers, and a director, including Constance, who was introduced earlier, and Nii, Kwesi, and John, whom you will meet throughout the manuscript.

I officially began participant observation as an intern/researcher in September 2015. I usually sat in the Accra office two to four days a week and attended at least one event per week, including staff meetings and workshops. Part and parcel of office life was sharing meals, coffee, and running errands with GAFP staff. While a majority of the work I conducted with GAFP was in Accra, I also traveled with program staff a number of times to the economic hubs and communities around Kumasi, Kintampo, Tamale, and Paga.

In an attempt to better understand the farming communities that made up GAFP's membership, I conducted three weeks of field interviews with farmers in and around the Bono East and Upper East Regions. In Bono East, I was joined by my trusted friend, social studies teacher and professional farm manager, Francis. Francis served as a research assistant, and we conducted interviews in Dagbane, English, Kasem, and Twi. Interviews were translated by Francis and transcribed by QuickScribeGH. In the Upper East Region, I was assisted by a GAFP volunteer, Samuel, and interviews were conducted in English and Kusaal. Michael Awimbilla of the Ghana Institute of Linguistics, Literacy and Bible Translation translated and transcribed these interviews.

In our interviews with farmers, we asked open-ended questions about what farmers grew, if and how their farms (including soil health, weather patterns, and yield) had changed over the years, and what farmers thought about Akin Adesina's axiom "agriculture is not a way of life, it is a business." I noticed that respondents seemed bored with me and my questions, and I soon learned that I was one of many outsiders who had arrived in towns with questions and nothing to offer in return. Many respondents told me of past researchers, NGO professionals, and extension officers who had presented enticing projects, but had little to show for their efforts. Others spoke about past agricultural modernization attempts gone astray, whether it was the introduction of fertilizer or improved varieties of crops.

Chapter 1 explores the historical basis of these critiques. I begin by describing how a violent past of enslavement, imperialism, and later colonial rule radically re-shaped agriculture and foodways in Ghana. Across these eras, new crops, agricultural technologies, and tools were introduced. I show how colonial officials established racialized hierarchies around food and agriculture in Ghana, standards that lasted through independence and to the present day. Moreover, I sample a few major agricultural development projects that have come and gone through Ghana's northern regions. This history is important because it forms the collective memory of communities—both farming and otherwise—across Ghana. I describe this collective memory as recipient fatigue, the absolute and embodied multi-generational exhaustion of being a subject of the development apparatus. I introduce this idea in chapter 1 and build it throughout the book.

But recipient fatigue is not simply experienced by farmers and farming communities; it helps explain the growth of the Food Sovereignty Platform, which grew out of opposition to the everyday materiality of development schemes, new seeds (GMOs) and policy (the Plant Breeders Bill). I explore the deep background of these connected initiatives in chapter 2. In particular, I examine how international development agencies, agribusiness companies, and US officials came together to bring GM crops to Ghana. To support this effort, the same donors set up a network of organizations to help Ghanaian officials write new seed policies, train journalists on reporting (favorably) on biotechnology, and establish a new government regulatory agency. As I discuss in this chapter, understanding this foundation—and the political reconfigurations that went into it—is essential for understanding the story of GM crops in Ghana (Rock and Schurman 2020).

With this foundation in mind, chapter 3 examines the emergence and growth of the Ghanaian Food Sovereignty Platform, which I argue was borne in part of recipient fatigue: activists were ready to take back development planning from international donors. For many, this goal had existed long before GMOs came on to the scene, but it was GMOs, along with its associated Plant Breeders Bill, that provided a platform for organizers to publicly take a bold stand. Chapter 3 explores the early days of organizing, along with how strategies and alliances have ebbed and flowed over time, and how activists took on a well-resourced, well-connected global network of GMO boosters.

GMO Boosters

Being embedded in GAFP and food sovereignty networks in Accra opened up opportunities to interact with a wide variety of individuals and institutions, including the country's GMO boosters, many of whom were headquartered in the capital city. I use "booster" to refer to organizations and individuals whose roles are to garner support for biotechnology in both public and political spheres. This category includes individual scientists as well as organizations like those listed earlier, PBS, ABNE, and so on. It also includes organizations created explicitly to act as brokers, or intermediaries, between donors, industry, and African institutions, such as AATF. While researching the officials, scientists, and advocates working to bring GMOs to Ghana was not my original intention, entering this world greatly expanded my analysis. In addition to conducting interviews with boosters, I also attended non-public events, such as a meeting of the National Biosafety Authority, a training of Ghanaian journalists, and a workshop with Ghanaian parliamentarians. These events, and the casual conversations I had in and outside of them, allowed me to better understand the complexities of the PPPs that constitute GMO projects in Ghana.

Chapter 4 explores the stances of the Ghanaian scientists and officials working diligently to commercialize GMOs. Through interviews, conference presentations, and observations, I show how Ghanaian scientists embraced GMOs in part due to the patents they hoped would accompany the seeds, allowing scientists—all working within state research institutions—to gain profit and recognition for their work. This prospect becomes complicated with PPP that underlie all GMO projects in Ghana, which are reliant on an industry "partner" to license their proprietary technology. I use the example of a GM rice PPP to demonstrate these complexities. Ultimately, I argue, Ghanaian officials were unenthused about genetic modification as a technology—they largely saw it as unexceptional—but driven by the possibility of patents. This is an important aspect of the GMO story in Ghana, because, as I argue in chapter 5, it is part of what bonds scientists and activists: the belief that Ghana currently lacks sovereignty in part due to the over-sized influence donors have on development policy and priorities. By elevating GM crops for their potential patents, rather than their supposed superior technology, Ghanaian brokers and boosters chip away at the discourse of GMOs as a revolutionary, life-saving, food security-ensuring technology (Lynas 2018; Paarlberg 2008). In doing so, Ghanaian

GMO advocates flip the script and demand space—both in and outside Ghana—to define agricultural priorities and futures.

Donors

The final group I researched were development donors. With the power of funding, donors are able to shape research agendas, NGO advocacy, and discourse. Donors are an essential aspect of the "new" Green Revolution and biotech stories, and I gathered data from this group in three key ways. First, I interviewed officials from various donor organizations. Second, to understand the discourses that circulate publicly regarding GMOs and the "new" Green Revolution, I spent time in *agricultural development spaces*, the meeting spaces, offices, and social and professional events of Ghana's major development actors: government institutions, multi- and bilateral development agencies, and NGOs. My access to these spaces was mostly mediated by gate-keepers and snowball sampling; an interview with a well-placed person (gate-keeper) would alert me to another person I should connect with or a meeting I should attend. Attending events in these spaces was pivotal for participant observation: I collected handouts, took notes, schmoozed during coffee breaks, and, importantly, waited for the question-and-answer (Q&A) section of each event. Q&A periods were often full of data; it was here that officials went off script, that audience members stopped being polite and asked what was on their mind, and where development—as an ideology, a practice, an embodiment—was contested.

Finally, to understand the basic discourses that key donors utilize in support of both GMOs and the "new" Green Revolution, I gathered, coded, and analyzed organization literature, news articles, policy documents, and public interviews using MaxQDA. I took a critical discourse approach in analyzing the discourses of donors, as well as farmers, activists, and biotech boosters. Following Norman Fairclough (2012) and Ruth Wodak (2012), I analyzed texts not simply considering them as standalone objects. Instead, I sought to understand the broader socio-cultural, political, and historical contexts "within which discursive events are embedded" (Wodak 2012: 529).

Working with donors, farmers, food sovereignty activists, and biotech boosters allowed me to probe commonalities and differences across and between these groups. Ultimately, as I conclude in the Epilogue, so much of the conversation that surrounded GMOs in Ghana was underscored by recipient fatigue and a drive for freedom from donors. In seeking this freedom, Ghanaians demanded to shape the systems and policies in which they are embedded, and used intersectional, deeply political lenses to analyze food, sovereignty, and agricultural development.

CHAPTER 1

Agricultural Development and So-Called NGOs

In the spring of 2017, I was sitting at my home in San Francisco when I received a call from Matthias, a farmer in his mid-sixties whom I had met in Ghana's Bono East Region. Matthias had called me that day to update me about a neighborhood borehole. The borehole—a metal water pump—had been provided by a major development organization and conveniently sat in the middle of the community. Donor-funded (and branded) boreholes and other sorts of infrastructure are ubiquitous across the Ghanaian countryside. The problem was, however, that the borehole was close to inoperable.

Matthias had first told me about the borehole as we sat outside his home, discussing the types of actors—government, non-profit, or otherwise—that were engaged in agricultural projects in his community. He used the borehole as an example of something he thought the government should deliver—access to water—but was instead provided by non-governmental organizations (NGO), who, he noted, were difficult to hold accountable. The borehole, he explained, was a good example of this. According to Matthias, the borehole exhibited problems soon after it was installed. Matthias chalked it up to the long metal hand pump used to extract water; it was so heavy, Matthias and his neighbors told me, it was nearly unusable.[1] Desiring easier access to water, the community had alerted the major development organization to the problem and asked them to install a mechanical device to assist pumping. A fair ask, many might agree, but according to Matthias, officials of the major development organization responded that the community raise its own funds for mechanization, quoting a cost of 3,000GHC (approximately US$750). Such a sum was simply out of the question for town residents, and so community leaders secured the pump with a chain, safeguarding it from anyone who might cause harm, hoping that someday it might be of use. However, when Matthias called me a year later, he told me that the borehole was now completely inoperable. "The so-called NGOs," he said, "some of them are just killing us."

Matthias had been instrumental in orienting Francis—my friend and research assistant—and I around rural Bono East, where we spent two weeks interviewing farmers and their families. During this time, Matthias walked us through town, pointing out dusty signboards on the side of the road that advertised old development projects. One sign marked a yam project, which, according to Matthias, was only evidenced by the signboards and the 5GHC (US$1.25) that project officers gave out to residents instead of actually executing the project. Back at his home, Matthias showed us more material he kept from development projects that had come to town. His archive was impressive; he kept old signboards, including one advertising a 1997 US Agency for International Development (USAID) project, and a black briefcase full of old project documents and agricultural magazines.

"You see this thing?" he asked, pointing to the USAID signboard. "When I came during the time my father lived here, I saw this signboard. You see? Funding agency, USAID. This one, since 1997. How much impact has gone to the farmers now? Nothing." One by one, Matthias pulled documents from the briefcase and told us about the often unsatisfactory outcome of each project. Matthias collects these signs and old brochures from development trainings, archaeological records of promises unmet.

How did this happen? What historical, economic, political, and climactic forces coalesced so that "development" appears to be more of a relic than a reality in agrarian Ghana? As archaeologist Amanda Logan (2020) writes, any contemporary discussion of food and agriculture in Ghana requires a historical perspective. As such, I start this chapter with Matthias to explore the historical archive of agricultural change, attempted modernization, and development in Ghana. As we will see later in the chapter, many interlocutors described agricultural modernization efforts in racialized terms, using the Twi word for "white person," *oburoni*, to describe newly introduced seeds, chemicals, and so-called experts. Such language use instructs us to consider agricultural practice and development outside of strict lenses of productivity. As such, I place my historical analysis of Ghanaian agriculture and foodways explicitly in political-economic processes—slaving, colonialism, independence, structural adjustment, and neoliberal capitalism—to demonstrate the racialized, colonial roots of the massive undertaking of the "new" Green Revolution for Africa, and to establish a foundation for, as we will see later in the book, how and why Ghanaians explicitly link contemporary agricultural modernization with the colonial era.

Doing so provides two key themes that continue throughout the book. The first is that agricultural modernization has long been a goal of the Ghanaian state, and one intimately tied with state making (Amanor 2011; Nyantakyi-Frimpong and Bezner Kerr 2015). However, attempts at modernizing the agricultural sector—whether by colonial officials or NGOs—have long, contentious legacies. As I explain in this chapter, mementos of failed development efforts—like the ones Matthias keep—loom large in the minds and collective memory of Ghana's farmers and farming communities. This reality, one I capture in the theoretical concept of *recipient fatigue*, is the second underlying theme that runs through the book and which I establish here. For the historical, social, and embodied legacies of colonialism and attempted development are crucial for understanding genetically modified crops and agriculture in Ghana.

From Ship to Staple

Agricultural change is shaped by economic, environmental, social, and political forces. In contemporary Ghana, one of the most significant events to impact agricultural production and consumption was the trans-Atlantic slave trade. The arrival of European forces, crops, and goods and the kidnapping of millions of Africans marked five centuries of political-economic changes that dramatically altered Ghanaian social, economic, political, and food landscapes (Carney and Rosomoff 2009; La Fleur 2012: 2). By beginning my historical discussion of Ghanaian agriculture and foodways here, I am not suggesting that there were not cultures, tastes, or politics surrounding food prior to European contact. Instead, beginning with the arrival of European powers—starting with the Portuguese—allows us to track the origins of what would become major changes in the agricultural landscape we see today: the introduction of crops that eventually became major staples, the reconfiguration of class and power, and the changes in agricultural practice that accompanied these processes.

The Portuguese began what would be almost four hundred years of intensive *precolonial* European contact (roughly 1500–1850). Drawn to the land they would call the "Gold Coast" (a name that remained during British colonial rule), Portuguese traders began establishing forts along the coast and purchasing captives in the late fifteenth century (Reynolds 1985). Soon, other European forces—notably the Dutch and British—began trading in humans along the Gold Coast, a violent extraction that would persist until the mid-nineteenth century. Along the fortressed coast, "European companies . . . codified coastal residents' immunity from enslavement in order to ensure their cooperation" (Holsey 2007: 45). European traders relied on groups in the interior of the country, such as the Asante Kingdom in Kumasi, to capture and transport Africans to the southern coast. Asante "had established a trade with northern territories prior to the arrival of the Portuguese" and "received slaves from the North from Hausa and Mossi traders" (Holsey 2007: 29). It is difficult to know exactly how many people were captured from the area we now know today as Ghana. The Trans-Atlantic Slave Trade Database at Emory University estimates that enslavers transported 1,209,322 enslaved Africans through forts along the Gold Coast, and historian Walter Rodney notes that at its height, anywhere from 5,000 to 6,000 people were kidnapped per year in the Gold Coast alone (Emory University 2013; Rodney 1982: 99).

The slave trade resulted in significant changes in agricultural production and diets on both sides of the Atlantic. To the Gold Coast, Portuguese brought what historians would later term "New World" crops to sustain troops, animals, and kidnapped Africans. Two of these would eventually become staples throughout the country: maize and cassava (La Fleur 2012: 9). Maize spread along the coastal regions, where farmers began experimenting and developing new varieties. Maize was attractive to farmers for numerous reasons. One was that it is "quicker to fruit than either sorghum or millets and therefore can be planted twice a year, to take advantage of the tropic's two rainy seasons, thus producing significantly higher yields than the older grains" (La Fleur 2012: 4). Farmers also began growing maize for both personal consumption and commercial sale, mainly to ships that were to transfer kidnapped Africans across the deadly Atlantic (Carney and Rosomoff 2009;

La Fleur 2012; Stahl 2001). To facilitate this trade, an elite entrepreneurial coastal class emerged, working as middlemen between European slavers and African farmers (La Fleur 2012: 107). And inland from the coast, cassava became a crucial crop for communities living in fear of kidnapping and raids. Amanda Logan explains how some farmers adopted cassava as a survival strategy:

> The pressures brought on by the slave trade and the new ways of living it engendered had multiple impacts on food security... Monocrop grain fields were particularly vulnerable during raiding: they were not only highly visible as distinct from nearby vegetation, but also required the presence of a farmer at very specific times of year for care and harvest. One adaptation... was to switch to the cultivation of cassava, which blended in with the surrounding vegetation, required little care, and could be left in the ground for several years and be harvested at any time of year. (2020: 87)

Across the region, whether around coastal trade centers or further north, centuries of kidnapping, trans-Atlantic trade, and political struggle resulted in profound culinary and agrarian changes throughout the region for generations to come (La Fleur 2012: 14). Moreover, slaving practices (and later, formal colonial rule) solidified ideological, political, and economic divisions between what would become the southern and northern halves of Ghana. For while kidnapping would eventually spread beyond the northern territories, along the coast, "Europeans and southern Ghanaians alike began to argue that... northern groups were not fit for anything but slavery" (Holsey 2007: 45). This discourse, and continued marginalization of the northern territories, would last beyond the slave trade and have lasting implications on foodways.

Colonial Configurations

After centuries of European trade and occupation of the coastal areas, Great Britain declared colonial rule over the Gold Coast from 1821 to 1957. Colonizers moved quickly to build internal industries to both self-fund the colonial project as well as fill the coffers of Great Britain. In addition to gold, for which the colony was named, British officials poured resources into palm oil and cocoa, which became the colony's star exports (Duncan 1997: 37; Berry 1993: 27).[2] Soon, at the direction of a state cocoa board that controlled the price, inputs, and methods of production, the Gold Coast became one of the world's largest cocoa producers. Agriculture was solidified as an essential aspect of statecraft: both essential to the making *and* the imaginary of the state.

The cocoa industry created incredible wealth for the Gold Coast colony, but it also had adverse socio-economic implications (Mikell 1989). First, the British invested resources in the southern, cocoa-growing part of the country—such as agricultural research, cash crops and commercialization schemes, and education for elite classes—at the detriment to the northern sectors, whose residents were encouraged by colonial officials to migrate south to provide labor to southern farms (Sutton 1989: 638, 643). While northern labor was key to the rapid growth of cocoa farming, the emigration of farmers and laborers to the south also "diminished agricultural production in the north" (Logan 2020: 105). As a result, cocoa was a part of a larger legacy of unequal development and marginalization of the northern territories (Holsey 2007; Sutton 1989). Second, support for producing cocoa and other commercial crops was mainly relegated to men (Duncan 1997: 38).[3] As state subsidies, family capital, and migrant labor went into cocoa (and other exportable goods), food production waned considerably (Berry 1993: 27; Logan 2020: 104–5). As Jonathan Robins writes, the drop in food production raised alarms for some officials:

> In 1926 the undersecretary of state for the colonies, William Ormsby-Gore, toured West Africa and produced a report identifying new directions for Britain's colonial administrations. He argued that cash crop production among Africans, especially in cocoa-growing regions of Nigeria and the Gold Coast, had been too successful: "The development of economic crops at the expense of production of food for local consumption is most undesirable, and a plentiful supply of cheap food, both for the native and non-native inhabitants of the countries, is the first essential." He succinctly concluded: "Food comes first, and economic crops for export should come second." (2018: 173)

While some officials like Ormsby-Gore drew direct links between the explosion of cocoa and decrease in food production, overall, colonial agricultural policy was, as Gwendolyn Mikell argues, marked by "disdain for traditional diets[,] and what [officials] considered inefficient cultivation techniques" (1989: 58). For example, a report on nutrition in the colonies lamented that "starchy roots" that made up must of the Ghanaian diet, such as rice and maize, were "low quality" and "unsatisfactory

... staple foods" (Advisory Committee 1944b: 1; 1942).[4] To counter, the (British) Advisory Committee on Imperial Questions proposed a thirteen-point guide to "correct feeding," including the consumption of "mixed grain staples, ... ground nuts and ... soya," expansion of meat production, and consumption of milk and milk by-products (Advisory Committee 1944a: 1–4). Missing from these reports are structural causes of malnutrition and (what colonial officials considered to be) low agricultural production. For, rather than consider the links between cocoa and food production, as Ormsby-Gore did, or the impacts of centuries of slaving and political upheaval on agricultural practice, colonial officials blamed Africans (Logan 2020; Robins 2018). Maintaining nutritional standards was not so much a moral imperative for colonial officials as it was an economic one; nutrition was seen as "critical for nurturing a productive labor force" to continue to labor for colonial profit (Logan 2020: 117). In addition to a disdain for staple crops, colonial officials were perplexed at the rising consumption of imported foods by Africans living in urban centers. Robins explains that "Europeans saw African consumption of imported foods as a form of conspicuous consumption, a subversive move across the 'color line' that formally and informally segregated European and African bodies in the colonies" (2018: 171). Accordingly, colonial preoccupation with nutrition and food consumption must be understood in the context of race and racialization, as well as global capitalism.

As colonial officials debated what to do about food crop production and consumption, the cocoa industry forged ahead. A key component of the colonial cocoa project was uniformity, as a uniform product was easier to sell in bulk on the global market. To ensure uniformity and thus profit, colonial officials sought to homogenize and discipline Ghanaian farming practice, which they believed to "[have] no scientific basis, [and] to be wasteful, inefficient and environmentally destructive," and therefore ill-suited for commercial enterprise (Sumberg 2011: 295). One way in which colonial administrators sought to remedy this was through the use of trainings, propaganda film, and literature. *Kofi the Good Farmer*, a fifty-one-page booklet published in 1950 by the Gold Cocoa Coast Marketing Board, is one such example. I first came across the booklet in the library archives at the University of California, Berkeley, and was drawn to the similarities between *Kofi the Good Farmer* and the handouts Matthias collects. Though I never encountered the booklet in the field, I do know that it was "republished in 1957 and 1987" (Blaylock 2020: 72), and that the Gold Coast Film Unit produced a film by the same name in 1953 (British

The cover of *Kofi the Good Farmer* (1950).

Film Institute).[5] *Kofi the Good Farmer* thus serves as a material and historical vessel through which to understand early colonial efforts at boundary work around "good farming" and, later, "agriculture as a business."

The text follows cocoa farmer Kofi on his quest to obtain the best price for his crop. The story begins by introducing Kofi in relation to his status to the state: "[Kofi] has a cocoa farm. He is an important man because he is part of the main industry of the Gold Coast" (Gold Coast Cocoa Marketing Board 1950: 3). The pages that follow depict Kofi, his wife, Ama, and their son, Kwame through a whole growing season: plucking ripe cocoa pods from their trees, extracting and fermenting the beans, and teaching Kwame how to identify good and bad beans.

Kofi and Ama seem to have a daughter as well, as there is a young girl that appears in family scenes, but she is neither named nor mentioned. Kwame, on the other hand, plays a main role in the family's cocoa production. In addition to learning about the family business, Kwame is shown in school clothes and with books on his head, suggesting that a good (commercial) farmer is not only male but also educated. Thus, if Kofi was an "important man because he is part of the main industry of the Gold Coast," then by extension Kwame is too.

With each page, Kofi moves closer toward his ultimate goal: obtaining top price for his cocoa from the state board. Price depends on quality grade, judged by state cocoa agents. These agents serve as experts, creating an artificial barrier between that which is "good" farming and that which is not. Kofi first goes to his local, Ghanaian cocoa-buying agent, but is displeased with the original price offered. This is where the appeal—and disciplining—process begins. Kofi petitions to the produce examiner, who also appears to be Ghanaian, but like the agent before him, the produce examiner offers Kofi a price he feels is unfair. The final option Kofi has is to appeal to the British inspector of produce, who is white, presumably a British colonial officer, and has the ultimate say. To Kofi's relief, the inspector offers a price Kofi feels he deserves. Kofi turns to leave, a smile of satisfaction on his face. On his way out, he sees his friend Kwabena, who has also decided to appeal to the inspector of produce. Unfortunately, Kwabena "did not take so much trouble" and thus receives a lower price for his crop than Kofi. Kwabena appears disappointed, and the final page of the book shows a triumphant Kofi returning home to a happy, smiling family.

Given the importance of the cocoa industry for maintaining the financial coffers and relative power of the British Empire (Sumberg 2011), interrogating the text of *Kofi the Good Farmer* illustrates a racialized foundation of agricultural statecraft;

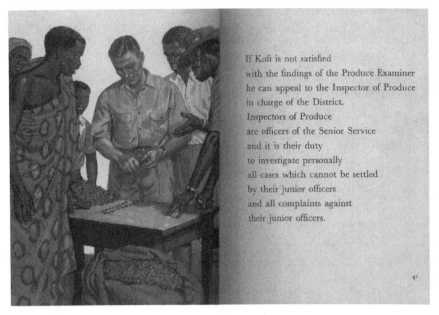

Kofi and the colonial inspector.

"good farming" was predicated on Ghanaian farmers producing commercial—not food—crops for the white colonial class under strict conditions and pricing. Through the example of Kofi appealing the price he was offered by Ghanaian agents, the Cocoa Board sets British official(s) as the official arbiters of cocoa, quality, and expertise. Moreover, Kofi is the colonial state's illustration of the "good" (right) way to be a farmer-citizen: growing cocoa, sending children (or at least sons) to school, and including the family in the entire production process. The opposite of this—the bad farmer, and thus bad citizen—is exemplified by Kwabena, who, like Kofi, appealed all the way up to the colonial official but was ultimately denied the price he desired. Kwabena acts as a disciplinary and boundary-making device, establishing a clear counter to Kofi's "good" practices.

Discourses of "good" farmers and farming, like those illustrated in *Kofi the Good Farmer*, continued well beyond both the colonial era and cocoa production. Colonial preoccupation with "correct feeding" and "good farming" established a discourse of agricultural modernization wherein Ghanaian staples were marked unhealthy, and "good" farming entailed commercial crops and using modern inputs: chemical fertilizers, "improved" seeds bred at research councils, irrigation, herbicides, and pesticides. Agricultural production and food consumption, like so many aspects of colonial rule, were racialized, relegating expertise, development, and so-called modernization with colonial models of farming. Such a vision of agricultural development would continue past independence.

Food and Farming in Postcolonial Ghana

After a long struggle, on March 6th, 1957, Ghana declared independence. Addressing a crowd of revelers gathered in Accra, Dr. Kwame Nkrumah, who had led the campaign for Ghanaian independence, proclaimed, "We have awakened. We will not sleep anymore. Today, from now on, there is a new African in the world! That new African is ready to fight his own battles and show that after all, the black man is capable of managing his own affairs." Nkrumah was an avid supporter of the Pan-Africanist movement. Championed by black intellectuals such as W. E. B. Du Bois, Pan-Africanists sought to create a free and unified African continent, a respite for those who had suffered under European conquest, and for those in the diaspora to return "home." For Nkrumah, establishing a Pan-African, de-colonial state was an explicitly racial project; colonial rule had been the dominance of white Europeans, and thus he envisioned Ghana to demonstrate to the world that "African people can build a state of their own based on democracy, tolerance and racial equality" (Nkrumah 1961: 110).

Nkrumah served as president of Ghana from 1957 to 1966. Agriculture was a core focus of the newly independent state, and a mix of state subsidies and foreign investment marked Ghana's early development policy. Ghanaian officials quickly set out to build roads, agricultural storage facilities and markets, infrastructure, and state farms. To support agricultural growth, the state established the Council for Scientific and Industrial Research in 1959 (CSIR n.d.; Nkrumah 1961: 117). Research was an important aspect of Nkrumah's tenure, and one beneficiary of this was S. La Anyane, the chief agricultural economist in the Division of Agricultural Economics in the Ministry of Agriculture. In the 1960s, the state awarded Anyane research funds to study Ghana's agricultural history. In his results, published in 1963, Anyane wrote:

The export industry, which emerged in its present-day form in the middle of the nineteenth century, and attained a high level of development by the end of the century, produced obvious difficulties for the local farmer. The rate of advancement was too rapid for him. He was illiterate, and the crops were new to him. Of all the export crops only oil palm was locally processed and consumed; and it was impossible at the initial stage for the farmer to form precise ideas on the final uses of his product, and therefore the quality of produce best suited to the world market. (1963: 17–18)

Anyane's conclusion that Ghana's agricultural export sector remained underproductive, due to "illiterate" farmers for whom the "rate of advancement was too rapid," marked the continuation of colonial discourse that demonized the average small-scale farmer. Discourse about, and orientation to, Ghanaian agriculture and agricultural producers is one of the many areas that was never fully de-colonialized by Nkrumah's government (Pierre 2012). Indeed, it was not only colonial discourse that carried over into independence. Some agricultural policies, too—such as an overt focus on commercial and export crops—similarly marked Ghana's early years (Robins 2018: 179). By Nkrumah's final year in office (1966), 62 percent of state farmland were cultivating commercial crops, with just 38 percent land being used for "food crops (mainly maize and rice)" (Benin 2019: 175).

Nkrumah's quest to build a strong state founded in socialist ideology and his ardent criticism of global financial systems garnered him many enemies. In his book *Neocolonialism: The Last Stage of Imperialism*, Nkrumah wrote: "The struggle against neo-colonialism is not aimed at excluding the capital of the developed world from operating in less developed countries. It is aimed at preventing the financial power of the developed countries being used in such a way as to impoverish the less developed" (1965: x). Just a year after publication, the United States and its allies, who believed Nkrumah's Pan-Africanist policies reflected "strongly pro-Communist leanings," orchestrated a coup d'état while Nkrumah was out of the country on state business (Komer 1966; Pierre 2012). Nkrumah would not again set foot in Ghana. In a memo addressed to US president Lyndon Johnson, US acting special assistant for National Security Affairs Robert W. Komer wrote: "The coup in Ghana is another example of a fortuitous windfall. Nkrumah was doing more to undermine our interests than any other black African" (1966). The coup was the first of successive efforts by the United States to chip away at the Nkrumahist, socialist underpinnings of early Ghana, and provides a sort of historical context for contemporary discourses about "enabling environments."

Any gains made during the first decade of Ghanaian independence were stalled by Nkrumah's overthrow, the first of a series of coups that would destabilize the country politically and economically for decades to come (Pierre 2012: 63). While Nkrumah envisioned both public and private streams of investment into the country's industries, agricultural policy following the coup increasingly "shifted to the private sector," state subsidies were funneled toward larger operations, and many state farms were shuttered (Amanor 1999: 33). Though agricultural policy changed, the pervasive discourse of an illiterate peasant class would continue. As successive governments took power, state officials and agronomists grappled with how to complete the task set out in *Kofi the Good Farmer* and establish a nation of "good farmers." In books and journals, agricultural professionals and state officials anxiously debated the best way to turn an "illiterate" peasantry into commercial farmers, like Kofi.

For instance, in *The Ghana Farmer*, a biannual publication from the Ministry of Agriculture, officials remained concerned about "planning for" farmers, and often in an irritable tone. In a 1973 publication, J. K. Osei, an officer at the Ministry of Agriculture, argued that many Ghanaian farmers considered agriculture "a way of life," which was holding the country back from mass agricultural production:

> There is enough evidence to show that the greatest proportion of [Ghanaian] farming is not directed to making the greatest profit. In many cases they farm just enough to feed themselves only. To some, farming is still a way of life. Some think that farming is a virtue ... That is why it is very important to consider the interests of the Ghanaian farmer when planning for him. (1973: 71)

To remedy this, Osei suggested that Ghanaian farmers approach "farming as a business[:] That a farming undertaking be regarded as an economic enterprise. As an economic enterprise the aim of farming is to make the greatest possible profit" (1973: 71). Kojo Amanor shares a similar discursive example:

> As one project manager informed Konings (1986: 308) at the Tono irrigation projects in the Upper East Region, "You cannot allow peasant farmers to continue growing millet, for the large investment in the project does not justify the cultivation of

a crop which is not worthwhile. Economics is the watchword. You have to bully people with a traditional mind to grow cash crops because it is ultimately in their interest." (Amanor 1999: 36)

Frustration and a need to "[plan] for" and "bully" Ghanaian farmers seemed to be foundational preoccupations of some Ghanaian state officials and scientists. Discourses that circulated among professionals marked Ghanaian farmers as poor stewards of the environment, under-productive, and not necessarily valued collaborators, but rather hindrances to national development. To tackle this, Osei argued, Ghanaian farmers needed to approach agriculture as a business rather than "a way of life." Forty years later, a group called the Alliance for a Green Revolution in Africa (AGRA) would take up the mantle of "making agriculture a business," in their question to spark a "new" Green Revolution for Africa.

Jimmy Carter Farms and Making Agriculture a "Business"

In 2015, Dr. Akinwumi Adesina became the eighth president of the African Development Bank. An agricultural economist by training, Dr. Adesina arrived at the bank from his former position as the Nigerian Minister of Agriculture and Rural Development with an impressive resume, including a PhD from Purdue University and previous positions held at the Rockefeller Foundation and AGRA. A few months after he took office, Adesina published an article on the Bank's website entitled "Agriculture as a Business: Approaching Agriculture as an Investment Opportunity." The text served as part-manifesto, part-introduction to how he thought about agricultural development. Adesina (2016) wrote:

> I wear my banker hat, and not my development hat, when I speak about agriculture. Agriculture is not a way of life. It is not a social sector or a development activity, despite what people may claim. Agriculture is a business. And the more we treat it as a business, as a way to create wealth, the more it will promote development and improve people's lives to boot.
>
> One way to treat agriculture like a business is to get the private sector more involved in it. When I was Nigeria's Minister of Agriculture, the most important thing I had to understand was that government can't create agricultural transformation;

it can only enable it by making more room for businesses to intervene. We could do this by putting the right policies and regulations in place, by creating strong institutions, and by building sufficient infrastructure. But there is not much else government can do with a reasonable measure of efficiency. Agricultural transformation has to be led by the private sector.

By the time Adesina had published this text, the phrase "agriculture is not a way of life, it is a business" was circulating throughout global and local development circuits. I heard it in meetings with government and donor officials alike, interviews with agricultural extension officers, and conversations with farmers groups.

When I first encountered this phrase, I found it abrasive and strange in how it essentialized diverse practices and created a sort of dialectic: that which is, that which is not. Such a discursive mechanism works as an ideological tool, suggesting a "right way" to approach agriculture (Althusser 1971); a map for how to establish the physical, economic, and political infrastructure necessary to achieve making agriculture a business (Sturgeon 2010); and a boundary-making device (Gieryn 1983). And as I explored in the earlier, maintaining such a boundary—between what is agriculture as a business ("good farming"?) and that which is not—is a matter of finance and potential gains. To better understand the interface between the Ghanaian government, donors, and the Green Revolution project of making agriculture a business, I went to the Ghanaian Ministry of Food and Agriculture (MOFA) to meet with the office in charge of managing donor relations.

When I walked in, I was immediately struck by how small the room was. Given the office's mandate—to oversee the entirety of donor projects related to food and agriculture in the country—I imagined a bustling, multi-person operation. However, at the time, the office was staffed by just three: a director and two program officers. Overseeing donor projects in a country like Ghana, where dozens of organizations and agencies operate on any given day and where until very recently donor funding comprised over half of MOFA's budget, seemed herculean. The enormity of this task was solidified when a program officer showed me an Excel spreadsheet of donor projects the team was developing, information not required by the government of Ghana, and thus only gathered by self-reporting.

I met with the director of the office and asked about the mantra of "agriculture is not a way of life, it is a business." Where did this come from, what is the history behind this kind of positioning, and what are your thoughts on it? I asked her. The director responded:

> The whole idea is, if you want to transform the sector, if you want to transform the livelihoods of those people, then you have to teach them that . . . it's not just getting up and that is your way of life, going to do whatever you can and feed yourself, if it is even enough to feed yourself and save up a little that is there. You must invest your time and little resources in a way that can bring you profits and change your life so that you will be able to educate your children, you will be able to buy things that you don't have, and things like that . . . Times are changing and we realize that people cannot just do anything and call it "farming." You must farm with a commercial mind [meaning] you must farm with the market in mind.

I remarked that the plan seemed very private-sector intensive, and the director replied, "That is what it is supposed to do because . . . in this part of our world, or for Ghana, we haven't had good experiences of government doing business." The director overall gave the impression that "agriculture as a business" was a relatively recent construction (despite the archival evidence I would find years later that suggested otherwise), and that Ghanaian farmers were largely "do[ing] whatever" they could to feed themselves, and that they instead needed to adjust and adopt a "commercial mind." Indeed, the director's comments echoed much donor and government rhetoric circulating at the time.

What happened in the decades between Osei's article and my meeting with this official? What transpired in Ghana politically, agriculturally, and socially, that created the condition wherein government officials described farmers as just doing "whatever"? In this section, I trace more contemporary attempts at "agricultural development" first by reviewing a number of major projects that preceded the "new" Green Revolution for Africa, and later by injecting the experience of farmers like Matthias and his neighbors, who, as "recipients" of such projects, may be the ultimate judges of their outcomes.

As the decades passed after the ousting of Nkrumah, so did state agricultural initiatives (Boafo and Lyons 2021). These projects, often large in scale and scope, ranged anywhere from the development of massive irrigation schemes, the creation of new state agencies to tackle development in the northern regions, and the establishment of home gardens (Nyantakyi-Frimpong and Bezner Kerr 2015: 16). However, Ghana's vulnerabilities were exposed in the 1980s, when "a combination of factors, including government over-spending, a fall in cocoa prices, severe droughts, and global oil price increase, led to a complete collapse of the economy" (Nyantakyi-Frimpong and Bezner Kerr 2015: 17). To counter these economic troubles, in

1983 Ghana signed on to what would be the first of eventual back-to-back structural adjustment policies, which slashed state funding and privatized or semi-privatized numerous state projects and services.

Publicly, the "Bretton Woods institutions and their supporters [hailed Ghana] as the most successful case of structural adjustment in Africa" (Konadu-Agyemang 2000: 469), even going as far to entitle the country as the "star pupil of the World Bank" (Adjei et al. 2014: 48). However, in Ghana and elsewhere, advocates of structural adjustment reforms relied on racialized constructions of African governments as somehow "uniquely dysfunctional" and corrupt to argue that state spending, policy and officials needed to be disciplined (Wilson 2012: 136, 141). In a 1994 interview with the *Los Angeles Times*, one Ghanaian official lamented, "At times you feel you are giving away your sovereignty and your independence. You wonder if it's not going too far, especially when some of their [World Bank and IMF] staff take on this patronizing approach to Africa—the impression that we can't get our act together and that they have to step in and set everything right" (Darton 1994).

The same article interviewed "27-year-old lawyer, writer and ardent feminist" Monique Ilboudo, who, while "sipping a drink in the marched shade of a baobab tree in Ouagadougou," described the "World Bank as some kind of monster. It sits on top of Africa like an octopus, sucking us dry. It never looks to see the effects on the lives of the people. It treats us like numbers, economic agents" (Darton 1994).

On the ground, structural adjustment policies radically altered everyday life for many Ghanaians. Prior to structural adjustment, Ghana's agricultural sector had received considerable public support. However, agricultural subsidies and services were slashed under structural adjustment (Benin 2019), which, combined with "excessive devaluation of the Ghanaian currency[,] ... reduced ... purchasing power dramatically" (Konadu-Agyemang 2000: 480; Ewusi 1989: 26–27; Pearce 1992: 42). The slashing of agricultural subsidies was a significant breech from the Nkrumah-days of state farms and subsidized inputs. Importantly for the larger story of GMOs and global plant breeding collaborations, state disinvestment during the structural adjustment era had considerable impacts on agricultural research and breeding efforts. For instance, the state-run entity entreated with breeding and disseminating seeds, the Ghana Seed Company, "was closed down, restructured and divested in 1989," leaving "seed growers (previously) employed by the state" to instead be "self-employed seed breeders contracted by the state to provide seeds" (Amanor 2019a: 46).

As the example of the Ghana Seed Company suggests, structural adjustment in Ghana (as elsewhere) was not a clean nor clear-cut process. Furthermore, as Kojo Amanor argues, to simply describe the era of structural adjustment as one of "privatization" misses the way in which the neoliberal reforms transformed the agricultural sector, further enmeshed Ghanaian scientists—and farmers—into global markets, and situated Ghana as a site for global capital:

> agricultural divestiture is not essentially about the transfer of state farms to private farmers, but the gradual transformation of state agricultural research services into integrated units that can be subsumed under international agribusiness, or which create the space to facilitate the growth of international agribusiness. (1999: 41)

Indeed, as the Ghanaian state exited the agricultural sector, donors, along with their industry partners, entered.

One project whose legacy echoes throughout the countryside is Sasakawa Global 2000 (SG 2000). In the early 1980s, Ryoichi Sasakawa, a Japanese businessman who made his fortunes from boat racing, was "shaken by the sight of famine in [Ethiopia]," and decided to allocate his philanthropy's resources toward improving agriculture on the wider continent (Sasakawa Africa Association 2015: 21).[6] With a desire to bring similar changes he had witnessed in Asia and Latin America during the Green Revolution, he sought out American scientist and Green Revolution pioneer Norman Borlaug and "asked him whether such a revolution could . . . be achieved in sub-Saharan Africa" (Sasakawa Africa Association 2015: 19). Initially, Borlaug hesitated, replying, "I don't know anything about sub-Saharan Africa and I'm too old to do anything about it" (Brinkley 1996: 57). But Sasakawa wasn't deterred. As the story goes, the next day Sasakawa apparently replied, "I'm 13 years older than you are, Dr. Borlaug. The central African initiative should have been done much sooner. No excuses; let's get to work" (Brinkley 1996: 57). Soon after, the two joined forces with US president Jimmy Carter, and in 1986, SG 2000 was born.

At the urging of Borlaug, and the invitation of then Ghanaian president Jerry John Rawlings, SG 2000 "opened its first office in [Ghana] . . . [with] two agronomists" from Mexico at the helm (Brinkley 1996: 59; Sasakawa Africa Association 2015: 25). Given that Borlaug "viewed food insecurity in sub-Saharan Africa as fundamentally a problem of inadequate food production" (Sasakawa Africa Association 2015: 22), SG 2000 followed a similar framework of the first Green Revolution: donors advocated for the use of "high yielding seeds, moderate amounts of chemical fertilizer [and] improved planting[, weeding, and insect control] methods" (Ewusi 1989: 29; Sasakawa Africa Association 2015: 22). To convince farmers to adopt these new technologies, project facilitators established over one hundred thousand demonstration plots across the country (Sasakawa Africa Association 2015: 48) and offered inputs (seeds and chemicals) on loan, to be paid later "in cash or in kind at harvest time" (Ewusi 1989: 29). These demonstration plots are memorable: over the years I have encountered people throughout Ghana who told me Jimmy Carter had a farm in their hometown.

Officials believed that chemical inputs—like fertilizer and herbicide—would help farmers improve not only their yields but also environmental stewardship. Fertilizer, officials believed, could be an alternative to slash and burn cultivation, which they viewed as environmentally destructive. In an interview, Jimmy Carter justified SG 2000's use of chemical fertilizer through a blunt dismissal of African knowledge and farming practices: "It's impossible to get people in poverty to worry about environmental issues. [So,] first we try to show the farmers how to triple or even quadruple production of grain per acre. When we show a direct benefit to the people, that gives them enough confidence to listen to environmental discussions" (Brinkley 1996: 57). Similar to discourse from colonial administrators and early Ghanaian agriculturalists, Carter constructed African farmers as poor environmental stewards and in need of planning for. SG 2000 was an intervention, not a collaboration.

In addition to chemical fertilizer, SG 2000's rollout in Ghana included a partnership with the CSIR-Crops Research Institute and US agri-giant Monsanto. Together, the two "advised [farmers] to buy" Monsanto's glyphosate herbicide Roundup "even though it was more expensive than other presentations" (Ekboir et al. 2002: 27; Boafo and Lyons 2021). Though officials hoped farmers would buy Roundup to reduce manual labor, the cost proved to be prohibitive, especially as cheaper products from China entered the market (Amanor 2019b: 15).

Though only briefly summarized here, Sasakawa Global 2000 is an early example of the types of philanthropic, humanitarian, and industry collaborations that mark the neoliberal era of agricultural development. Scrutinizing SG 2000 also provides insights into the types of legacies that such projects leave behind. For example, a friend of mine, Suraj, clearly recalls when Sasakawa Global 2000 came to his community just outside of Tamale, the agricultural and administrative hub of the Northern Region. Though Suraj was just a boy at the time, he remembered his father and uncles eagerly joining the project. Using the seed and fertilizer provided by SG 2000, Suraj's family initially experienced high yields: "The short-term glories were very good, everyone was hailing, 'Fertilizer has come! At long last farmers can breathe!'" Suraj explained that given the foreignness of the project, farmers initially trusted Sasakawa officials and inputs: "Now, as we said, the white man brought the fertilizer. You brought the oburoni fertilizer! And they said, 'Oh, this thing is coming from oburoni, it's good, it's good.' So they hailed it, and welcomed it." But after a short period of time, Suraj remembers, the project transitioned and fertilizer became expensive. Many, including Suraj's family, were unable to afford fertilizer, either upfront or in kind after harvest. Without cash to purchase inputs, Suraj's family found that the fertilizer that had once provided such good yields had left the soil weak from its use. The soil, Suraj told me, never recovered, and he considers his father and uncles worse off than before.

Suraj's story echoes what other researchers have found regarding SG 2000. Though initially farmers participating in SG 2000 programs reported high maize yields, Hanson Nyantakyi-Frimpong and Rachel Bezner Kerr (2015) note that problems regarding loan repayment and soil fertility emerged just a few years into the program.[7] By the program's own accounting, one issue was that maize yields were *too* high, in that supply outpaced demand. Worried that "an oversupply of maize to the local market could depress the prices being received by farmers," Borlaug "urged [Ghanaian officials] to cut back on the number of demonstration plots in maize and to . . . include other important food crops for which improved technology existed" (Sasakawa Africa Association 2015: 31).

As a result, the following year officials announced a drastic decision: they would no longer direct funds to maize demonstration plots. Once the star of the program, maize farmers were now left in a lurch without support to purchase inputs for the upcoming growing season. After an uproar from farmers and extension agents, the Agricultural Development Bank (AfDB) of Ghana decided to step in and offer loans for maize farmers participating in SG 2000 (Sasakawa Africa Association 2015: 32). But there was one problem. Previously, in-kind loans through SG 2000 were partially subsidized through the Ghanaian government. But those "elements of subsidy were removed in the 1990s," and subsequently "loan recovery faltered" (Amanor 2019b: 15; Al-Hassan and Poulton 2009: 12). In 1990, nearly 60 percent of farmers defaulted on their loans (Sasakawa Africa Association 2015: 32).

Sasakawa Global 2000 was just one of many projects/NGOs that has attempted to shape the Ghanaian countryside over the past decades. While interviewing farmers in the Bono East and Upper East regions, many shared vivid recollections of their introductions to chemical fertilizer. Under the shade of a mango tree, John shared a story similar to Suraj's. A farmer and an evangelist, John inherited his land—about twenty-five acres in the far Upper East Region—from his father, who taught him how to farm. John, now sixty-five, told me about chemical fertilizer arriving in his community:

> I still remember the time my father was alive, the whites, they will bring the fertilizers, . . . I remember, it was one agriculturalist . . . from Holland. He was working the Agric station in Garu, he was the station manager there. Then he even started with my fathers, training them how to do this Agric . . . So, before he brought them newly to test and see, he said we should take for free. So, it was free.

Fertilizers remained free for a few years thereafter. With fertilizer, John's father and uncles were achieving higher yields than before—"plenty harvest!" But, like Suraj's story, the free fertilizer ride soon ended. After a few years, the Dutch supplier began to sell fertilizer through the local church for 20 pesewas (US$0.05) a bag: "Every year, the man will bring with the car, and they were in groups, the church members, you send it to them. And they were able to influence others of the goodness of the fertilizers [laughs]—it was very harmonious! [laughs] *That* was marketing!"

A few miles down the road, Maebel, an elderly widow and grandmother, had a similar story about her introduction to fertilizer: "When they brought the fertilizer, they said some white people brought it for the government to give to farmers." She recalled feeling misled: "When they introduced fertilizer, they deceived us that it was free. We started applying it on our farms and after some time, they said we had to buy it." Eventually, both John and Maebel stopped being able to afford fertilizer to cover the entirety of their farms. John described his soil as "dead," killed by what he described as an "addiction to" chemical fertilizers. At the time of our meeting, he was embarking on his tenth year of attempting to rehabilitate his soil.

While we don't know whether John and Maebel participated in the SG 2000 program, their stories, along with Suraj's, track with larger research on fertilizer and soil fertility in northern Ghana. Writing on soil fertility in the Ashanti and Northern Regions, two areas where SG 2000 was active, a report by IFPRI describes farmers as "unanimous in their views about yield trends, indicating that land was very fertile in the 1980s, no fertilizer was used, and yields were very good, and at least sufficient to meet their subsistence needs" (Johnson et al. 2019: 150). Though "little inorganic fertilizer was used in the 1980s, . . . today its use is widespread, largely because the fertility of most of the farmed lands has declined" (Johnson et al. 2019: 149). In both the Ashanti and Northern Regions, inorganic fertilizer application nearly quadrupled between 1998 and 2012 (Johnson et al. 2019: 150).

The narratives presented here, as well as countless others in my notes, all had common themes: that agricultural modernization attempts—whether technology, inputs, or value chain schemes—had come and disappointed. In some cases, interlocutors described their experiences as Suraj and John did, as explicitly racialized ones. Whereas colonial propaganda booklets like *Kofi the Good Farmer* suggest a harmonious relationship between farmer, technology, and (colonial) expert, the stories I heard throughout Ghana suggest a legacy of disappointment, confusion, and distrust.

The Growth of NGOs in the Countryside

Structural adjustment reforms mandated that the Ghanaian state withdraw their support from social services. But the private sector did not simply step in. Huge gaps were left in areas such as education, health, and social work. These very real needs, coupled with characterizations of African governments as unable to fulfill them, created an opening. To fill it, donors and financial institutions positioned non-governmental organizations (NGOs) as "vanguards of civil society and as more dependable partners in economic and social development" (Laird 2007: 470). In Ghana, the rapid growth of NGOs was remarkable. From 1990 to 1996 alone, the number of registered NGOs almost tripled from 350 to 900, and between 2004 and 2011 the list of registered NGOs grew from 3,000 to nearly 5,000 (Laid 2007: 470; WASCI 2005: 25).

The rapid growth of NGOs reverberated across the country. Tamale, the city Suraj grew up outside of, became not only the administrative hub of the Northern Region, but also of NGOs serving Ghana's northern zone. By the mid-2000s, Tamale had earned double titles of the "fastest growing city" in West Africa and the "Headquarters of NGOs in Ghana" (Ziem 2013). Today, a dizzying number of NGOs and donors are operating at any given time in Tamale and, indeed, across much of the country (Vercillo 2020). Some funders, like USAID, contract out large projects to US-based organizations, who in turn are tasked with forging relationships and collaborations with other NGOs, industry partners, and state institutions. The following passage from Kojo Amanor provides a sense of the complex number of actors that might be active in any given project:

> In 2008, the Ghana Grains Partnership was established between private sector input suppliers, including YARA and Wienco, the African Enterprise Challenge Fund, farmer organizations organized by Wienco, the NGO Technoserve, the Ministry of Food and Agriculture, commercial banks, and food processors and retailers to provide farmers with credits and packages of inputs and seeds. These established a farmers' association, Masara N'arziki, in the three northern regions and Brong Ahafo [now Bono East]. Farmers entered into contract agreements with Wienco and YARA, which specify the terms under which farmers are provided with access to inputs and conditions of repayment. The seeds supplied under the programme were Pannar hybrid seeds from South Africa (Guyver & MacCarthy, 2011). With the takeover of Pannar by Dupont Pioneer, a new partnership has developed among USAID, the US NGO ACDI/VOCA, and [Dupont Pioneer] to actively promote the uptake of Pannar varieties in Ghana. Building upon the Ghana Grains Partnership, this also uses farmer associations to build market avenues and contractual arrangements. (2019a: 46)

I discuss details of USAID and DuPont Pioneer's work in Ghana later, but my point here is twofold. First, as the examples of SG 2000 and the Ghana Grains Partnership demonstrate, agricultural development projects in Ghana are sites of global convergence of funding, capital, and labor.

Second, there are broad, historical arcs connecting efforts to transform the Ghanaian countryside across time and space. *Making agriculture a business*—the pinpoint of the "new" Green Revolution in Africa, the crux of Dr. Adesina's writings, and a core focus of Ghanaian scientists—has long been a goal of officials in Ghana. And while fertilizer schemes of the 1980s live in the memory of many, there have been dozens, if not more, of major agricultural initiatives carried out by donors over the past forty years. The Ghana Grains Partnership, mentioned earlier, is one. The Millennium Village Project, a four-year, $15 million, 3,900 household project—with contested, if any, impact—was another (Masset et al. 2020). Feed the Future, President Obama's ambitious food security program, funded multiple projects in Ghana that targeted commercial crops like maize, rice, and soybean (Boafo and Lyons 2021). The list of major initiatives and actors is long, and when large state initiatives are added, the list becomes even longer.

As the number of NGOs and projects expanded throughout the country, so, too, did a particular type of neoliberal discourse, one that put responsibility—and blame—on citizens for improving their conditions, and one that dangled "modernity" as the opposite of tradition (Hausermann 2018; Hodžić 2017; Li 2007). Yet, as I've noted throughout this chapter, discourse that blamed individuals—their actions, knowledge, and technology—for their supposed lack of development is not unique to the neoliberal era; there is a direct arc from the precolonial era through today. For instance, writing on her work with NGOs in Ghana's northern regions, Saida Hodžić noted how government agencies characterized inequalities in the north:

> governmental regimes have winnowed the pool of explanations for northern scarcity and regional inequality down to the notions of "harsh environment" and "patriarchal traditions," or what we might refer to as "harsh culture." Northerners are hungry, officials say, because they hold on to traditional food taboos; their land is infertile because they are hostile to their own environment, burning and overpopulating it. (2017: 117–18)

Similar pathologies are found in Ghanaian social studies textbooks, where Ghanaian pupils learn that "poor countries do not change fast because they do not assimilate and use new ideas and new ways from other cultures that will help improve their way of life as fast as possible" (quoted in Rock 2018a). In the Aki-Ola Series *Social Studies for Senior High Schools*, first printed in 1999, students learn about "problems of agriculture" that impact "economic life," including "unwillingness to accept new technologies: due to illiteracy and ignorance on the part of the farmers, farmers still use old tools like cutlass and hoes and are not prepared to use fertilizers for higher yields" (2014: 201).

The excerpts from Hodžić and state social studies curricula are uncomfortably similar to discourse that circulated during the colonial and immediate postcolonial eras.[8] Thus, it would be inadequate to suggest that development discourse in Ghana is a product of just that—development. Instead, through examining texts across a large span of time, we find that discourse about African farmers as lazy, destructive, unprepared, and techno-skeptical are more familiar than strange. Such a blame obfuscates political economy and structural inequalities. For despite "more than half a century of pursuing . . . [similar] agricultural intensification initiatives, there continues to be deepening inequalities between northern and southern Ghana," inequalities that cannot be simply explained away as lack of trying on the part of farmers (Nyantakyi-Frimpong and Bezner Kerr 2015: 18–19). Such inequities—and histories—featured heavily in conversations I had with farmers throughout northern Ghana.

Recipient Fatigue in the Countryside

When I set out to conduct research in Ghana's northern regions, it was not necessarily to learn about the history of agricultural development over the decades. Not initially, at least. As part of my research with Ghana Association of Food Producers (GAFP), I decided to conduct a month of research with some of the group's farming base in the Bono East and Upper East Regions. I chose to focus on these two areas because they were geographically and agriculturally different, and because GAFP considered them member strongholds. My goal was not to conduct a comprehensive study, or compile profiles of farmers (for this has, and continues to, be done by many excellent scholars). Rather, my goal was to understand GAFP's farmer base and if and how their advocacy was representative of those they purported to serve. I worked with GAFP to identify a few of their membership strongholds and connected with GAFP leaders in those areas: Aunty Sarah in Bono East, and Mohammed, a GAFP board member, in the Upper East. I was joined by Francis, my friend and research assistant. I had planned to spend two weeks each in Bono East and Upper East, but ended up spending just one in Upper East due to research complications. With a question guide in hand, we set out to interview people about their farms (size, crops and vegetables grown, strategies they used for combating pests, weeds, and soil infertility), the weather, food taste and preference, and chemical use. We soon learned people were tired of such questions.

Aunty Sarah, who lived in Kintampo and whose family lived throughout the surrounding area, was our guide in Bono East. In addition to having a farm outside of Kintampo, Aunty Sarah also had a cosmetics side-business. Climate change, she said, had forced her to look elsewhere for income, but also for new technologies to assist with the lack of rain she and her neighbors were experiencing. While we were there, she was trying to negotiate the purchase of solar-powered borehole pumps for herself and her neighbors. Given her family ties, Aunty Sarah knew the area intimately, and suggested that we first start our research in a community about a five-minute drive outside of Kintampo. But first, she explained, we would need to get permission from the town assemblyman.

We met the assemblyman on a sunny morning. He welcomed us to begin research, but first, he said, we would need to have a town meeting. An announcement in Twi was made over a loudspeaker in the center of town, close to the taxi stand. Francis started laughing; apparently the announcer said that we had arrived and everyone "should stop whatever they're doing and come now!" Eventually, close to forty people gathered, and it was time to begin. After a group prayer and introductions by Aunty Sarah, Francis, and myself, the floor was open. At first, the group debated the best time for us to come for interviews—either early in the day before folks left for the farm, or later, once people had returned home. After a few minutes of deliberation, a man indicated his desire to speak. He told us that the town had seen plenty of researchers and nothing so far had come out of it. So, he said, the community would be hoping to see quick results from my research. Before I had time to react, Aunty Sarah jumped in and explained that we were doing academic research, the results of which would take time to emerge. The man seemed unconvinced.

Over the next few days, we walked through the community in the evening after people had returned from the farm, sampling every other house. On our second day conducting interviews, we ran into Mr. Boateng, a fifty-six-year-old farmer who was born and raised in town. We had met him the day before when we interviewed his mother. We stopped and chatted with him for a while. He mentioned that in the early 1990s, a white woman who worked for an NGO had lived in town for a bit. I recognized the name of the NGO immediately and my mouth dropped—it was the same organization my mom had previously been employed with (albeit a decade later). The following day while walking through town, a man approached Francis and I and asked if we were an NGO. It took me a moment to understand that I was a walking embodiment of an NGO, a nebulous term used to describe any sort of organization that worked generally within the realm of "development." We told him we were not, and he was disappointed; he needed funds to prepare for the planting season. We apologized and went our separate ways. In one interview, a long-time resident ended our conversation with a word of caution:

> People [have] been coming here now as you are here now. They'll be asking the questions and you'll be answering them. They will give you promise, they are going

A dusty road. Francis Adi Sabara sits near the road adjacent to Matthias's home, which had recently been expanded by a political candidate.

to come, but when they go, they don't come. They don't even turn and see whether the questions they've asked have been helping or not. And so, you too, are you doing the same thing, or . . . ?

Though I had naively thought of my position of a researcher as distinct from that of an employee of an NGO, these interactions told me that I was wrong. Rather, they all pointed to the obvious: that my arrival was not the first time an oburoni had come to town, asked questions and taken up people's time, and then left. In pointing this out, folks like Mr. Boateng flipped the script and put me on the spot, interrogating my intentions and forcing me to grapple with my role in continuing the extractive relationship between researcher/NGO/outsider and communities. Such moments became constellations in my field notes, pointing to a larger ecosystem of the ways the countryside and the people who work and live within it had been altered by decades of attempted "development." This legacy shaped how people viewed the state and the development apparatus, for the two are intrinsically bound (Ferguson 1994). The story about how the road next to Matthias's home came to be exemplifies this.

After a week working in and around Kintampo, Francis and I traveled to a nearby town. There, Aunty Sarah introduced us to Matthias, who would become our guide for his community and the surrounding area. Matthias had spent most of his life outside the community, working various jobs in Kintampo and Bolgatanga over the years. It was after his father's death that he returned to his hometown and took over his familial farm. Matthias spoke fast and with conviction, never shy to share an opinion.

Francis and I spent many days sitting with Matthias near the road adjacent to his home. This road was important, as it connected all the towns in the area with Kintampo, an economic hub about a forty-minute drive away. And as with any infrastructural project, especially those in rural areas, this road was the site of hot political contestation. Primary elections for Parliament had recently been held, and, according to Matthias, two hopefuls of the ruling National Democratic Congress (NDC) had campaigned hard in the area. As part of his campaign promise, one candidate hired Caterpillar tractors to widen the road, felling trees and kicking up dust as they went along. His shoddy work would cost him the campaign. Shortly after the road was widened, the First Lady of Ghana drove through the area with a caravan of SUVs whose speed kicked up clouds of dust. She was apparently so disturbed by the dust that she went straight to Kintampo and had the district chief executive, who happened to be the same candidate who hired the tractors to grate the road in the first place, fired for such shoddy work.

The remaining NDC candidate's victory in the general election was almost guaranteed, as her opponent from the New Patriotic Party (NPP) was missing in action. His absence was due to a scandal rocking the nation; the candidate was part of the "God Is Love Fun Club," a pyramid scheme (or, as Matthias referred to it, a "microfinance syndicate") that had stolen money from hundreds of clients (MyJoy-Online 2016). However, not complacent in her de-facto victory, the NDC candidate decided to dig a borehole and pump to make a final point to the community that she was a worthy candidate. On the day the pump was inaugurated, Matthias told us, "not a single drop of water" came out. It now sits with a bag over the top, like a hood of shame. Between this and the Major Development Organization borehole, Matthias and his neighbors have limited access to water.

Matthias used this road to orient us to the everyday realities farmers work within. The hours passed and we watched life go by: neighbors came and went, young men with rifles strapped on their backs drove by on motorbikes (hunters, Matthias told us), and timber trucks rattled past (Francis swore he could hear the sound of distant chainsaws). Occasionally, a neighbor or visitor would stop by. In one instance, a state agricultural extension officer arrived by motorbike and greeted a neighbor across the street. He turned around sheepishly, saw Matthias, and quickly sped off. I asked about this odd behavior, and Matthias explained the officer had forged his signature on papers saying Matthias had completed a donor-sponsored training. The trainings never took place.

Extension officers like this one were a point of ire for Amina, Matthias's neighbor. As we sat talking outside her home, she told us how some years back "Agric"—a term used interchangeably to refer to both state and private extension officers or NGO officials—came to town promoting beans they promised would produce "three bowls" of yield, high yielding compared to other beans available. For those who wished to take part in the project, the Agric officers provided farmers with beans and fertilizer on credit. However, as luck would have it, the rains were bad that year, and for many, yields were disastrous. Amina harvested not more than a fourth of a bowl of beans. She is now skeptical of Agric and wants nothing to do with their technologies. Amina's neighbor, Ama, said it's for this reason that she does not speak with Agric extension officers: "When they bring seeds for us to plant and we grow and the seeds don't grow, they demand money from us. That is why we don't talk to them."[9] Agric "are criminals!" another neighbor stated emphatically.

Amina's story highlights the complexities of farming in a rapidly changing climate. For she is first dealing with erratic weather patterns and uncertain rains. Many Ghanaian farmers, like Amina, rely mainly on rain to water their farms. This fact, and lack of irrigation or other sort of water supplies, make adopting new technologies that require application of certain levels of water and potentially other agrochemicals—such as the fabled beans—risky business (Boafo and Lyons 2021; Nyantakyi-Frimpong and Bezner Kerr 2015). Moreover, as Amina suggests, climate change and neoliberal capitalism have brought another uncertain element into the mix: Agric. Though the flexibility of the term sometimes makes it difficult to know exactly who the speaker is referring to (state extension officer? NGO official? Agribusiness representative?), the interchangeability of the word suggests the speaker is more interested in evaluating one's outsider-ness than their actual title. While the term "Agric" is often used to denote someone who possesses some sort of "expertise," the speaker does not always (positively or negatively) evaluate said expertise.[10]

In addition to providing—either through sale or sample—new technologies/commodities, Agric officers are also known in town to organize workshops and other events. Across the road from Amina, we met Opoku, a senior high school graduate who had opted to farm with his father rather than continue schooling. Opoku told us about an article that was recently published in the local newspaper. The article detailed a workshop held by local agricultural extension officers that supposedly trained farmers on high-yielding seeds. To his surprise, Opoku's father's name and signature printed in the paper, indicating he was a workshop participant. However, his father never attended the training, nor signed a paper signaling that he did.

Trainings and workshops are events where people come into contact with what we might consider the "development" apparatus (Hodžić 2017: 96). It is here, at gatherings led by so-called experts, where farmers meet in offices, on fields, and in hotel conference rooms, and development materials circulate. Such materials might be printed handouts like the ones Matthias keeps in three-ring binders, t-shirts, or the cash *soli* participants receive at the end to reimburse their transportation costs, and then some. Often, a workshop organizer will identify a junior officer or intern to take photos of the event, to be later uploaded to social media accounts and web pages to show donor funds were well used.

Such events were also the object of critique of some of my interlocutors. One day, Aunty Sarah invited me to meet her and some fellow farmers in Kintampo. She had just returned from a workshop where she learned about a national fund that allocates returns from the state oil company to the agricultural sector. The most painful thing, she said, was that the fund was going into training as opposed to programming.

"Training for what?" she asked the group.

"Empowerment!"

"Capacity building!" Two male farmers shouted out, shaking their heads.

One followed up: "After you have built capacity, then what?" The group continued joking, code-switching between English and Twi. At one point, the group erupted in laughter. I had missed the joke, but Francis filled me in: "the Flagstaff House [the presidential office in Accra] has sprinklers for ordinary grass, but won't provide [them] for food. It is beautiful and we are hungry."

From jokes to stories, we heard time and again stories of agricultural interventions gone astray. In fact, tales of failed development projects were often the first narratives farmers would share, a warning, perhaps, to us strangers who were asking them for their time. I approached such stories not as claims that needed necessarily to be verified, but rather as *moral geographies*—reflections of a speaker's understanding and evaluation of the world around them—stories that live and operate in community imagination and discourse (Gombay 2010; Leap 2010; Thomas 2002). Moreover, as these stories accumulated over time, and as my interviews began to reach saturation, it became clear that these experiences were essential for understanding the other types of questions I was asking, of seeds, of farming techniques, of crops.

Now, to be sure, not every initiative, project, or technology failed. For example, *Obaatanpa*, one of the most widely grown maize varieties in Ghana today, was developed in 1992 by a joint initiative between the state research council and Consultative Group on International Agricultural Research (CGIAR) centers, and distributed in part by SG 2000 (Poku et al. 2018; Ragasa et al. 2013; Sasakawa Africa Association 2015). Nor am I suggesting that there isn't value in analyzing particular projects. Instead, considering the legacy of development projects as moral geographies allows us to take farmers' stories at face value. For in discussing failed development projects or disappointing NGOs, farmers were placing their farms, their lives, their experiences, within larger histories and political economies. In other words, jokes about the presidential palace, stories about evangelizing fertilizer purveyors, and remarks about seeds that don't grow were more than simply discursive moments; they were farmers insisting that I redirect my inquiry to focus on the structures in which they were entangled.

Such moral geographies take a particular salience in the context of the international development industry, wherein professionals talk often of "donor fatigue." The phrase has multiple uses and meanings, one of which is to connote the hesitancy of donors to continue making investments into projects or initiatives that they feel have so far produced small or undesired returns. And yet what I experienced throughout my travels throughout agrarian Ghana was almost the opposite, or perhaps the different side of the same coin: the fatigue of the communities who are on the receiving end of donor projects and funding, or what I came to term *recipient fatigue*. This became apparent in small acts of refusal that popped up in the field; some farmers denied interview requests, while others told me they were hesitant because they had talked to outsiders like myself many times before and participated in projects with NGOs, and yet nothing had come out of it.

These small moments of refusal were generative (Simpson 2007: 78; McGranahan 2016). Through them, I began to notice how farmers—and later activists, scientists, development officials, and so on—worked on and against dominant political, economic, and ideological structures they found themselves in. In other words, many Ghanaians I encountered were engaged in *disidentification*, opting "neither... to assimilate within such a structure nor strictly [oppose] it" (Muñoz 1999:11; Althusser 1971; Pêcheux 1982). Ashanté Reese (2019a, 2019b) asks how ethnographers might think about refusal as care, both from the point of the interlocutor and the ethnographer. I read people's hesitancy to speak to me as a refusal to be a part of the larger extractive oburoni system of both past and present. Such refusal reflected of everyday realities, which, in the areas I moved throughout, was influenced, understood, and organized by development and its discontents. In a sense, Matthias and others—who collect physical, emotional, and historical mementos of empty promises and outcomes—were expressing recipient fatigue, opting out, even if momentarily, of a system that they deemed was not working for them, of a system that had proved too risky in the past to continue in the present (Simpson 2007). This fatigue, I soon found, also underscored the work of Ghanaian activists, scientists, and officials in the cities of Accra, Kumasi, and beyond.

Conclusion

"This one will come with a different topic, and this one will come with a different topic, but you won't see them again," Matthias said, in reference to NGOs and other actors engaged in agricultural development work. We were sitting outside his home, surrounded by old workshop handouts, signboards, and flyers he had pulled out of storage to make his point. "So, at times, when they come like this, the farmers are fed up. 'Yɛabrɛ.'" We are tired.

In this chapter, I set out to establish a number of historical legacies that permeate everyday life in contemporary Ghana. For, as I and my interlocutors argue throughout the book, agricultural modernization—whether as a set of discourses, goals, or technologies—cannot be understood without a long view of the destruction and changes slaving, colonialism, and neoliberalism have left in their wake. Rather than considering these as three distinct eras, in this chapter I have instead shown how they are deeply interconnected. I focused particularly on discourse, and the ways in which state officials (from colonial inspectors to scientists), donors, and outside experts view and talk about farmers. In doing so, I was able to establish one of the themes that weaves its way throughout a long history of agricultural modernization in Ghana: a discourse of farmers as lazy, skeptical of new technologies, and unreasonable. This discourse can be traced from colonial nutrition reports to contemporary social studies textbooks.

In establishing this long discursive arc, I set out to do four things. First, to provide historical background to the comments and conversations that line the remainder of this book, and to show how colonial legacies are present in everyday life. Second, and relatedly, establishing a longitudinal discursive arc challenges the category of "development discourse" or even neoliberal discourse as unique and/or standing on its own. Instead, in demonstrating how discourses present in the current neoliberal, development-focused present are direct descendants of the colonial era, I argue that such discourse is more familiar than strange.

Third, I sought to challenge discourse of the "new" Green Revolution in Africa as being just that: new. While proponents utilize a discourse that Africa was left out of the first Green Revolution (Annan 2004), as this chapter has shown, there have been many iterations of attempts to make agriculture a business, and to spark a Green Revolution, in Ghana throughout the past century. However, these attempts—including SG 2000, which was spearheaded by the "father" of the Green Revolution himself, Norman Borlaug—are obfuscated in contemporary narratives of the "new" Green Revolution.

And finally, I demonstrated how the legacy of the state looms deep. As farmers and rural Ghanaians made clear, even in its absence, the state is always present. Busted roads and wells from a MP race, the largely unregulated movement of NGOs in the countryside, and fertilizer subsidy schemes are all routine reminders of the state. However, unrealized promises of development have resulted in an increasingly skeptical populace. Interviews, observation, and refusal revealed that, for many, modernization ventures have been bad business for Ghanaian farmers. This history has resulted in a countryside of fatigued so-called recipients of development aid. Such concerns were only magnified with the arrival of genetically modified seeds.

CHAPTER 2

From Peasantry to Prosperity

On a sunny day in December 2015, the Ghana Association of Food Producers (GAFP) held a year-end conference at the Gold Star Beach Hotel.[1] Nestled against the Gulf of Guinea, the hotel is both luxurious and massive, and is popular with weekend revelers, travelers, and conference hosts alike. Boasting a nationwide membership base and over a decade of work, GAFP occupies a unique space in the Accra development scene. They are at once a fierce lobbying force for the nation's farmers, but also enjoy strong relationships with some of the country's top donor and civil society groups. It was GAFP who introduced me to the development world of Accra and provided an "in" for the Food Sovereignty Platform. For close to a year, I spent three to five days a week in their headquarters in Accra assisting with their online presence in exchange for permission to conduct participant observation and interviews in their office, at events, and on trips throughout agrarian Ghana.

The association's December meeting was an important convergence. They had invited many of the association's "stakeholders" to the Gold Star—farmers, government officials, NGO representatives, and allied organizations—to share findings from their annual report. Over one hundred participants filled long tables, each seat denoted by a complimentary folder, pad of paper, writing instrument, water bottle, and small candies to pass the time. A handful of farmers sat at the front of the large ballroom, guests of honor for the day. Organizers buzzed around, making last-minute changes and adjustments, anticipating the arrival of the keynote speaker, the minister for food and agriculture. Ministers and dignitaries are often invited to events like these, but don't always attend. Today was to be different; the organizers were told the minister was *actually* coming.

Sure enough, forty minutes after the program was slated to begin, a police officer entered the room with the minister in tow. Constance, GAFP's head program officer, rushed to a podium in the front of the ballroom and excitedly announced the minister's arrival. To her dismay, the audience showed little fanfare, and she mimicked toward the crowd, encouraging us to clap. Some complied but most sat silently. I leaned to Kwesi, a program officer at GAFP, and whispered, "We have to ask people to clap for the minister?"

"Can you imagine?" he responded, apparently more dismayed than I was.

Undeterred, the minister delivered his keynote. He spoke broadly about the "new" Green Revolution theme of making agriculture a business. The minister acknowledged that agricultural growth was lower than the government desired—a point GAFP and many others agreed with—but attributed limited growth to the weather. While there's no doubt that changing weather patterns and climatic events were mounting challenges for farmers (Antwi-Agyei et al. 2012; Kumasi et al. 2019), this explanation was largely unsatisfactory for those at the Gold Star. Many groups and representatives gathered there, not least GAFP, spent a considerable amount of time and budget lobbying government for increased spending in the agricultural sector, the passage—or delay—of legislation that would impact farmer livelihoods, and a general re-investment in the sector, which had yet to recover from the structural adjustment era. These themes, or even an acknowledgment of this work, were largely absent from the minister's comments. The minister concluded by telling farmers they should not expect only the government to "bring changes," but rather "accept issues that we can resolve on our own." He continued: "Mindset change must happen, so that we can change from peasant farmers to prosperous farmers."

The audience sat quietly and a tense air reverberated around the room. Had the minister really just come to an event organized by a farmers' association and rather than acknowledge them, engage with them, or even thank them, had instead chastised them? A cruel irony hit as someone's cell phone began to ring with the whistling intro to Bobby McFerrin's "Don't Worry, Be Happy." Soon after, the minister finished his remarks and left the stage. The audience again provided little applause, remaining quietly in their seats.

Indeed, as already demonstrated, implications that farmers are lazy (evidenced by the minister's inference that farmers wait on government) or in need of "mindset change," are more standard than they are strange. In spite of this, GAFP was an ardent believer in the state. It was the ministry, not donors, that organizations like GAFP wanted to see take the reins of the country's agricultural development. For, as previously discussed, the heyday of state agricultural interventions under Kwame Nkrumah was thought by many to be a pinnacle of state success. On the flip side, many Ghanaians also felt that close to forty years of concentrated donor "interventions" had little to show, and that continued donor investment was an embarrassment to the state, an indication that the promise of decolonization was yet to be achieved.

There was another tension that the minister did not acknowledge, a tension that might help explain both his comments and the cool audience response. And that is, by the time of the Gold Star meeting, GAFP was locked in a contentious multiyear battle with the ministry and other state institutions over the arrival of genetically modified crops and a piece of legislation entitled the Plant Breeders Bill. The bill was designed to establish intellectual property rights (IPRs) for plant breeders, a long-term goal of both the state and its development donors. For it is IPRs, along with other liberalization schemes, that organizations like the Ministry of Food and Agriculture, the US Agency for International Development (USAID), and the Bill & Melinda Gates Foundation (BMGF) believe are key to sparking a "new" Green Revolution in Africa.

In Ghana, the Plant Breeders Bill was just one example of the many legal and policy mechanisms the state—and donors—envisioned would help move farmers from "peasantry to prosperity." The Plant Breeders Bill, Plants and Fertilizer Act, and the Biosafety Act are essential for understanding the story of genetically modified organisms (GMOs) in Ghana. Together and apart, these three policies significantly reconfigured Ghanaian legal and agricultural landscapes in a relatively short amount of time. While the structural adjustment era began the dismantling of state agricultural systems and subsidies, the project of liberalization has continued long after. Key to this project has been the creation of *boosters*, new organizations whose missions were to build public and political support for biotechnology and sometimes act as intermediaries between donors, national governments, and industry. Thus, while much of the literature on GMOs in Africa focuses on what the outcomes of growing genetically modified (GM) crops might bring, I draw attention here to the changes already well underway, ones that will last regardless of whether GMOs ever reach Ghanaian farmers (Rock and Schurman 2020).

Creating an Enabling Environment

In the summer of 2013, Marietta Brew Appiah-Oppong, Ghana's minister of justice and attorney general, submitted a piece of legislation entitled the Plant Breeders Bill for the consideration of Ghanaian Parliament. The bill had been developed with the support of the Alliance for a Green Revolution in Africa (AGRA; and perhaps others; AGRA 2013: 14), and its purpose was relatively straightforward: to "establish a legal framework to protect the rights of breeders of new varieties of plants or plant groupings . . . by making available to them an exclusive right on the basis of a set of uniform and clearly defined principles" (Plant Breeders Bill 2013: i). In other words, the Plant Breeders Bill sought to allow breeders to obtain IPR protections for new and novel plant constructs.

The Plant Breeders Bill was brought to parliament for consideration the same year that government authorities approved field trials of a number of genetically modified crops. If the Bill's sponsors had hoped for a smooth legislative ride, they were in for a surprise. For though the Bill's contents are relatively straightforward, there was nothing routine about the Plant Breeders Bill. Soon after the bill was introduced to parliament, activists caught wind of it, and turned it in to a national debate. Whether intentionally or not, the decision to introduce the Bill the same year as field trials began set the stage for what would be the ire of GMO proponents: activists' insistence that GMOs be considered for their political, as well as scientific, merits. To that end, the Plant Breeders Bill is key to the story of GMOs, food sovereignty, and activism in Ghana.

Adikanfo: The Forebearers

A few months after GAFP's meeting at the Gold Star Hotel, I traveled to a small town in the far northeastern corner of the country, where the Ghanaian border hugs both Togo and Burkina Faso. I had come at the invitation of Mohammed, a board member of GAFP and a self-described commercial farmer. As one of the more resourced farmers in his area, Mohammed took it upon himself to bring new ideas, projects, and technologies to his neighbors, including some that were essential to the ministry's efforts of transitioning the Ghanaian countryside from peasantry to prosperity. On the day I arrived, the sun was unbearably hot—well over 100 degrees—and Mohammed's town was going on three days without electricity. He was in no mood to take me to farms as we had originally planned, and I happily agreed when he suggested we sit in the shade of a nearby mosque and talk.

As we sat drinking warm fruit cocktail from Togo, I asked him about a nearby signboard advertising a demonstration plot of DuPont Pioneer hybrid maize. The signboard, similar to those Matthias had showed me, stood in a fallow field. There was no maize left, just the signboard and the details it provided about the project's sponsors: the Agricultural Development and Value Chain Enhancement Project (ADVANCE), a USAID-sponsored program carried out by the DC-based organization ACDI/VOCA; the agrochemical company Yara; DuPont Pioneer, one of the world's largest agribusiness giants; and the Ministry of Food and Agriculture.

I asked Mohammed about the project. Were farmers included in the demonstration? Yes, many. How were the yields? Fantastic, more than the average farmer was getting. How many farmers adopted the seed after seeing the results? None. Why? The seed was too expensive and needed to be purchased every year.

In 2014, USAID and DuPont Pioneer signed a Memorandum of Understanding (MOU) to launch a project called the (Ghana) Advanced Maize Seed Adoption Program. The initiative was a quintessential example of a "new" Green Revolution project: it sought to link farmers like Mohammed with global value chains and offer a market to DuPont Pioneer. The project built upon a similar initiative in Ethiopia, where USAID and DuPont Pioneer had partnered together from 2013 to 2018 to help "farmers move from open-pollinated to improved hybrid seed varieties" (USAID 2017: 53).The Ethiopian project would become a hallmark project of then-president Barack Obama's Feed the Future initiative, even garnering a visit from President Obama himself in 2015. During his visit, he addressed members of the press while donning a blue hat with USAID's logo emblazoned on the front and standing behind three open bags of DuPont Pioneer maize seeds.[2] In describing why the United States was focusing on smallholder farmers, he said, "With just a few smart interventions, a little bit of help, they could make huge improvements in their overall yields" (USAID 2015).

However, the view from Ethiopia wasn't all rosy. A report by USAID provides insight into how Ethiopian officials initially resisted the USAID/DuPont Pioneer partnership:

> USAID brought the Regional Head of Commercial Activities, the Ethiopian Ministry of Agriculture and Natural Resources (MoA), and the Ethiopian Agricultural Transformation Agency (ATA) into the partnership conversation with DuPont, who was eager to build its own relationships throughout the Ethiopian Government. The Ethiopian government did not immediately buy in to the partnership vision. In initial discussions, MoA expressed concerns about supporting DuPont, a for-profit player, seeking to further their own business interests. Historically, Ethiopia had taken a state-led approach to food security and development, and questioned the intention and sustainability of private sector investment. MoA, however, acknowledged the importance of introducing new seed varieties and increasing production volumes and would later highlight that farmers prefer and demand the DuPont seeds. USAID . . . was instrumental in helping MoA and DuPont align on the vision . . . USAID did this in part through facilitating numerous conversations between the parties, taking advantage of their role as a respected third party with a long-standing history of working with the government and investing in Ethiopia's development, dating back to 1961. (USAID 2017: 52–53)

The report from USAID sheds light on the essential role US officials play in establishing so-called public private partnerships in countries like Ethiopia. As the excerpt demonstrates, it was USAID who helped negotiate agreements between the government of Ethiopia and DuPont Pioneer, who was "eager to build its own relationships throughout the Ethiopian Government" (USAID 2017: 52–53). Ethiopia's eventual acquiescence represented a loosening of the country's "state-led approach to . . . development," one which USAID hoped to replicate elsewhere.

For decades, numerous African countries such as Ghana and Ethiopia had stringent policies in place regarding seed production and distribution. While structural adjustment policies chipped away at state breeding practices in Ghana, some believed the reforms hadn't done enough to set the stage for incentives and protections for the private sector—especially the foreign private sector—to intervene. Though the Ghana Seed Company was disbanded under structural adjustment, there were still breeders and research scientists employed by the state research council who would "partner" with donors and multinationals, such as the example of Sasakawa Global (SG) 2000 and Monsanto (Amanor 2019a; Boafo and Lyons 2020). But, in the eyes of those who wanted pure liberalization, there was still more that could be done. The irony—like many neoliberal reforms—is that it would require additional legislation, or, in other words, more (not less) state intervention.

In the early 2000s, USAID had identified laws in Ghana and other West African countries that the agency considered too protectionist. Such policies, USAID argued, not only stifled global competition, but also blocked African farmers from accessing (e.g., purchasing) "improved" seed. Agency officials decided that such polices needed reform and awarded Iowa State University and Cultivating New Frontiers in Agriculture (a Washington, DC–based contractor) a multimillion-dollar grant to carry out the West African Seed Alliance (WASA; Rock and Schurman 2020: 22; Rock and Park 2019). WASA was focused on getting hybrid seeds, mainly from American companies (DuPont Pioneer and Monsanto were official partners in the project), into West African markets. WASA's mission revolved around working with multiple governments to "[draft] new seed laws or [revise] existing ones to be in conformance with . . . 2009 ECOWAS seed regulation,"[3] and "helping link" African plant breeders and local seed companies with "international seed companies . . . [to access] hybrid seed directly from them" (USAID 2012: 12). Though officials recognized that "assistance to government breeders [was] absolutely essential," the project's aim, and "strategy for sustainability," was "to gradually turn over as much of the seed production business as possible to the private sector, as is done in much of the world" (USAID 2012: 16, 24). The emphasis on hybrid seeds was as agronomically informed as it was economically minded. Internal documents justified the focus on hybrids in part because they "must be replaced annually compared to [open pollinated varieties]" (USAID 2012: 12). Officials deemed this—purchasing new seed each year—as best practice (indeed, this is a larger theme within other "new" Green Revolution initiatives), and also one which guaranteed a steadier market for WASA's industry partners, like DuPont Pioneer and Monsanto.

Through WASA, officials enacted policy reform in five countries including Ghana. The Ghanaian outcome was a piece of legislation entitled the Plants and Fertilizer Act (2010). The multi-part law enacted several changes to the seed sector, two of which are important for the discussion of GMOs. First, whereas prior to the act seed production and breeding was almost exclusively in the hands of the public sector, the new law expanded the scope of who can breed and export seeds, "allow[ing] the production of any class of seed by any approved entity and permits both domestic private sector activity as well as access to foreign (public and private) varieties" (USDA FAS 2020b: 12). Second, the act outlined new guidelines for plant variety registration and established a "national variety list" of seeds that "conform[ed] to distinctness, uniformity, stability" (Plants and Fertilizer Act 2010: 21).

Actualizing the 2009 ECOWAS harmonization law via the Plants and Fertilizer Act was a major win for WASA. The next step was to begin linking farmers, breeders, and agro-dealers with private seed companies. As the case with Ethiopia, that's where DuPont Pioneer came in. Just a year after the Plants and Fertilizer Act was passed, "hybrid maize seed [was made] commercially available in Ghana for the first time" through DuPont Pioneer and its subsidiary, Pannar (USAID 2012: 13).[4] Internal USAID documents celebrated this as "a major breakthrough for Ghana" (USAID 2012: 13). A few years later, DuPont Pioneer and Pannar imported two hybrid maize varieties, Pioneer 30Y87 and Pannar 53, for farmers working within the USAID project. The varieties were given names in Twi: *Adikanfo*, "forebearers," and *Sika-Aburo*, "money maize" (Van Asselt et al. 2018: 2). ACDI/VOCA, a US contractor overseeing the ADVANCE program, circulated the hybrid maize to demonstration plots around Ghana—such as the one on Mohammed's farm—to convince farmers that the high-yielding seeds would be worth the investment.

The project hit a snag in 2015. A report by the USAID contractor overseeing the ADVANCE project stated: "Pioneer and its partner firm, Dizengoff, have not been able or authorized to continue importing the seeds in Ghana, due to an issue related to the enforcement of local seed laws" (ACDI/VOCA 2015: 44). Soon after, the situation seemed to be improving. In 2016, Dizengoff, DuPont's Accra-based agri-supplier, tweeted excitedly, "It's finally here! The #Pioneer #Edikanfo 30Y87 #hybrid #seeds are available at Dizengoff Ghana,"[5] with a link to their Instagram account featuring a photo of a bag of Adikanfo (Dizengoff Ghana 2016). But what happened next is unclear. A dissertation by PhD student Jasmin Marston (2017) suggests that Ghanaian officials stipulated infrastructural investment from DuPont Pioneer—apparently a seed factory—in exchange for permission to operate in the country. DuPont Pioneer supposedly declined. And it is also likely that, as was the case on Mohammed's demonstration plot and as it has been well-documented throughout the country, the seed was too expensive for the average farmer to justify purchasing (Nyantakyi-Frimpong and Bezner Kerr 2015). WASA encountered problems in other countries too. USAID's own reporting indicated that "while WASA had some notable accomplishments," such as the introduction of hybrid seed in Ghana, "they were not as large as expected" (USAID 2012: 14). One issue that arose was that some partners "viewed [WASA] as being too 'American,' dominated by USAID and US seed companies" (USAID 2012: 14). "Any future alliance," the document concluded, "should be African led" (USAID 2012: 14).

Regardless of whether WASA accomplished its total goals in Ghana or elsewhere, the project left an important legacy in Ghana: the Plants and Fertilizer Act. With the act on the books, multinational companies were able to really eye the Ghanaian market. In other words, the policy reform supported by WASA helped subsidize market entry for international seed companies, like DuPont Pioneer. This legal reform offered a significant boost for those advocating for the adoption of biotechnology. For at the same time Ghanaian officials were debating the Plants and Fertilizer Act, they were also deliberating a law to allow GMOs to enter the market too. That law was the Biosafety Act.

The Biosafety Act

In January 2000, after intense rounds of negotiations, members of the Convention on Biological Diversity adopted the Cartagena Protocol on Biosafety (Buttel 2003). The adoption of the protocol (which would go into effect a few years later) established global standards for how states should regulate emergent biotechnologies, including procedures for "the safe transfer, handling and use of living modified organisms resulting from modern biotechnology" (Secretariat of the Convention on Biological Diversity 2000: 3). The protocol was heavily shaped by activists and representatives from the Global South who sought to curtail the rapid expansion of GMOs. Many involved in protocol negotiations, happening at the height of the liberalization and free-trade era, sought to implement further, rather than less, state control on the movement of GMOs and their multinational purveyors (Buttel 2003; Schurman and Munro 2010). The regulatory framework required signatory states to implement a variety of oversight on GMOs, including the identification of a national body to oversee matters related to biotech.

For many countries, this meant the need to develop *new* state institutions specifically to regulate the movement, research, and commercialization of GMOs, what are commonly referred to as *biosafety* regulations. Developing such institutions, often called national biosafety authorities, required financial, technical, and political resources (see Schnurr 2019 for a robust discussion on the development of biosafety laws and authorities across the African continent). The Program for Biosafety Systems (PBS) was created by US officials in part to fill that void. The program, which grew out of the George W. Bush–era Initiative to End Hunger in Africa, has a mission to "support ... countries in Africa and Asia in the responsible development and use of biotechnology" (IFPRI 2017).

Ghana was an early signatory of the Cartagena Protocol (2003). A year after Ghana joined the protocol, a Ghanaian chapter of PBS was inaugurated "to promote the judicious use of modern agricultural biotechnology in Ghana in order to increase agricultural productivity with linkages to regional and global markets" (WikiLeaks 2005b). Housed within Ghana's Biotechnology and Nuclear Agriculture Research Institute (BNARI), the chapter turned its attention to assisting the government of Ghana to get in compliance with the Cartagena Protocol. To do so, PBS, as well as officials from the United Nations Environment Programme, partnered with Ghana's newly established National Biosafety Committee (2002) to get to work. This new regulatory body was meant to take the "impartial role of [a] neutral broker," or, in other words, be seen by the public as an institution of expertise that could fairly judge matters of biotechnology and biosafety without a bias one way or another toward the technology or its products (UN Environment 2018: 67).

With the establishment of a regulatory authority, the next order of business was to turn a draft biosafety policy into law (USDA FAS 2011b: 3). Ratifying the Biosafety Act was essential for a few key reasons. First, the regulations laid the groundwork for the testing, importation, and eventual commercialization of genetically modified crops. Second, the Biosafety Act would set the legal groundwork to transform the National Biosafety Committee into an *Authority*, providing the body with legal means to oversee all matters related to GMOs in Ghana, including importation, research and design, and commercialization.[6]

However, transforming the act from draft into law was not easy. Reports from the US Department of Agriculture (USDA) reveal a long, arduous process. In 2005, "the United Nations Environment Program and the Global Environment Facility provided financial and technical support towards the drafting of the" Biosafety Act (USDA FAS 2005: 3). That same year, USAID "planned to fund a sensitization workshop on biotechnology/Biosafety Bill around October 2005 for parliamentarians in order to facilitate sensible and dispassionate debate as the bill is moved forward" (USDA FAS 2005: 7). The government of Ghana, the report noted, "would pass the Biosafety bill by the end of the year, according to the Minister of Environment and Science" (USDA FAS 2005: 7).

But behind the scenes, there was more disagreement than the USDA report let on. In June of that same year, the US State Department sent a senior advisor for

Agricultural Biotechnology to Ghana to meet "with [Government of Ghana] officials, Parliamentarians, and private sector to discuss the state of biotech in Ghana" (WikiLeaks 2005a). Afterwards, the US Embassy in Accra drafted a diplomatic cable describing the senior advisor's visit:

> There is some appreciation in Ghana for the possible benefits of biotech, especially among private research institutions and at the Environment Ministry, which has the lead on biotech and biosafety issues. However, other Ministries—particularly Agriculture and Trade—and Parliamentarians expressed reservations or displayed sheer ignorance on the issue. . . . The Agriculture and Trade Ministries were particularly cautious, with Deputy Ministers from both emphasizing that there is insufficient awareness and has not been enough debate on potential benefits and risks [of biotech]. Both questioned the safety of transgenic crops, raised concerns about Ghana becoming dependent on foreign (read U.S.) seed companies, and worried about risking their European export markets. Although both acknowledged the potential benefits—better quantity and quality, fewer pests, less soil erosion—they argued that major education is needed before sending the biosafety law to Parliament, and then Ghana must ensure the regulatory system is strict to limit environmental, health, and food safety risks. (WikiLeaks 2005a)

The report concluded that "it is not clear that there is sufficient support to obtain Parliamentary approval" for the Biosafety Act "this year" and described "many Parliamentarians [as] poorly informed on biotech" (WikiLeaks 2005a). In addition to skeptical officials, civil society groups, including Friends of the Earth Ghana, mounted public opposition to the bill (Black et al. 2011). Needless to say, the Biosafety Act did not pass in 2005.

In February 2006, USAID funded the workshop they had proposed the year before, but again the act was not passed, and frustrations among US officials mounted (USDA FAS 2006: 5). USDA reported in 2007 that "the process has been slow and it is not clear as to when the draft Bill will be passed" (USDA FAS 2007: 3). To "circumvent the delay[,]" in 2008 the National Biosafety Committee submitted a Biosafety Legislative Instrument to Parliament to allow for "the conduct of confined field research [and] trials of genetically engineered products" (USDA FAS 2008: 3). Parliament agreed to the exemption, but the question of passing the larger Biosafety Act remained important, for it was the larger act that would need to be in place before the country could commercialize any GM crop.

In 2007, 2008, and 2009, USDA reports on Ghana's agricultural biotechnology program reveal that the US Embassy in Accra desired to "arrange a biotechnology program for high-ranking, policy level officials from the Presidency, Ministry of Agriculture, Education and Science, Rural Development and Environment, Health, legislature, and the academia" to place pressure on Parliament and government officials to "fast-track the creation of an enabling regulatory environment for biotechnology" (USDA FAS 2009b: 6). Finally, after almost a decade after the first biosafety guidelines were drafted, Parliament passed the Biosafety Act in 2011 (USDA FAS 2011b: 8).

With the Biosafety Act in place, Ghana was officially open for biotechnology business. US officials "anticipated that biotech cotton, sweet potato, cassava, cowpea, corn, soy, and rice [would be] developed for the Ghanaian market over the next few years" and noted that "some U.S. companies [had] begun the processes of requesting permission to engage in trials in country" (USDA FAS 2011b: 1; WikiLeaks 2010). That same year, global biotech boosters traveled to Ghana on two separate occasions to attend high-level meetings on biotechnology hosted by the African Union's Forum for Agricultural Research in Africa: the first Annual Dialogue of Ministers of Agriculture, Science and Technology (April 28–29) and the first Pan-African Conference on Stewardship of Agricultural Biotechnology (November 29–30). At the latter, Sir Gordon Conway, the former president of the Rockefeller Foundation and a strong supporter of the first Green Revolution, gave the keynote speech in which he presented a dark picture of agriculture in Africa through a PowerPoint presentation. One slide entitled "Food Riots" contained a single image of a woman carrying a child through a street surrounded by burning tires, while another slide labeled "African hunger" showed a map of hunger rates by country. "The crisis is getting worse," another slide warned (FARA 2012). Though a later slide would say "biotechnology is not a silver bullet," the combination of image and word choice present an insight into how Western counterparts viewed the potential benefits of biotech crops for Africa. As the Introduction discussed at length, proponents utilized racialized images of Africa as violent and starving to build support for a biotech intervention.

As donors continued to build a case for biotech crops, they also continued to provide support for Ghanaian biosafety officials. The UN Environment Programme awarded Ghanaian officials a $1.4 million grant to "implement" the Biosafety Act, build the National Biosafety Authority, and educate the public on matters related to biosafety. By 2014, Ghanaian officials had approved research of GM cotton, cowpea,

TABLE 1. Overview of GM Crop Projects in Ghana

CROP (VARIETY IF KNOWN)	TRAIT(S)	FACILITATOR	TECHNOLOGY PARTNER	GHANAIAN PARTNER
GM sweet potato	High protein	Tuskegee University	n/a	CSIR—Crops Research Institute
Bt cotton	Insect resistance	Monsanto	Monsanto	CSIR—Savanna Agricultural Research Institute
GM cotton	1) Insect resistance; 2) herbicide tolerance	Monsanto	Monsanto	CSIR—Savanna Agricultural Research Institute
Bt cowpea (Songotra)	Insect resistance	AATF	Monsanto	CSIR—Savanna Agricultural Research Institute
NUE rice (NERICA)	Nitrogen use efficiency	AATF	Arcadia Biosciences	CSIR—Crops Research Institute
NEWEST rice (NERICA)	1) Nitrogen use efficiency; 2) water efficiency; 3) salt tolerance	AATF	Arcadia Biosciences	CSIR—Crops Research Institute

Note: Adapted from Rock and Schurman (2020: 14).

sweet potato, and two types of rice at state scientific institutions across the country.[7] Scientists applying for research permits also had to request permission to import seeds, as no genetic modification was happening within Ghana. Bt cotton came from Monsanto warehouses in South Africa; Bt cowpea was genetically modified by scientists in Australia working as part of a large international consortia researching the maruca pest (Ezezika and Daar 2012; Rock and Schurman 2020); and nitrogen use efficient rice zigzagged across the United States and Colombia before arriving in Ghana.

Half of the GMO projects were overseen by the African Agricultural Technology Organization (AATF). As described earlier, AATF was created by donor and industry officials to serve as an intermediary, a *broker*, between industry, donors, and African scientific councils. Instituting a broker organization was how officials imagined they would get around the tricky issue of patents: industry would lease their patented material, have a say in how it was used (and what the terms were for its use), and would have a trusted organization implementing the terms of engagement and shielding industry via indemnification clauses. As I examined earlier, donors envisioned AATF to be seen as an African force on the front lines of biotechnology. Doing so, a Ghanaian official close to the GM cowpea project in Ghana (a project initiated by AATF, housed in a Ghanaian state research institution, and partnered with Monsanto) told political scientist Jacqueline Ignatova, allowed companies to more easily gain the trust of farmers: "If Monsanto was the one pushing it, I'm sure that farmers would be a bit hesitant. Because it's being pushed by their indigenous research institutions, through a government negotiation, that's easier to accept" (Ignatova 2015: 105).

Understanding the AATF model is essential to understanding GMO projects not only in Ghana, but across the African continent; AATF currently works in Burkina Faso, Ethiopia, Ghana, Kenya, Mozambique, Nigeria, Tanzania, South Africa, and Uganda. AATF oversees biotech *projects*, comprised of actors, technologies, and processes. In any given project, AATF pairs an agribusiness company and a "transformer"—a lab where the genetic modification takes place. The company sends the leased genetic material to the transformer, who also receives the crop at hand—rice or cowpea in the case of Ghana—through AATF. After the genetic modification (*transformation*) takes place, the crop might be sent for testing before in-country field trials take place.

Once a crop is ready for in-country field trials, it is sent to the national research council of the project country. From there, the country project team, headed by a primary investigator, oversees confined field trials of the crop. Laborers might be hired to plant the crop, security guards hired to watch the fields, and, occasionally, nearby farmers are recruited to monitor the trials in anticipation of good performance results. During and after the field trials, AATF and donor partners require that crop samples be sent elsewhere for testing, presumably to ensure quality control (for example, NUE rice was sent to the United States for testing). Most of the projects AATF oversees are comprised of not one, but multiple countries. For instance, the Bt cowpea project takes place in Burkina Faso, Ghana, Malawi, and Nigeria, while the NEWEST rice is in Ghana, Nigeria, and Uganda.

In Ghana, though the GM rice, cowpea, cotton, and sweet potato projects began around the same time, cotton trials moved fastest. This could be due to the fact that cotton was overseen directly by Monsanto who already had infrastructure in place to import seed, chemicals, and experts quickly into the field. It could also be because, unlike AATF, Monsanto did not have multiple project partners and thus was not limited by bureaucratic considerations. Thomas, a Ghanaian scientist who worked with a biotech booster and was involved in early policy debates and biotech strategy, explained that GMO boosters had originally envisioned commercializing cotton before other GM crops. In an interview in 2016, before the cotton trials abruptly ended, Thomas explained:

> Now there are multi-locational trials [of cotton] in the north.... And then there's also cowpea in the north, which is *so* successful, and within the next two years I'm sure it will be commercialized together with the cotton. But the strategy is to start with a non-food crop like Bt cotton so that people, the farmers, will have confidence in the technology.

I asked Thomas why starting with Bt cotton would inspire confidence among farmers. He referred to the belief that GMOs are unsafe for consumption and explained, "It will bring confidence because they have been told when they eat [GMOs], it will give you cancer. You don't eat cotton, you use it for textiles. So, when they see, you know, our textiles being produced and the cost reduced because we are producing, then they will [feel confident]." Thomas didn't offer any more details, and from his comments it is difficult to know the actors and deliberation involved in developing such a strategy. But his comments reveal an interesting insight into how Ghanaian GMO boosters thought about activists and farmers in relation to their own work.

As Thomas and other boosters worked to sway public opinion and Ghanaian scientists worked with their global counterparts to research GM seeds in Ghanaian fields, biosafety officials were also hard at work. They collaborated with the Ghana Standards Authority to establish what would eventually be a detection lab (as of the time of this writing, the lab was still in development). Additionally, in 2019 Ghanaian Parliament passed into law an additional measure, the Biosafety (Management of Biotechnology) Regulations, a legislative instrument that provides the National Biosafety Authority with further authorization to enact the full scope of the previously passed Biosafety Act. But biotech advocates did not stop there. For there was one final legislative hurdle donors wanted to pass; they wanted the Ghanaian state to implement a new IPR law for plant breeders.

The Plant Breeders Bill

By the time I began fieldwork in Ghana in 2014, the Plants and Fertilizer Act and the Biosafety Act were both old news. They were passed by Parliament, in the books, and while perhaps still points of contention, all eyes were turned toward the Plant Breeders Bill. The bill, a standard copy of the International Union for the Protection of New Varieties of Plants (UPOV) draft framework, sought to take the broad changes laid out in the Plants and Fertilizer Act a step further. If the Plants and Fertilizer Act opened the commons for new plant breeders to enter, so to speak, the Plant Breeders Bill sought to enclose it by offering those new breeders exclusive rights to any new nor novel plant they might develop. As I will later discuss, IPR legislation, like the Plant Breeders Bill, has been a core way multinational corporations have been able to gain global dominance in seed and agrichemical markets (Cleveland and Murray 1997: 486). Though the title of "plant breeder" invokes images of people, perhaps in the field, perhaps in the lab, the Plant Breeders Bill proposed to define a "plant breeder" as "a citizen or resident in the country [or . . . a] legal entity with its registered office in the country or within the territory of a State which is a party to an international treaty to which the Republic is a party" (Plant Breeders Bill 2013: iv–v). A legal entity could be a co-op, it could be a corporation. The definition was geographically broad as well: it could be a legal entity registered in Ghana or any state that belongs to an international treaty that Ghana also belongs to. A "plant breeder," it turned out, could be a Ghanaian scientist employed by the national lab, or a multinational company headquartered in the United States.

In this section, I provide some groundwork for how the state and its donor partners first presented the bill and its components, and how they tried greatly—though unconvincingly—to persuade the public that the Plant Breeders Bill had nothing to do with GMOs. Important for this discussion is understanding how the bill's drafters presented the document to be an integral aspect of national development. In a memorandum that accompanied the bill to Parliament, Attorney General Appiah-Oppong argued that the bill was an essential component for the state's efforts to "[create] and [promote] *an enabling environment* for the stakeholders in the agricultural sector, especially the seed industry, through [in part] the development of policies," like the Plant Breeders Bill (Plant Breeders Bill 2013: ii–iii; emphasis added). Providing exclusive patents for plant breeders, she argued, "will encourage investment in plant breeding since plant breeding requires long term investment and efforts," and would result in "the development of new varieties adapted to the environment and specific needs of the country" (Plant Breeders Bill 2013: ii). Switching to a first-person voice, Appiah-Oppong contended that the bill would "encourage" plant breeders to develop "better seeds" that are "high yielding ... [and] are not only adaptable to *our* environment but have good taste and nutritional qualities" (Plant Breeders Bill 2013: ii–iii; emphasis added).

Scientists within Ghana's state research councils had long been breeding crops "adapted to the environment and specific needs" of Ghanaian farmers. The issue, at least according to supporters of the Plant Breeders Bill, was allowing these same scientists to be properly recognized for their efforts. The memo continued:

> Recent breeding initiatives by the [CSIR] and other private plant breeders have failed to yield the required dividends to the owners as the new varieties were appropriated and used by persons who failed to recognise the investment and effort of the breeder and the need to pay the necessary royalties to the breeder due to the absence of protection. (Plant Breeders Bill 2013: ii)

I heard this argument often throughout my fieldwork, and almost always in reference to Obaatanpa. Obaatanpa, as discussed earlier, is one of the more popular maize varieties in Ghana. Developed by Ghanaian plant breeders in the early 1990s, Obaatanpa caught the attention of the SG 2000 initiative officials, who were already actively working with Ghanaian scientific councils. Given its success in Ghana, SG 2000 officials decided to distribute the seed elsewhere on the continent. This—the global expansion of a Ghanaian-bred seed—is not necessarily a point of contention. But what is, at least for some boosters I encountered, was that the Ghanaian breeders of Obaatanpa were not able to patent, and thus financially benefit, from their construct. Thus, the story of Obaatanpa is used by some in Ghana to argue for why Ghana needed protections for its breeders. Justifying his support of the Plant Breeders Bill, one parliamentarian said, "[Obaatanpa] is being grown in the whole of West Africa. Ghana invested in the scientists at Crop Research Institute to produce it. But everyone is taking it free without paying a dividend to Ghana. That is what we are saying that we have to protect" (Gakpo 2018b).

The tension here, of course, is that Obaatanpa was developed through a development project not unlike the projects Ghanaian scientists are currently engaged in with GMOs. And the broader memo laid out another tension that would play out in street protests, courtrooms, and NGO workshops, and that is the question of who the Plant Breeders Bill was designed to protect. While the memo stated that the state hoped the bill would attract foreign breeders, it also used the example of state breeders to build an argument for the bill along nationalist lines (Plant

Breeders Bill 2013: ii–iii). And to this end, proponents repeatedly stated that the bill was unrelated to GMOs or the field trials that had begun the same year the bill was introduced to Parliament. Instead, proponents cited the Biosafety Act, which they contended was *the* law on the books related to biotechnology. This sort of argumentation was replicated in the media, shared in articles such as "Breeders' Bill Has Nothing to Do with GMOs—CSIR" (Ghana News Agency 2013).

While technically the Biosafety Act was the main law dealing with biotechnology, it did not preclude the Plant Breeders Bill from being deeply integral to Ghana's larger biotech journey. And in fact, as will be detailed later, it was the possibility of patents that made GMOs alluring for many politicians and scientists alike. To understand how certain actors deployed particular arguments, it is essential to know the boosters advocating for the adoption of GMOs.

Brokering Biotech

"Farmers in my country . . . they do their own thing—they don't listen to simple instructions. . . . When they have learned something, they don't apply exactly what they have been taught. They sometimes find their own way of doing things."

"Is that a bad thing?" I asked Kweku, a seasoned Ghanaian journalist and GMO booster.

"It is a bad thing!" Kweku replied emphatically. He explained further: "You've been to the hospital? A doctor has given you prescriptions, right? . . . The prescription is one in the morning, one in the afternoon and one in the evening. So, you said, 'Okay, because I am a big woman and I know everything on my own, I will not take the morning one, I will not take the afternoon one, I will only take the evening one.' And you want to be healed. So, if you are not getting well, it is whose fault? Is it the doctor's fault? Is it the hospital's fault? It is your fault."

"But is a farmer not also a professional in what they do?" I asked.

"It is not about professionalism. It is about *facts*."

"It's also about knowledge, no? And skills—"

"If you think you are so knowledgeable, why didn't you develop your own hybrid seeds?" He retorted, in a reference to farmers.

"Farmers have developed other sorts of seeds."

"It didn't work. It *didn't* work."

"Oh really?"

"For instance, when the Fall Army Worm broke out, do you know the chemicals they were using here? Kerosene, Omo [a washing powder], pepper. And it didn't work! So, are you saying that if you are so knowledgeable and your technology didn't work, and someone else is giving you another technology, won't you embrace it? You are sick, you had your own prescription, it didn't work. You've come to my hospital and I've given you medicine, and you don't want to use it because you think you are so knowledgeable. Then why did you come to my hospital in the first place?"

Kweku is one of many Ghanaians advocating for the adoption of GMOs through a booster organization. In this section, I explain the various boosters—groups who are generally donor-created, and whose goal is to generate public acceptance of biotechnology—that exist within the Ghanaian, and larger African, biotech ecosystem. While not every booster might agree with Kweku's metaphor of plant breeders as doctors, improved seeds as medicines, or the agro-mart as the hospital, the group *was* bonded by a unifying goal of commercializing GM crops; a small group of shared donors that supported their work; and a resolve that farmers needed to grow better seeds. Given that, as Kweku alluded to, there was little demand for GMOs, at least at the time donors were building massive infrastructural projects (e.g., policy reforms and transnational seed research) across the continent, boosters play an important role in the quest to build public support and commercialize GM crops.

In fact, the slow, seven-year process of passing the Biosafety Act revealed to donors and proponents alike that establishing so-called enabling environments was not going to be easy. While PBS was already on the ground and assisting countries like Ghana to create biosafety policies, the inclusion of US officials in creating official state policy—whether directly through US development workers or indirectly through groups like PBS—was a tricky task. US development officials did not want to be seen as lobbying on behalf of a certain policy, let alone American companies (though, as discussed in the Introduction, this does not stop US officials from doing so). This is where boosters like CAS and Open Forum on Agricultural Biotechnology in Africa (OFAB) play a particularly important role.

OFAB was created in 2006 by AATF, who envisioned the group would serve as an in-house communications booster. Like PBS, OFAB's self-described mission is to "explore new avenues of bringing the benefits of modern biotechnology to smallholder farmers in Africa" (Otunge et al. 2017: iii). To do so, OFAB arranges meetings and trainings with different "stakeholders"—"scientists, policy makers, legislators, journalists, farmers and the public"—to create consent, demand, and excitement around GM crops (Otunge et al. 2017: iii). And they've been somewhat successful; since their establishment, OFAB claims credit for at least six countries establishing biosafety regimes (Otunge et al. 2017: iii). As part of these efforts, officials work to place OFAB chapters within already established government institutions to ensure access to personnel and appear "homegrown": "OFAB is 'co-hosted' by the National Biotechnology Development Agency and the Agricultural Research Council; in Burkina Faso, OFAB is housed within the Institute for Environmental and Agricultural Research; [and] in Ethiopia, OFAB is hosted by the Ethiopian Institute for Agricultural Research" (Rock and Schurman 2020: 23). And OFAB chapters have hosted numerous trainings for journalists, state officials, farmers, and more. In a ten-year reflective of OFAB's work, Dr. Denis Kyetere, the executive director of AATF, warned, "the anti-GMO movement is strong and relentless in its pursuit for total ban of genetically modified foods and crops. They continue to instill fear amongst the public on the potential risks of modern biotechnology products. It is important that the public gets to know the truth about biotechnology and also about these negative activism [sic] by others. OFAB and its partners can contribute to this" (Otunge et al. 2017: iv).

The OFAB Ghana chapter was launched in August 2011 and is housed within the Council for Scientific and Industrial Research (CSIR), the state institution that, at least at the time, oversees all GMO research in the country. Upon their creation, OFAB quickly got to work, organizing "seeing is believing" trips for farmers to visit the field trials of GM crops and hosting events in Accra. For example, in May 2013 OFAB and CSIR hosted a talk entitled "Unraveling the Great GMO Divide: Perspectives from a Former Global Anti-GM Activist." The keynote speaker for the day was Mark Lynas, a British environmentalist who that same year had received quite a bit of press from transitioning from a confessed anti-GM activist to an outspoken GMO advocate. In addition to the public talk, OFAB organized a meeting for Lynas (and OFAB officials) to meet with parliamentarians. Their access to lawmakers showcases OFAB's embeddedness with people and institutions in positions of power.

With OFAB affiliated with CSIR and PBS with BNARI, biotech boosters were officially integrated within Ghana's top scientific bodies. In addition to being housed within influential Ghanaian institutions, these groups were also connected to powerful donors, including USAID and the BMGF, and preeminent higher education institutions, including Cornell University and the West Africa Centre for Crop Improvement (WACCI) at the University of Ghana. WACCI, founded in part through a major grant from AGRA, provides MA and PhD programs in plant breeding, genetics, and seed science for students from throughout the continent. WACCI is considered to play an important role in increasing the number of African plant breeders on the continent. Alumni from the program have gone on to work within national research centers and work on projects that have won grants from some of the same agencies that fund WACCI, such as AGRA and USAID, including the NEWEST rice project in Ghana and the Next Generation Cassava project in Nigeria (WACCI 2014).

With OFAB and PBS working with parliamentarians and the public, and WACCI training plant breeders, one last, albeit integral, group remained: farmers. Many of the boosters I spoke with, such as Kweku, saw farmers as needing to be convinced of the efficacy of GM technology. They were a group to be won over, rather than understood or partnered with. One way to do so, Thomas explained, was to organize "seeing is believing" trips: "We organize 'seeing is believing' trips. We organize to Burkina Faso for some of the farmers to go and look at the cotton fields. And in fact, when they came back, they were asking, 'So, when, when, when do they start?'" Similar to demonstration fields like that of Mohammed's, described earlier in this chapter, "seeing is believing" trips are organized around a simple premise: that, if shown proof of success with their own eyes, farmers—and in some cases regulators and politicians—will be more willing to adopt a certain intervention (Schnurr and Gore 2015). These trips are big bets on behalf of the organizers; they must arrange transport, lodging, meals, and sometimes visas and per diems, depending on the destination. And these are bets being hedged in light of the fact that, as Mohammed described, farmers may very well like what they see, but it doesn't mean they will automatically invest their often-limited resources in it.

As activists built up their campaign in 2013 and into 2014, biotech boosters saw a need to directly counter the messages activists were sharing. One way of doing so was to organize workshops and meetings with farmer groups. Thomas explained how these sorts of meetings were an opportunity for organizations like his to address "rumor-mongering" from activists:

> the activists are giving out information which is . . . let me say, rumor-mongering among the farmers. So, the farmers are scared to adopt the technology, even though they don't know much about it. So, we also go and educate them on the technology so that they will understand it properly. And then we give them evidence, because it is evidence-based, we don't just talk. Because the activists tell them that we remove fluid from lizards and inject into tomatoes, that is why the tomatoes is looking

fine, and then they eat it and they get cancer.... So, we allay their [farmers'] fears and tell them the right thing, and show them through PowerPoint presentations of crops, you know, in other countries.

While I did not encounter arguments pertaining to lizard fluid in the field, boosters would often reference the idea of farmers, or consumers, as being scared of the technology. This stood in contrast to the arguments that activists made in public around seed companies, IPRs, and food sovereignty.

PowerPoint presentations and talking points were key to two other strategies used by biotech advocates to reach farmers as well as the general public: public media campaigns and journalist trainings. The Alliance for Science is especially active in this area. First founded at Cornell University, the the Cornell Alliance for Science (CAS), a self-described "pro-choice" "grassroots global network of . . . 'science-allies'" that seeks to "depolarize the GMO debate" (OFAB Ghana 2016; Cornell Alliance for Science 2015; Shackford 2014). CAS was founded, and is sustained, by a multimillion-dollar grant from the BMGF and is one of the many booster organizations that exists in the United States, and Africa, to form a link between industry, state institutions, and the public.[8] CAS hosts an annual Global Leadership Fellow Program, a twelve-week intensive training course at Cornell's Ithaca campus. Fellows receive training from scientists, professors, and communications specialists such as 270 Strategies, a firm comprised of former Obama administration staffers, in the areas of plant breeding, biotechnology, and communications. The program's directors are able to tap into Cornell's relative social and political capital in the United States to gain access to high-profile spaces. For instance, program organizers arranged for the 2015 global fellows to present at the United Nations in New York City, where they made passionate pleas to an audience of ambassadors and allies to support biotech.[9] And in November 2018, CAS sent a delegation of current and former fellows to the UN Biodiversity Conference in Egypt (Gakpo 2018a).

At the time of writing, Cornell had hosted cohorts of fellows in 2015, 2016, 2018, and 2019, with Ghanaians attending each year. Kweku, the journalist I introduced at the beginning of this section, had been a fellow. He explained how he was handpicked by Lucy, a previous fellow, to start a Ghanaian chapter of the alliance:

When Lucy came back [from the fellowship], . . . she called a meeting and made her intentions clear that she believes there's something we should and can do in this regard with the fight around the challenges farmers are facing regarding new innovations.... The reason why [I was chosen] wasn't because there weren't other competent journalists around the country, but what was unique about me was that I was with this association called the Ghana Agricultural and Rural Development Journalists Association (GARDJA).... It's a network of rural development journalists, and ... we are about 350 journalists across the country.

With Kweku and GARDJA onboard, the pool of journalists who could potentially produce pro-biotech coverage ballooned overnight. Kweku explained that he and Lucy quickly got to work and "started putting plans together to see how [they could] organize regular events." Funding was an immediate issue. While GARDJA was funded independently by a variety of private and public donors (including a Ghanaian agrochemical company and a Dutch development agency), according to Kweku, CAS offered no financial support to the Ghanaian chapter. Already connected to other biotech boosters through their journalistic trade and Cornell fellowship, Kweku sought out meetings with WACCI, OFAB, CSIR, PBS, and CropLife (an agribusiness industry association) "to see how they could help us in our programs and activities." The latter, according to Kweku, became official partners of the chapter, offering funding and resources here and there when available. The chapter also occasionally asks for, and receives, funding from people they've met through Cornell fellowships, "individuals who love the alliance."

Today, members of the Ghanaian chapter of the Alliance for Science are active participants in pro-biotech spaces. Joseph Opoku Gakpo, the journalist highlighted in the Introduction, regularly publishes articles and essays for his employer, Joy News (one of the largest media outlets in the country) as well for CAS. In addition to media publications, the Alliance for Science Ghana occasionally holds public events. For instance, in 2017 and 2018, returned Cornell fellows organized "March for Science" contingents in Kenya, Nigeria, Uganda, and Ghana (Gakpo 2018c). Though the March for Science was originally planned to be a rallying cry for climate science, the message of localized marches varied. In marches led by CAS fellows, most placards and signs carried contained messages about biotechnology and plant breeding. In 2019, Kweku and colleagues organized a march, this time in Tamale.

I was in Tamale for two weeks.... And I spoke to the people. "I'm not here to get anything from you. I'm not here to force you to agree to what we are saying, but the point is, do you want to see yourself in poverty and hunger in this twenty-first century? And you see your MPs and ministers driving in [SUVs]. And when they are going, they give you ten cedis, twenty cedis, and you are happy. Is that what you want? Why can't you feed yourself?" So this is the conversation I had with most of the farmers. And they were like, "So, Kweku, how can we do this? We now understand what you are saying, but *how* can we do this?" And I said, "That's why I'm here. There's an upcoming event called March for Science. I want us to speak and tell our stories."

Kweku estimated between six hundred and seven hundred people attended, but this number is hard to verify, as there was little coverage of the event outside of CAS sources. While I did not have the chance to observe conversations between Ghanaian boosters and farmers, insights from Kweku and Thomas present an interesting image of how Ghanaian boosters view their work and the political economy of GMOs. "Why can't you feed yourself?," as Kweku asked his farmer audience, represents a narrow view shared by many GMO advocates; that fighting hunger and poverty is an individual choice based in consumption—in this case, the purchase of improved seeds and necessary agrichemicals.

In interviews with various boosters, a complicated picture emerges of transnational networks unified around a single goal—the commercialization of GM seeds—with differing ideas on how to get there. For example, the CAS arranged for their Ghanaian colleagues to get a copy of, and rights to stream, the pro-biotech documentary *Food Evolution*. Kweku explained:

> Lucy came back with a movie called *Food Evolution*, which Alliance for Science had put together, giving the history of [agricultural biotechnology].... Lucy brought this movie and I saw it... and I said, "Lucy, we can do a lot of work with this movie." And so we organized University of Ghana Association of Agriculture students... about five hundred of them. We watched it at the Silverbird Cinema [at the Accra Mall].

While Kweku described the screenings as a success, Appiah, a colleague from another booster organization, was a bit more skeptical. According to his own account, after the Accra screening, Appiah approached CAS requesting the film be translated into some of Ghana's eighty-some languages to reach non-English-speaking populations. CAS counter-offered and suggested Appiah organize theatre troupes to travel to communities and instead perform the core tenets of *Food Evolution* "to demonstrate how they [the farmers] are going to profit and all that." "I thought it was also a good idea," Appiah said, "but in the absence of that, I thought we could do the translation and then use it."

Many of the boosters I encountered spoke about financial challenges. OFAB, PBS, and the CAS Ghana chapter are all reliant on outside sources to fund the work they do. Hosting events for parliamentarians and journalists, taking farmers to visit farms in Burkina Faso, and hosting media events is not cheap. Appiah described the booster he works for as a "project." When I asked what that meant, Appiah laughed and explained that a *project* "has a short lifespan. A project for us is anything that has a cost and benefit stream. But this one has a short period; when funding ends, [the] project may end." And when funding streams do dry up, folks ask each other, and a small group of organizations, for help: OFAB, PBS, the African Biosafety Network of Expertise, USAID, and the USDA.

Boosters, though connected with some of the world's largest development financers, recognize the limitations to their work. One described the obvious fact that most boosters are neither farmers nor plant breeders, the two groups supposedly meant to benefit from GMOs and the Plant Breeders Bill. And in one candid interview, Thomas lamented that the technology their organization was promoting—GMOs—was not only expensive but also required incredible resources and infrastructure, most of which Ghana did not yet have.

> The challenge is that [genetic modification] is expensive, and we need to be sponsored like they are doing now. Scientists need to be trained, and we need equipment, and they are bringing equipment. So, it's actually a challenge in certain areas where we don't have the equipment. Where the researchers have to go outside to go and do certain procedures.

At the time, I didn't push Thomas on what exactly he meant by "equipment" and the persons behind it. But in the years since our interview, the GMO projects in Ghana have stayed the same: "researchers have to go outside to go and do certain procedures." Crucially, though, it is not Ghanaians who "go outside" to oversee their projects. Instead, it is the crops that are sent "outside" for "certain procedures," such as genetic modification, performed by researchers elsewhere. As I will show, the uneven power relations between Ghanaian scientists, American donors, and multinational agribusiness companies was a common complaint, albeit a subtle one, among Ghanaian GMO supporters. For it is not just farmers who are tired of being on the receiving end of aid projects.

Conclusion

In the midst of efforts to spark a "new" Green Revolution for Africa, the Ghanaian state entreated its farmers to adopt high-tech agro-inputs to move from peasantry to prosperity. This project required at once liberalizing markets—opening them for competition—but also establishing intellectual property rights—an enclosure of the commons—so that companies were afforded protection. To facilitate such a transition, successive governments chipped away at state regulations designed to protect the Ghanaian seed sector. With the help of development agencies, researchers from US land-grant universities, and development contractors, the Ghanaian state passed a number of laws to liberalize the seed sector and open the Ghanaian market to multinational companies dealing in hybrid and genetically modified seeds (see table 2). Hoping to capitalize on this, one the world's largest multinational agribusiness companies, DuPont Pioneer, fashioned itself through its maize seeds as the "forebearer" to agricultural wealth. While the Plants and Fertilizer Act expanded the definition of a plant breeder to include the private sector, the proposed Plant Breeders Bill sought to afford plant breeders of new and novel varieties exclusive patents. The Biosafety Act, meanwhile, allowed plant breeders, either those working within or outside of the country, to begin importing and planting genetically modified crops.

The Biosafety Act was an important, and contested, piece of legislation. Unlike conventional breeding, biotechnology is governed globally by specific conventions, namely the Cartagena Protocol, which has its own rules for compliance. For countries like Ghana, signing on to the protocol meant that scientists and companies could not simply import seeds and sell them on the market. Instead, Ghanaian officials and donors had to develop a number of infrastructural projects that would establish an "enabling environment" for biotechnology. This included policy reform and the creation of a biosafety regulatory agency. Outside of what the protocol dictated, GMO proponents also set out to establish pro-GMO booster and broker organizations, embed their work within CSIR, and manufacture "demand" for GMOs via public relations campaigns (Schnurr and Gore 2015).

TABLE 2. Ghanaian Laws Related to Plant Breeding and Biotechnology

	THE PLANTS AND FERTILIZER ACT	THE BIOSAFETY ACT	THE PLANT BREEDERS BILL
SIGNIFICANCE	Expanded law to allow private sector to breed foundation seed, essentially opening the seed market to multinational competition	Established a national regulatory body to oversee the research, commercialization, and importation of GMOs in Ghana (Biosafety Act 2011: 4)	Enacted an intellectual property rights regime that provides exclusive patenting rights to plant breeders of new and novel varieties (Plant Breeders Bill 2013: i)

I spend time delving into the political history of biotechnology and seed policy in Ghana for a few reasons. First, to establish the ways in which development actors—mainly here the Rockefeller Foundation, BMGF, and USAID—leverage their political and financial clout to essentially lobby for the creation (or amendment) of laws deemed to be business friendly. And they do so under the auspice of *development*, essentially using gross global inequities to open and expand capital frontiers. While doing so, these donors and the booster organizations they've created argue that such legal and agronomic changes will be good for not only national development but importantly the country's breeders and therefore farmers. However, this argumentation stands in tension with the stated goals of USAID's WASA project: to move plant breeding entirely to the private sector.

These tensions are not necessarily hidden; rather, most live in plain view. Just as "ideology never says 'I am ideological'" (Althusser 1971: 175), neoliberalism never says, "I am neoliberal." The relative ease at which discourses about production, African hunger, and modernization circulate sets the stage for the reorganization of national laws, institutions, and farmland under the auspice of development. To ensure such reforms, and to confront any naysayers that may arise, international donors created a cadre of GMO boosters, organizations and individuals whose core purpose is to create the conditions wherein GM seeds can be bought and sold in Ghana. And yet, as the US government subsidized DuPont Pioneer's and Monsanto's entry into Ghanaian markets through so-called humanitarian ventures, the companies were not willing to significantly risk profit. DuPont Pioneer reportedly refused to set up a factory in Ghana, and Monsanto (and other agri-giants) required AATF to establish highly complicated international networks to protect their patented property.

In this case, property protection meant the passage of IPR laws, not investing in infrastructure (which could hypothetically lead to domestic competition), and keeping African scientists far from the actual genetic modification processes. As I will describe, it is precisely this type of convoluted set up that has Ghanaian activists, scientists, and farmers alike questioning the sustainability of a so-called sustainable technology. For, while GMOs may be a global technology, and while AATF's projects may be literal worldwide affairs, Ghanaian expertise—scientific, agricultural, regulatory, and otherwise—is both an integral and marginalized part of the equation. It was Ghanaian activists who brought these concerns to the light, and who first raised very public concerns over the dominant role donors play in Ghana's development trajectories.

CHAPTER 3

Our Stomachs Are Being Colonized

The Freedom Centre sits along a busy road in the neighborhood of Kokomlemle, close to the bustling economic and transport center of Accra. The center itself occupies the second floor of a red two-story building; below it, a provisions shop, and next to it, the offices of the *Insight Newspaper*. Established in 2007, the Freedom Centre serves as the official meeting site of the Socialist Forum of Ghana and regularly hosts public lectures, film screenings, and study groups. The office is decorated with portraits of revolutionaries—Kwame Nkrumah, Martin Luther King Jr., Che Guevara, Harriet Tubman, Fidel Castro, Bob Marley, and Fela Kuti—and bookcases with works by the latter. Inside, a sign on a donation bin appeals to visitors: "Your genuine contribution will advance the revolution."

It was here that Accra-based activists and NGO officials began discussing and organizing around the question of plant patents and genetically modified seeds in 2013. Out of these talks emerged two groups: the Food Sovereignty Platform—an umbrella network of already established organizations—and Food Sovereignty Ghana (FSG)—an organization primarily focused on stopping GMOs and the Plant Breeders Bill.[1]

It was at the Freedom Centre that I met Kofi, a young activist and spirited organizer involved with FSG. Born and raised in Accra, Kofi had been active in the early founding of FSG, which he referred to as "a movement . . . who have come together to call for the collective ownership of our national resources over that of foreign multinational corporations." Purposefully broad in his definition, Kofi viewed FSG as a force to tackle all matters of issues. GMOs were one.

On a sunny morning in August 2014, Kofi and I met to discuss FSG's campaign against GMOs. At one point during our conversation, I made a remark about maize and its various introductions to Ghana; first brought to West Africa to feed captured Africans, and now brought by multinational companies in the form of patented seeds (Carney and Rosomoff 2009; Stahl 2001: 134). Kofi listened quietly and, when I finished, told me kindly but sternly that I was wrong:

> It is not true that it was the white man who brought [maize] seeds to Ghana . . . because if you watch the history of the indigenous people of Accra, the Ga people, they have a festival called *Homowo*, and Homowo has lived with the Ga people long before colonialism. . . . That variety of crop has been with our people long before the white man came here. This is one thing we must get very clear.

The corrected anthropologist, I smiled and considered both the maize historicity that Kofi was describing, and that which I thought I knew. In particular, I was drawn to Kofi's understanding of maize as an indigenous crop to Ghana, or at least one that had been around "long before the white man came here." In contradicting my understanding of maize's origins, Kofi laid wider claims about what maize is, what maize means to Kofi and his community, and why FSG had centered maize in its activism. For Kofi's description of maize was not that simply of a "staple," but also a vessel of cultural tradition and continuity despite colonial and neocolonial ruptures, a claim to ethnicity, and, especially in the context of GMOs, an expression of nationalism and sovereignty.

During this time, preparations were underway for the Ga festival of Homowo, a holiday that "recalls a critical period in [Ga] history when there was a great famine" and celebrates the feat of this period by "hoot[ing] at hunger" (Yankah 1990: 8). A central component of Homowo is the offering of the maize dish *kpokpoi* to ancestors and gods, to ward off—that is, hoot at—future bouts of hunger. In the days leading up to the festival, FSG and senior Ga priests published a press release stating their opposition to the use of GM maize (GhanaWeb 2014). According to the priests, kpokpoi needed to be made from "indigenous" corn, and thus GM maize would be unacceptable for ancestral sacrifice.

Though at the time GM maize was not in circulation in Ghanaian markets or farms—at least there was no record of such—Kofi, FSG, and the Ga priests used Homowo and the hypothetical of GM maize to make explicit claims about maintaining "tradition" in contemporary Ghana, maintaining Ghanaian-ness in a globalized world, and maintaining access to a variety of seed and crop varieties. The latter—access to seed—was especially important for the farmer groups that made up the Platform. I gained access and insight to the Platform mainly through the Ghana Association of Food Producers (GAFP) and their project officers I spent a majority of my time with—Kwesi, an experienced project assistant in the NGO world who had recently joined the association; Nii, a seasoned official within the association who was also a farmer; John, a full-time volunteer with the association and a skilled orator (once, John, in expressing his anger at the amount of power and influence donors have in the country, asked me, "Does Bill Gates love Africa more than me? Does Bill Gates love my children more than me?"); and the organization's head, Constance, who was a force to be reckoned with.

"From time immemorial—I may sound philosophical or whatever it is—from time immemorial, we have always traded between ourselves, exchanging seeds." Constance said one day, as we sat in the GAFP office.

> Even up to this minute I'm talking, with all the improved seed, high-yielding seed, the biotech seed, hybrid seed, we still want to exchange seed. Why? Because it still maintains our traditional, indigenous *taste* of the food that we eat. And we feel safer with the seed we *know*. We know that this is a traditional seed handed down from time. We feel safer. There's no uncertainty about it, we feel safe. And we don't pay almost nothing. It's cheap for us. But with the coming of GMO, . . . they will make sure that whether you are poor [hits desk], [whether] you can afford it or not, you will come and buy GMO. By killing the exchange of seed, indigenous seed, they will just make sure.

Similarly to Kofi, Constance spoke of seeds and foods not simply as productive things, but also as items with deep significance, particular taste, and knowledge regimes. In this chapter, I use insights from Kofi and Constance as springboards to detail the development of, and distinctiveness within, the Platform. Though the Platform is made up of complex organizations and figures, as this chapter will demonstrate, members are bonded by many commonalities, including a strongly held belief that the state, not donors, should drive development; that agriculture (knowledge, practice, outcomes) today are deeply tied to historical legacies of slaving, colonialism, and structural adjustment; and that GMOs are representative of both this historical legacy and the letdowns of development so far. Later in the chapter I offer a vignette of a public forum held by the Platform that featured Indian scholar and activist Dr. Vandana Shiva to illustrate how activists operationalize these critiques, and how they frame their struggle within local and global contexts.

And while the Platform shared a common goal of halting the introduction of GM crops into Ghana, groups within the collective differed greatly in their strategies of how to reach such a goal. As I demonstrate later in the chapter, strategic tensions came to a head in 2015 when the Platform splintered, with some groups, led by FSG, choosing to sue the Ghanaian government over GMOs, with others, including GAFP, opting not to join. Finally, this chapter will demonstrate how, in the midst of internal disagreements and accusations of being "anti-science," Kofi, Constance, and the groups they belonged to remained firm in their analysis of agriculture and development being structurally and symbolically violent.

Much of the data presented here was gleaned through participant observation and interviews with Platform members. As an embedded intern with GAFP, I was able to attend meetings and workshops throughout Accra. It was on the sidelines of these events, during informal chats and meals shared with colleagues, where I learned the most. During a break at one workshop in Accra, for instance, I stood with Constance, Kwesi, and Osman—a union official engaged in the Platform—and chatted while we ate finger sandwiches and sipped on tea.

"I [studied] sociology and read about the spread of capitalism and it is so bad. It is all the Americans," Constance said in reference to agribusiness, which she then compared to the 1884 European partition of Africa. I flexed my arms, using my body as a stand-in for American imperialism, and Osman jokingly put his hands around my neck. Constance continued, explaining that while the British "took our resources, [and] made us slaves," they did not bring "culture." Americans, on the other hand, did, by which Constance meant capitalism. I pointed out that we were drinking tea and eating biscuits, which felt pretty British to me. Constance laughed and conceded my point. However, she was steadfast in her overall analysis that the US imposition of capitalism was a crime equal to British imperialism. The point here is Constance's exasperation with the (agricultural) development field and her explicit links of race, history, power, economics, and labor. These are essential to the discussion of GMOs in Ghana.

A Movement Begins

Sometime in 2013, after the attorney general introduced the Plant Breeders Bill to Parliament, activists got their hands on a copy. In Ghanaian parliamentary procedure, when a bill is submitted to Parliament floor for consideration, the bill technically leaves backroom negotiations and enters the public domain. If and when the public learns about, or has access to, the bill is another question. That's part of what makes the story of the Plant Breeders Bill so interesting. There are many accounts, but little consensus, about how the bill traveled from Parliament to the Freedom Centre. Some say it was a journalist at the *Insight Newspaper*—a left-leaning independent publication whose offices are next door to the Freedom Centre—who first got hold of it. Others say it was a source from Third World Network's Ghana office—an international organization involved in campaigns for seed sovereignty among other things—who passed the bill on. Whatever the case, the bill ended up at the Freedom Centre, whose regulars, including members of the Socialist Forum of Ghana, began concerned talks over the bill's contents. Slowly the talks expanded to include representatives of other groups, some of whom had also heard of the bill or were already interested in genetically modified crops.

Eventually, the Platform emerged, whose membership included the Centre for Indigenous Knowledge and Organizational Development, the Christian Council, the Catholic Bishops Conference, FSG, the General Agricultural Workers Union, the Ghana Muslim Association, the Peasant Farmers Association of Ghana, the Rastafari Council, and the Vegetarian Association of Ghana. Much of the initial organizing took place within Accra, but Platform members with nation-wide bases began generating debates in other constituencies. These networks allowed the Platform to grow quickly, both in and outside of Accra.

Through consultations with lawyers and policy experts, activists concluded that the Plant Breeders Bill was linked to field trials of the GM rice, cotton, and cowpea that had begun that same year (2013). Though proponents of the bill sought to separate its contents from GMOs, activists not only considered them to be inextricably connected, but fought to keep the two synonymous in the public sphere. "You know, the two things are related," Constance remarked, "but they try to separate them. I think it's . . . a 'red herring' as they call it, it's a way to deviate or divert people's attention from the main issue, which is the Plant Breeders Bill."

Activists argued that the researchers and companies behind the technology required legislative and intellectual property right (IPR) protection before they brought their product to market. They concentrated on Clause 9 of the Plant Breeders Bill, that which would establish the broad, legal definition of a plant breeder to be an individual or entity in country or "within the territory of a State which is a party to an international treaty to which the Republic is a party" (Plant Breeders Bill 2013: iv–v). Clause 9 became one of the main contention points for activists. Platform members, especially those with farmer memberships, were well aware of the global concentration of agribusiness, with the market for seed and agrochemicals dominated by just a handful of companies. Given the fact that a majority of the GMO projects in country at the time, including the GM cowpea, cotton, and rice projects, included an industry "partner" licensing patented material, activists worried that the bill would allow companies such as these to apply for breeding rights and patents, and eventually dominate the market. In a policy brief published by three Platform members, activists "demanded" that a "consensus" be reached "on the fact that the [Plant Breeders Bill] . . . is highly skewed in favour of a few local breeders and multinational seed companies as against local subsistence/smallholder farmers" (CIKOD et al. 2014: 6).

At some point in these early organizing stages, activists circulated US diplomatic cables discovered on WikiLeaks that described US-backed support of the Biosafety Act. For many activists, these cables described what they viewed as interference from USAID in the internal affairs of Ghana. One cable outlined the work of USAID-funded Program for Biosafety Systems in the country: "USAID will soon sign an agreement with the International Food Policy Research Institute (IFPRI) to undertake a three-year program in Ghana—the Program for Biosafety Systems (PBS)—designed to assist the Government of Ghana to develop policies, training and details that will support Ghana's biosafety legislation" (WikiLeaks 2005b). Indeed, as outlined earlier, the PBS Ghana chapter had been active since 2004, working with officials and other boosters to support the passage of the Biosafety Act and other biotech-related activities. Activists later discovered that, in addition to USAID, the Bill & Melinda Gates Foundation was also involved in funding and promoting the GM projects, and thus built their public campaign around the political economy of the seed industry, the influence of international aid donor, and what the latter meant in terms of state sovereignty.

Within their first year of organizing, the Platform had attracted organizations with national membership and began a public campaign that forced conversations that were already happening within academic, government, and donor circles into the public sphere. Each member of the Platform had their own expertise to bring: the three farmers/agricultural organizations were able to organize farmers throughout the country; the Rastafari Council was skilled in quickly recording, editing, and publishing media content; Christian and Muslim organizations drew upon their symbolic capital as leaders of faith-based communities to bring more attention to the cause; and FSG, arguably the most vocal group of the Platform, rallied international supporters. This work was undertaken mainly by a Ghanaian member living in Europe, who, with access to cheap, high-speed internet, provided "air force" for the group, using social media outlets to build a base by tapping into communities of Ghanaians living abroad and global anti-GMO networks. Twitter and Facebook allowed the Platform to craft and control its own narrative, and to do so cheaply. Platform members were also invited to television and radio debates and public forums, the proceedings from which were reproduced in print and online media. Activists regularly published statements and manifestos on online media sites, such as ModernGhana.com (Rock 2018c). Through these public campaigns, the Platform grew quickly both in membership and in public awareness. And importantly, according to Kofi, the Platform had informants within government institutions—including the scientific research councils hosting GMO field trials—who were sympathetic to the cause but afraid to speak publicly. With each member of the Platform playing a specific role, the group was able to keep GMOs in the public spotlight and make their case.

A Vicious Cycle

At the core of the Platform's contention against GMOs and the Plant Breeders Bill was a deep historical analysis. It wasn't that Platform members were against technological or scientific advancement; rather, activists, farmers, and civil society members raised concerns about a particular technology dominated by multinational companies, and a piece of policy that proposed to protect those same companies. For some Platform members, like Constance, who had watched both the agricultural sector and the state transform over the decades, GMOs represented a techno-fix for a sector badly in need of structural support. Constance grew up in northern Ghana and, like many of the officials who worked in GAFP's office, came from a family of farmers. As she moved through school, eventually leaving her hometown to continue her education, she remained observant of how life was changing for her friends and family and their farms.

"When I was growing up, they were using hoe and cutlass," she explained, but over time, farmers began to mechanize, using tractors to prepare their soils. However, while mechanization saved time and manual labor, new challenges emerged. "Now people are using tractor, and . . . the tractor scientifically disturbs," she explained, in reference to soil nutrients. "And that is the other thing! You see, as I said, it's a very vicious, vicious, vicious cycle. You use the tractor, you *deplete* the soil, and then you have to go and buy fertilizer, and the soil becomes poorer and poorer, and then you keep buying fertilizer. You see the sense in it? So, yeah, agriculture in Africa has not always been poor."

The image of the hoe and cutlass is commonly invoked by speakers as a temporal mechanism, and often a negative one, to indicate an age-old technology that African farmers continue to use despite technological advancements. At a conference of horticulturalists I attended in Kumasi, the keynote speaker, a vice chancellor at the Kwame Nkrumah University of Science and Technology, decried that the "continued use [of the hand hoe] should be considered a crime against humanity." But what Constance is doing here is different. Rather, by charting the progression of tools used by farmers, from hoes as a child to tractors as an adult, and the impacts of that progression (soil depletion, in this example), Constance is challenging linear notions of progress and advancement that underline so much of development thinking and discourse. For Constance, the failed promise of clean, linear progression was something she observed not only in farmers' fields, but more generally, in everyday life in postcolonial Ghana.

As Constance moved through university and the workforce, she eventually ended up at GAFP, working with colleagues across the country to advocate for equitable policy and programming. Given that GAFP was already deeply embedded in Accra's vibrant civil society and policy circles, when the issue of the Plant Breeders Bill arose, it was something Constance and her colleagues studied seriously. One day in GAFP's office, I asked Constance why GAFP took the stance it did against the Plant Breeders Bill and GMOs. "Let me take you back a bit to the Structural

Adjustment Program," she responded. John, sitting nearby, let out a loud "hmmm" in agreement. Constance continued:

> Before the Structural Adjustment Program, farming was a pleasure. I mean, a lot of things were subsidized and the North was a food basket. Then the structural adjustment came. What did the structural adjustment do? It stopped any subsidies that was going to farmers, that is one. The structural adjustment led to the laying off of lots of civil servants, that is two. Three, . . . the other side of the structural adjustment, at the same time, . . . *coincidentally* or whether it was planned, you had the trade liberalization coming in at the same time.
>
> So here was the case that farmers were not supported to grow more food any longer, and then they will open our doors . . . for the influx of food coming from highly subsidized countries like your country. So eventually the two sides of the coin was that production fell, and the little that was produced *koraa* was not getting anywhere. . . . We fell back, instead of progressing. We went back ten years, and that ten years cost us a lot.

A skeptical reader might dismiss Constance's description of farming as a "pleasure" before structural adjustment. But by beginning at structural adjustment when asked why GAFP was opposed to a specific "improved technology" and liberalized IPR laws, Constance was deliberate in her problematization. She drew parallels between "improved technologies" and liberalized policies of the past and present. And importantly, she argued that what the development industry might describe as "agricultural" issues or chokeholds affecting Ghana are actually political-economic ones. Constance's analysis of the structural adjustment era, along with her experience living through it and watching farming change in her hometown and amongst her family and friends, helped form her view of GMOs and the Plant Breeders Bill. In other words, her views are shaped by recipient fatigue in that failed development schemes inform her skepticism of *new* development schemes.

When I asked Constance why GAFP was against GMOs, she provided me with three broad reasons: their relative expense compared to locally available seed varieties (and the ways in which some actors use [white] saviorism as a cloak to disguise these costs); GAFP's prioritization of infrastructural improvement to improve the agricultural sector; and finally, GAFP's worry about Clause 58 of the Plant Breeders Bill and its potential impacts on seed saving. I'll discuss the first two here, and address Clause 58 later in the chapter.

"GMO," she explained, "it's not cheap. "If you are able to develop the GMO seeds, you have to pay back the money you have used for the research and other things. And most of all, the Monsantos are doing business, they have done business from time immemorial, making huge, huge, huge money from less privileged people with their new inventions and other things. We cannot say that introducing GMOs into the country is a *charity*; it's for money. And all those people who are supporting GMOs, if you look well and you read properly, it is a very *vicious* cycle in that they think, "Okay, so, Africa is suffering, they are hungry, they need food. This is a quick fix, this is a quick fix for African hunger." Constance hit her desk to emphasize "quick fix."

"So, it appears to us we are looking for want of a better word, salvation. We are hungry, we need food, so our salvation may lie in the GMOs which they say is high producing, it's pest resistant and *all* these things are things farmers are already facing. . . . Right now, I want to just assume that there are no GMO seeds [on the market in Ghana]. But there are improved seeds, hybrid seeds, high-yielding seeds, and all those things. And those that are brought in from outside are very expensive. And even local improved seeds are very expensive, and the farmers cannot afford."

Constance's comments here echo those of other farmers we met earlier. Remember the story of the farmer who hosted a DuPont Pioneer hybrid maize test plot on his farm; though yields were impressively high, the cost of the seed was so prohibitive that not a single farmer in his community purchased it. In other words, farmers and members of the Platform remember being promised what Constance refers to as "quick fixes" before, and these experiences in turn inform their opinion on GMOs. Memories of quick fixes—both good and bad—inform GAFP's insistence on championing the importance of infrastructure, but which I mean roads, storage, and markets. High productivity, Constance told me, is meaningless without the structures to support the crop to move from farm to market, and without a robust market to absorb an influx of products:

> And lastly, . . . we have problems with storage facilities, we have problems with infrastructure, [and] accessing market. . . . So, let us assume that GMOs are actually very high yielding, so we grow GMO [and] we get so much . . . rice, so many beans. Where are we taking them to? Where will you take them to? Why don't you solve these existing problems?

Embedded in Constance's comments is a critique on the idea that productivity (or lack thereof) is *the* issue facing Ghana's agricultural sector. In Ghana, news stories about farmers losing an entire harvest because they were unable to move their crop from farm to market due to washed out roads, lack of buyers, or other infrastructural concerns are common. For example, that same year, Ghanaian news reported that there was a "watermelon glut" in the country; so many farmers had grown watermelon that the market was saturated (Bokpe 2016). "The thing with watermelons is, if you make some money in one year, then everybody wants to join the party," one farmer told a reporter (Bokpe 2016). That year, the price of watermelon fell over 50 percent compared to the previous year (Bokpe 2016). Moreover, annual estimates of post-harvest loss are high too; the country "is estimated to lose about 20 to 30% of cereals and legumes and about 20 to 50% of tubers, fruits, and vegetables in storage, during transport or at the market" (Rutten and Verma 2014: 5; Nyo 2016). With full knowledge that farmers often faced difficulty selling their harvest, GAFP had made (infra)structural improvements a top priority. As discussed earlier, Ghana's farmers had seen promises of miracle seeds and technology come and go before. By placing questions of infrastructure squarely in the conversation of GMOs, Ghana's food sovereignty activists were shifting the conversation away from individual choice of seed to the collective good.

We Are Made to Believe Our Food Is Not Good

In Ghana, a relatively young country, the message that the Plant Breeders Bill represented a possible loss of seed and food sovereignty resonated with many. "We don't control our economy. We don't control the prices of our commodities . . . so can't we even control our food?" mused Samia Nkrumah, a prominent politician and also the daughter of Kwame Nkrumah, at a street protest in 2014 (CGTN Africa 2014). Nkrumah, who at the time was the chairperson of the Convention People's Party, a political party established by Kwame Nkrumah, had joined the Platform, and was the only politician to openly do so. Her comments indexed a deep, historical political-economic critique of global power and food structures, a sentiment that is foundational to Ghanaian food sovereignty advocacy: activists center the growth of the state and state sovereignty vis-à-vis agricultural production, and not the other way around. To that end, the Platform used their original goal—halting the commercialization of GM seeds—as a springboard to draw attention to an agricultural sector already struggling: poor infrastructure (markets, roads, storage), high post-harvest loss, and a global economic system that works against a small country like Ghana.

"Very often, our politicians push some ridiculous arguments which make you wonder whether they understand the global trend of politics and whether their commitment to our country is actually even in existence," Kofi said to me as we sat at the Freedom Centre. "What is globalization when you as a country are not playing any significant role in globalization? As other countries in the world are pushing their scientists, they're pushing their companies to come and exploit your resources. What are we also doing as a country? And this idea of globalization is so stupid that it is very difficult to understand where it is coming from."

Comments from Kofi about Ghana "not playing any significant role in globalization" and Nkrumah's argument of "we don't control our economy" were especially salient in the Platform's first few years of existence, which coincided with an ongoing economic crisis. Beginning in late 2013 and early 2014, the national currency, the cedi, had descended into freefall. In light of an oil find in 2007, the state, it turned out, had overspent money it didn't have, predicting returns from offshore drilling would be more than they actually amounted to due to a global oil glut. As the cedi fell, other sectors were soon caught in its wake. In 2014 an oil shortage hit Accra; the government was grossly behind in its payments to oil distribution companies, who, due to this high debt, were refusing to deliver fuel to the nation's gas stations. The shortage frustrated many Ghanaians: how can we produce oil, but not have fuel at gas stations? A few days later, more bad news arrived; the government was millions of dollars behind payment to the private, Christian-run Mission Hospitals who served over 50 percent of the country, who stated they would no longer accept the national health insurance (National Health Insurance Scheme [NHIS]). To boot, in the middle of the fuel crisis and NHIS collapse (and dismal and controversial World Cup performance in Brazil), the government announced water and electricity price hikes, and the removal of fuel subsidies, meaning that when fuel *did* return, it would be more expensive.

During those same months, the Ghanaian state announced that it had agreed to lease out the state-run Electricity Company of Ghana (ECG) for twenty years as a stipulation of an agreement the state had signed with the United States under the Millennium Challenge Corporation. In other words, the government had effectively agreed to privatize one of the final state-run services left after three decades of structural adjustment and neoliberal dismantling. Upon hearing the news about ECG's leasing, a friend remarked, "Everything is gone, oh. We are gradually losing

Leave ECG alone. Sign opposing the privatization of ECG hangs outside an ECG office in Accra.

everything." In light of the water, currency, and electricity challenges, Reuters declared, "Once a Model for Africa, Ghana's Economy Loses Its Shine" (Bigg and Kpodo 2014). But at the same time, folks took to the streets to protest mounting hardships. On July 1, Republic Day, a group called the Concerned Ghanaians for Responsible Governance organized the "Occupy Flagstaff House" protest. In the hundreds, protestors "walked through the rain toward Flagstaff House, the seat of government, and presented a petition to" presidential staff (Daswani 2020: 104). Some weeks later, thousands of Ghanaians around the country took place in a labor-organized strike in protest of poor economic conditions.

In this context, the Platform's argument that the state lacked sovereignty was not a controversial position, but rather an everyday embodied reality. When I asked David, an early member of the Platform, why he became interested in IPRs and GMOs, he cited Paolo Friere's *Pedagogy of the Oppressed*. David described the colonial-era education system where, he argued, Ghanaians developed a consciousness on how to serve the colonial government. This relationship, David told me, continued into the independence era. The failure to decolonize Ghana's education system, David said, had created a contemporary "status quo" wherein the educational system today continues to "maintain" colonial structures by those who "[chop the] post of white man." To *chop* is to consume, and so what David described was a system where the elite literally *eat* to maintain racialized power relations.

Nii, an officer at GAFP and also an early Platform supporter, explained how the "status quo" David spoke of seeps into everyday life: "I think that people are brainwashed. They are made to think that what they own, everything about them, is bad." He continued, noting how this impacted agriculture: "It's the same with our traditional farming system. We are made to believe that our food is not good, the food that we used to feed our children is not nutritious, the food that we ourselves eat is not nutritious." In our same conversation, Nii described GMOs and other seeds purchased or provided by extension officers, NGOs, and agro-dealers as *oburoni*, and the seeds that farmers saved, passed down, traded, and obtained from the market as *local*. The question becomes, Nii asked, whether it is "possible . . . to actually get resources to be able to go by the conditions given by the oburonis using the oburoni seed?" Here, Nii links the oburoni designation explicitly with seed that comes with "conditions" for maximum growth, such as chemicals, water, and other inputs to grow properly. Similar to Constance's comment about improved seeds and quick fixes, Nii questions the efficacy of resource-intensive interventions for farmers who are largely resource-constrained.

Both Nii and David described Ghanaian agricultural and food systems as socio-political spheres racialized first during colonial rule and today by the educational system and development industry. They also expressed feelings of alienation that, as Frantz Fanon wrote in 1952, originate from the structural, racialized projects of imperialism and colonization, and continue today in the postcolonial, neoliberal world order (Fanon 1952: 80; Pierre 2012). This long arc, one that replicates and unfolds in classrooms, in farmers' fields, and in boardrooms in Accra, is part and parcel of recipient fatigue. For to be told over generations that one's food is not good, one's way of farming is not good, one's knowledge is not good; it is not surprising that an outcome of this is a rejection of—or at least a questioning of—new formations that seek to make global connections and *claim* to flatten global hierarchies, like globalization (Kofi), oburoni seeds (Nii), or plant breeders laws (Constance). For if these formations, if these technologies, have so far been a bad deal for you, for your parents, for your friends, for your aunties and uncles over generations, why not try something new? Why not look back to the things that you've been told are bad—your food, your farming, your knowledge—and begin to build from there?

Given the legacy of development programs and the violence they enacted—on landscapes, people, and communities (e.g., Nii, "we are made to believe that our food is not good")—the Platform insisted there had to be other ways to develop Ghana's agricultural sector. And this point is key; development, though critiqued, remained a goal. To this end, many activists and farmers drew on *sankofa*, the Akan philosophy of looking to the past to move forward in the present, as a baseline for designing alternatives. One way activists applied sankofa to their work was by grounding socio-components of food and agriculture and a pride in agri-*cultures*—foodstuffs and their various uses, agricultural knowledge, gastro-identities, and the oneness of food and seed. Mark, a food sovereignty activist and NGO official, made this point routinely when discussing his opposition to GM seeds:

> Food is also our identity. You can identify any group of people from the food they eat. . . . For the Ga people, food means *kenkey*. You give them anything apart from kenkey, they may eat it, but it's not food. . . . You will go to the north where I come from, food is about TZ, *tuo-zaafi*, you know. And I can eat anything, but if I don't eat tuo-zaafi, I haven't eaten food. . . . So, if you change my food, you change my identity.

In Ghana, as most places in the world, the preparation and consumption of food is not simply a production or caloric practice, but also a cultural one. Activists viewed attempts at altering such practices as personal, corporeal, and political. Thus, instead of emphasizing deficiencies in agriculture, activists rather began with the *lifeworlds*, the socio-economic aspects of farming that mark life across agrarian Ghana. Specific cuisines, as Mark mentioned, are one example. Seed was another. Juxtaposing the use of seed in industrial agriculture—maximum production—activists emphasized the various types and uses of seed in Ghana: organizational and social value; seed as a family heirloom; and, importantly, the ability to "reuse" seed, that is, the ability to collect seed or other reproductive material from crops grown. This capability—described by activists as "the miracle of a seed" and "how God has made it"—is an obvious part of everyday farming in Ghana. Farmer-members of GAFP who I met with in the Bono East and Upper East regions described the importance of achieving *minimal* or *predictable* yield as well. While many acknowledged that improved seeds might bring larger harvests, they were quick to clarify that this was only if the farmer was able to purchase adequate fertilizer and agrochemicals, and if the sky provided enough rain. For many resource-constrained smallholder farmers, in a country with rapidly changing and erratic rain patterns the likelihood of obtaining the "high yields" promised by improved seeds was uncertain at best.

In just the first few years of the Platform's existence, the group grew in size and reputation both locally and globally. As I will show in a vignette later in this chapter, during this time the Platform used various means, such as public forums, to build a case for their core beliefs: that GMOs and the Plant Breeders Bill threatened the state; that the state was to be defended; and that sankofa should guide future agricultural development efforts. However, what was seemingly a well-oiled machine hit a major roadblock in 2015 after an officer in FSG was accused of malpractice and forced out, and many of the original organizers quit in protest (I explain the full story later). The fight went public and got ugly. As a result, organizations within the Platform sought to distance themselves from the messiness, relationships were broken, and, according to Kofi, informants disappeared, declaring the work too risky. What resulted was a splinter: FSG largely operated on its own, some organizations quietly backed out of the Platform altogether, and those remaining vowed to continue the Platform's work. As I will discuss below, what resulted was a Platform 2.0, weaker than the original, though just as determined.

Building (Post-)Colonial Solidarities

"I'm so happy to be here in Ghana," Dr. Vandana Shiva said with a smile and twinkle in her eye, addressing the nearly one hundred people who had gathered at the Paloma Hotel in Accra.[2] "Because from a distance I've been getting the flavor of the food sovereignty movement in Ghana and I know it's very special. It's very special because it is fueled by the energy of people, and I know that energy is unstoppable, especially when it is energy that is informed by the priorities that matter."

In June 2014, Dr. Shiva traveled to Ghana to speak at a public forum organized by the Platform and the Alliance for Food Sovereignty in Africa (AFSA). The Ghanaian Platform was connected to AFSA primarily through Bernard Guri, the executive director of the Centre for Indigenous Knowledge and Organizational Development (CIKOD) who helped found AFSA in 2008. CIKOD was an early member of the Ghanaian Platform, and Guri was an important link between Ghana, continental, and international activists. Dr. Shiva was there, in her words, to offer solidarity to the Ghanaian Platform, whose anti-GMO and anti-Plant Breeders Bill organizing had begun to gain international attention. The struggle in Ghana, she noted throughout her talk, was a matter of postcolonial solidarity.

"So now they're [using] another trick—[to] make it illegal for people to have their own seed—which is what the new seed legislation is all about," Shiva continued, referencing the Plant Breeders Bill. "It's about criminalizing local biodiversity. It's the way the British tried to criminalize our languages—"

"Yes!" someone in the audience shouted.

"Our ways of dressing—"

"Yes!"

"Our ways of eating. Criminalizing what is ours has always been the way of colonialism—"

"Mmm!"

"But this time, we cannot afford a new wave of colonialism because it means extinction of life on earth. We know better, we can do better.... We don't need to be fooled to be colonized *again*. With our indigenous seeds, with our indigenous knowledge, with agroecology, with solidarity, the kind of solidarity that was brought forth when our countries fought for freedom and independence, we were *one*. We have to become one again; not just country-wise, but across the world."

Shiva's presence, and the global attention it garnered, provided a new type of spotlight for Ghanaian activists, and the chance to use a high-profile visitor to elevate their message. Dr. Shiva was joined by a larger speaker panel that day: Bernard Guri of CIKOD; Million Belay, the coordinator of AFSA; Samia Nkrumah; Kwesi Pratt Jr., managing editor of the *Insight Newspaper*; and Yaw Opoku, a lawyer and prominent member of Food Sovereignty Ghana who presided as the master of ceremonies for the day. Given the panel makeup, the Shiva event provides an opportunity to ask, how do Ghanaian activists frame their struggles within local and international contexts?

As the master of ceremonies, Opoku's job was to keep the audience entertained, draw connections between speeches, and, importantly, provide brief bios for each of the speakers. His excitement was palpable as he rose to his feet to introduce the first speaker, Samia Nkrumah:

> It is my privilege to introduce somebody, who, when I mention their name, I feel tears welling in my eyes because without him, I would not be where I am. Unfortunately, he's not around, but the daughter has taken the mantel to do what the father [did].... And so, for me, it's always a glorious moment when I see the daughter and it reminds me of what the father stood for. Anytime you are talking

about Ghana, we can never, never, never, never, never stop talking about the father, that is *Osagyefo* Dr. Kwame Nkrumah. And I'm privileged to introduce [his] daughter, who is also the chairperson of the Convention People's Party of Ghana. Please welcome Madame Samia Nkrumah.

The audience erupted in applause and Nkrumah rose, not in the front of the room, but from the middle of the audience. She walked to a table in the front of the room (the "high table") where the rest of the discussants were seated and took a chair to the left of Guri. Smiling, she greeted the audience and welcomed Shiva to Ghana:

> Thank you, and welcome, Vandana. . . . Of course, as Mr. Opoku rightly said, very often when I'm invited to events, or when I'm taking part in any program, I know that I'm not only around in my personal capacity, but rather more importantly for what I represent. And that I've come to understand is that what I represent is something much bigger than many of us. It's a vision that refuses to die. A vision for African freedom, African self-reliance, African self-sufficiency, and freedom for our self-confidence and our ability to manage our own affairs. . . . And this whole struggle, this struggle against genetically modified foods, against the laws that will make it possible, or make it easier to facilitate the entry of GMOs into Ghana, into our markets and our land, into our food chain, I think this whole struggle is closely linked to our struggle for genuine freedom, for our freedom to create wealth, to control our land, to control our resources, and many of us instinctively, many before many facts became apparent to us, we instinctively and straight away saw the danger to our sovereignty.

As Nkrumah noted, Ghanaian activists worried about the introduction of a patenting regime for seeds. In particular, the bill's broad definition of a plant breeder (Clause 9)—a citizen, resident, or registered entity in the country or "within . . . a State which is a party to an international treaty to which the Republic is a party"—was particularly malicious for activists. "Can you imagine?" Opoku asked the audience after describing the contents of the bill. Activists warned that the bill would allow multinational companies to require Ghanaian farmers to sign contracts vowing not to save, trade, or replant seeds protected under the bill. Here, activists referenced Clause 58, which established standards and punishment for those who were found to be in violation of the law, and concerned activists because it broadly defined a violator as "a person who willfully offers for sale, sells or markets the propagating material of a variety protected in Ghana" (Plant Breeders Bill 2013: 14). Activists interpreted this clause as criminalizing the regular practice of seed saving and trading.

"I do not understand why there is this huge rush into GMOs, as if our current methods of farming are responsible for our poverty and . . . our underdevelopment," Pratt mused at the public forum. "What is responsible for our poverty and underdevelopment is not our current methods of farming, but the capitalist system which ensures that people can only eat if somebody can make a profit." A staunch socialist, whose newspaper shared an office with the Freedom Centre, Pratt was firm not only in identifying causes of poverty (capitalism), but also in calling out common discourse that misrecognizes causes of poverty. In doing so, Pratt—along with Nkrumah and others—highlights the structural and symbolic violence of agriculture in contemporary Ghana. Pratt continued:

> One of the things that happened in the past that puts us where we are today is the fact of slavery . . . One of the reasons why we are here is the fact of classical colonialism. The fact that our resources were exploited for the benefit of others, and not our people. The fact that other cultures were imposed by us, that we were made to eat in ways that were alien to us is one of the reasons that we are here today. And this should become an important sounding post in the discussion that we have today.

Constance, too, would often remark on the structural and violent legacy of colonialism, as well as the slave trade, when she spoke about agriculture, GMOs, and the Plant Breeders Bill. "They think that we are against the Plant Breeders Bill *mainly* because it is going to open the way for GMOs. It's one of them, but that is not the only thing why we [oppose] the Plant Breeders Bill," Constance explained to me one day. She returned to Clause 58, the section that establishes offences for those found to trade or sell patented seed.

"Legally he's not allowed to share [the seed] with me! You understand? I mean this is just . . . some other people have described it as something colonial. It's a new way of colonizing us, you know, it's a new way of *taking over*, taking over everything. It's a new way of . . ." Constance trailed off and stopped talking. When she picked back up again, her voice was lowered and softened: "They were here, [they] took away our . . . great, great, great-grandfathers to go to America and farm and build their country for them. Now they are so developed they are coming back here with what they have got, just to take away the little that we have that we can call *our own*." It was an emotional moment, and we sat in silence for some time after.

The structural and symbolic violence (Bourgois 2009) of agriculture as it relates to West Africa and the United States cannot be understated. Constance spoke of ongoing violent processes; *structural*, the historic use of enslaved black labor to build white wealth, *symbolized* by enslavement of the past, the seed cartels of the present, and the loss of seed sovereignty of the future (Bourgois 2009). Following Constance, then, development is a violent practice. This logic forms the core of the Platform, for many of whom colonialism is not a distant past. Development as violence is also an essential component of recipient fatigue. Thus, the use of (anti) colonial arguments by activists are not simply discursive tactics; they are reflective of contemporary subject-making and subjectivity (Fanon 1952; Nkrumah [1965]).

Back at the Paloma Hotel, Bernard Guri drew broad connections to colonialism as a political force and an embodied experience. "So, if a country is so-called 'independent,'" he explained carefully to the audience, "and yet you cannot feed yourself, you have to depend on another country to feed you, then you are not independent, you are still being colonized. . . . Our stomachs are being colonized!" Here, Guri's mention of "feeding yourself" referenced both the individual and the nation-state, demonstrating the embodiment of coloniality and its entanglements in global processes. For Guri, the availability of food was as intimately tied to Ghanaian farmers as it was to the highly concentrated multinational seed industry, where only three companies "control more than half of the global proprietary seed market" (Howard 2015: 2489).

As speakers took turns on the mic at the Paloma, the audience buzzed, nodding, murmuring, and exclaiming in agreement. No one really talked about "development." A part of recipient fatigue are moments like the Shiva event, where speakers reframe larger conversations around agriculture and the state to reflect the outcomes of goals *they* would like to see, which necessarily involves flipping the frame of analysis. In other words, for activists, GMOs were not a question of agricultural development, but rather a question of the state and its ability to perform, compete, and exercise sovereignty in a global world.

Soon, the event was all but over. As a final word, Opoku asked the audience to observe a moment of silence for Maya Angelou, who had passed away a short month prior. Angelou was one of many black intellectuals who moved to Ghana in the 1960s, and to that day remained a "friend of Ghana," Opoku said. One by one, audience members rose to their feet and stood in silence.

Food Sovereignty Ghana Goes to Court

In 2014, the Platform seemed unstoppable. They had hosted Vandana Shiva, presented at academic conferences and NGO meetings, organized farmer marches, appeared on radio stations and newscasts, and generally put up a united, well-coordinated political front. And they had joined international networks, including AFSA, whose coordinator, Million Belay, spoke forcefully at the Shiva event of the importance of pan-African solidarity and reclaiming the mic—and gaze—from northern experts: "Some of you have been, I'm sure, traveling all over the world . . . and wherever you go, what you see is other people, other northern NGOs mostly, speaking on behalf of Africa. So, in 2008, . . . some of us came together and decided to speak together in one voice about Africa." However, by the end of 2014, the Platform had splintered. What happens when the solidarity that Belay, Shiva, Nkrumah, and so many others spoke of falls apart?

The collapse of the Platform was instigated by internal fissures within FSG, who at the time was acting more or less as the de-facto spokesperson for the larger movement. FSG was the most visible Platform group both domestically and internationally, using social media and their fairly youthful base to build support. FSG had always been a bit controversial; since they were relatively new to the scene, they had few friends and almost no financial donors, which meant they weren't beholden to people in power. Other organizations within the Platform, on the other hand, like PFAG and CIKOD, were older, more embedded in state and donor structures, and therefore more reliant on funds and contacts to continue their work. While some Platform members told me privately that they did not agree with the way certain FSG members handled business (some younger members were thought to be aggressive in their speak and actions), they nevertheless conceded that FSG was successful in garnering public attention with their diverse strategies.

But in the months following the Shiva event, the organizational structure of FSG collapsed. The fall was instigated after a cadre within the group accused the organization's leader of pocketing group funds, accusations he denied. Though FSG's leader decried the move as an internal coup, in the end, he resigned, as did many members of FSG loyal to him. Had FSG handled their matters privately, the damage may have ended there, but the organization made their infighting public, publishing articles and tweets about the leader's removal (FSG 2014). As the conflict went public, others in the Platform quietly distanced themselves from FSG. AFSA, who just months earlier had co-hosted the Shiva forum with FSG, booted FSG from the alliance. And, as Kofi told me with sorrow in his voice, allies in governmental and scientific institutions who had worked quietly and behind the scenes for the Platform soon disappeared, distrustful of a group so volatile and willing to publicize private matters.

Ever defiant, the new FSG leadership decided to press on without the backing of the Platform. They organized a march in Accra for the worldwide March Against Monsanto in May 2015, released an anti-GMO song and music video with Ghanaian reggae artist Bobo Shanti (2015), and stayed active in online campaigns. But after breaking off from the Platform, perhaps the most significant, and controversial, move FSG took was suing the National Biosafety Authority (NBA) and the Ministry of Environment, Science, Technology and Innovation (MESTI) in 2015 in an attempt to bring a permanent ban on GMOs. Long before the Platform splintered, its members had debated whether a legal battle was the right course of action to take. At the 2014 Shiva event, Pratt broached the subject and announced his opposition to using the courts to stop GMOs. Pratt believed that judges were likely to side with agribusiness and, in this case, the state institutions that were hosting GM field trials, and thus preferred collective action to pressure the state. And so, when FSG announced in 2015 they would be suing state institutions after all, their former allies were split. Though Platform members shared FSG's desire to stop the commercialization of GM crops, privately most organizations within the Platform did not agree with the premise and timing of the case. In the end, PFAG, GAWU, and CIKOD did not join as co-plaintiffs, while the Convention People's Party and the Vegetarian Association of Ghana did.

While FSG had many qualms regarding GM crops, from the partners developing them to concerns about their safety, FSG's suit was premised on a bureaucratic technicality; according to the National Biosafety Act (2011), the government of Ghana needed to establish a National Biosafety *Authority* before field trials of any GMOs could take place. At the time FSG filed their lawsuit, the country had established a National Biosafety *Committee*, but not an *Authority*. FSG argued that the lack of an authority violated the country's own law, and thus rendered ongoing field trials of GM crops illegal. The matter took on particular urgency for FSG, as they believed that Bt cowpea was soon to be considered by the National Biosafety Committee for commercialization. (At time of this writing, Bt cowpea still isn't commercialized.) FSG submitted their case to the Human Rights Court, arguing that food production and consumption were fundamentally human rights issues.

The case began with a dramatic start. On the same day as the first court hearing, February 17, 2015, MESTI announced the transition of the National Biosafety *Committee* to an *Authority*. The timing of the announcement was auspicious, to say the least, and one made no doubt in an attempt to quell FSG's legal arguments. Nevertheless, the change was made too late to sway the case's judge, who ordered a temporary injunction to be placed on GM cowpea and rice field trials while the case was being adjudicated. The injunction was considered a significant victory by activists within and outside of Ghana. However, the joy was short-lived: in October of that year, the judge overseeing the case, Justice Kofi Essel Mensah, along with twenty-nine of his colleagues were removed from the bench months after a viral exposé revealed judges, including Justice Mensah, accepting bribes from undercover journalists (BBC 2015). As a result, the case slowed down, but eventually resumed under the stern review of Justice Dennis Adjei, who had no patience for activists in his courtroom. "I'm bound by law and not public outcry," he warned during an initial hearing, "these matters concern food science and environmental science."

I attended two hearings of the case. Both times, I was struck by the juxtaposition of the Law Courts Complex, a newly constructed five-story building that hugged High Street and overlooked the worn, colonial-era Ministry of Food and Agriculture office buildings across the street. The court complex was brand-new—TVs and furniture were still wrapped in shipping plastic—a project financed by the Chinese government, the newest development donor on the scene. It's glam, especially compared to the decaying ministry buildings, seemed to speak to global donor priorities: the supposed rule of law and "good governance" versus food and agriculture.

On October 29, 2015, eight months after the case had been filed, I climbed a flight of stairs searching for the room hosting the hearing—the complex was so new, room number placards had still not been installed. I arrived to find a packed chamber, with only a few seats available in the front row. Everyone was there: FSG's new leadership and a dozen or so supporters; the CEO and board members of the NBA; and active proponents of GMOs, including Dr. Walter Alhassan, a Ghanaian animal scientist who is largely credited with working diligently for years to bring GMOs to Ghana.

By the time Justice Adjei entered the chamber, twenty minutes after the hearing was slated to begin, the lawyers for the NBA and MESTI had still not yet arrived. Judge Adjei began without them. (They would arrive later, toward the end of the hearing, and receive a stern warning from the judge: "I sit at 9[a.m.], so next time, don't do this.") He read his judgment quickly: the court disagreed that there was high risk involved with the ongoing GMO trials, and that likewise any risk was taken care of by the Biosafety Act and the NBA. Justice Adjei concluded that the "Defendant will suffer harm if application is approved" (or, in other words, that the defendant would suffer if the court were to ban GMOs), and dismissed the application "without merit." The room remained silent as people quickly filed out.

I followed the crowd out of the building to a large outdoor rotunda where a group of reporters were waiting. A crowd quickly formed around FSG members and their lawyer, George Tetteh Wayo. The disappointment was palpable. A reporter asked Wayo to react to the judge's ruling that the "Defendant will suffer harm if application is approved."

"I disagree. I wholly disagree," Wayo responded. "What does the defendant lose? The defendants will not lose anything! Fine, they will say that they put money into experiments. But . . . the defendants in this matter have not spent a dime. These monies have been given to us by so-called donors and corporate bodies who are fronting GMOs: Monsanto, Syngenta, and DuPont."

Wayo's use of "us" was in reference to the state institutions overseeing GM field trials in the country, mainly CSIR. And so, Wayo's larger argument was that since the defendants—the NBA and MESTI—were not the financial investors of the GM projects, they would not "suffer" if the court had ruled in FSG's favor. Wayo continued, arguing that the court's ruling essentially protected the "so-called donors and corporate bodies who are fronting GMOs" rather than Ghanaian citizens.

After Wayo made his comments, Edwin Kweku Andoh Baffour, FSG's communication director, stepped into the middle of the crowd. Sporting a pin of Kwame Nkrumah on the lapel of his shirt, Baffour promised to appeal the case:

> We are going to appeal. . . . Despite this action and this decision today, we remain confident that the people of Ghana are not going to be swayed by the argument of science, because there are no hungry people in this land. We produce more food than we need. Food rots. What we rather need is investment in roads, warehouses, manage post-harvest loss. But the fact that you want to say that we must genetically modify our foods, I want to ask the Ghanaian farmers that who in Europe is going

to buy your genetically modified orange juice on the shelf? Who will buy your genetically modified pawpaw in Sweden? Who will buy your genetically modified mango in Germany if we go ahead with this? This is not about feeding. It is not about efficiency in agriculture. This is about the control of the food supply of nations.

Baffour's comments provide insight into how FSG—and indeed some members of the Platform—thought about, and advocated against, GMOs. First, there was the infrastructural angle—"Food rots. What we rather need is investment in roads." Similar to my conversation with Constance earlier in the chapter, Baffour used the well-known example of post-harvest loss as an appeal to the average Ghanaian, whether in the capitol or in rural communities, who knew all too well of the structural issues facing Ghana's food sectors.

Similarly, Baffour's second core argument related to produce markets in the European Union (EU), where Ghanaian farmers exported vegetables and fruits. The previous year, the EU had placed a ban on the import of Ghanaian vegetables due to high levels of pesticide residue, effectively closing major export opportunities for many Ghanaian farmers. As such, Baffour's appeal that genetically modified crops would not be accepted in the EU—which already banned a number of Ghana-grown vegetables—was a realistic threat for Ghanaian farmers and policymakers alike.

While the latter were logistical, political-economic concerns, Baffour's third argument of was that of problematization. With his comment "we remain confident that the people of Ghana are not going to be swayed by the argument of science, because there are no hungry people in this land," Baffour is walking a linguistic tightrope. While GMO supporters like to suggest that opposition to GMOs is "anti-science," that's not what's happening here; Baffour is not suggesting that he or FSG are against the notion of science. Rather, he is trying to problematize the narratives biotech boosters use to justify the use of GMOs: that Ghana is hungry and therefore needs technologies to address hunger, and that GMOs are scientifically safe and therefore there should be no debate about them. Instead, Baffour engages in a political-economic analysis of food security and access in the country, pointing out both infrastructural concerns and the trickiness of export markets. In doing so, he not only highlights structural impediments of food access in the country, but also insists that GMOs be understood not simply in the context of "science," but within the political-economic sphere in which agricultural technologies, Ghana's food systems, and Ghanaian farmers operate. These complexities are crucial for any (agricultural) technology, yet are so often obscured in conversations about food security on the African continent that focus on urgency ("Biotechnology is so important and we can't develop without it" [Introduction]) and essentialist constructions of African food systems and farmers that mark the entire continent as starving ("The Europeans have decided they don't want to use it . . . which is fine, they're not facing malnutrition and starvation" [Introduction]). What Baffour, Constance, and others insist on is a structural critique.

Nearby FSG's press conference, Dr. Margaret Atikpo, who at the time led the Ghana chapter of the Open Forum on Agricultural Biotechnology in Africa (OFAB, the communications arm of the African Agricultural Technology Foundation), stood with Professor Kwabena Mantey Bosompem, a board member of the NBA. They kept their distance from the huddle around the FSG legal team and waited for the press to come to them. Out of the half a dozen reporters interviewing FSG, only one (and I) eventually made their way over. Where the courtroom and FSG's press conference had been tense, Professor Bosompem and Dr. Atikpo were in a celebratory mood. Professor Bosompem promised the reporter that Ghana had laws in place to safely regulate GM production and cultivation, and stressed that

> the few applications for genetically modified organisms that we have in the country today, like the one on GM rice, the one on GM cotton, or GM cowpea, have come from . . . recognized state research institutions of the CSIR who have been established by law and are mandated to look in to how to promote socio-economic development of this nation through the advancement of appropriate, reliable, safe, scientific technologies.

Professor Bosompem's emphasis on "recognized state research institutions" acted as a claim-making device in two ways. First, similar to activists such as Edwin and others, Professor Bosompem highlighted the role of the state and its supposed ability to handle an outside technology. But secondly, and related to the first, is that while marking GMOs as foreign, Bosompem also stressed their local handling. This type of argumentation is popular among GM proponents, especially those working within internationally based organizations such as OFAB (Dr. Atikpo). In such an argument, proponents contend either directly or indirectly that GMOs in Africa are "homegrown" as they are housed within state research institutions. And it is exactly the nature of the GMO projects—their foreign funding, direction, and promotion—that Edwin, FSG, and other Platform activists seek to highlight. Remembering back to Lawyer Wayo's comments—"the defendants have not spent a dime; these monies have been given to us by so-called donors and corporate bodies who are fronting GMOs"—FSG's case was as much about development funding and construction and its impact on state institutions (as evidenced by Wayo's use of "us" to reference donor funding to state institutions) as much as it was about GMOs and a new agricultural technology.

Members from FSG had slowly migrated to where Professor Bosompem and Dr. Atikpo were, and the scene quickly grew heated. After about five to ten minutes of intense group exchange, security guards demanded that everyone leave the premise. Members of FSG who were still there tried to organize a group photo, but the security guard insisted they leave. "The corruption never stops," a FSG member said, a double-reference to both the ejection and the court's ruling.

Throughout the day I exchanged messages with my contacts within the Platform and watched as conversations unfolded in WhatsApp groups. Generally speaking, there was a feeling of dread and disappointment. No one was surprised at the decision, but many worried that this closed a door to any future legal contests. Jacqueline Ignatova argues that by "bringing GMOs to the courtroom, activists have sometimes invoked and reinforced the same legal regime that enabled the introduction of GMOs in the first place" (2015: 41). I read these tactics a bit differently; by utilizing state institutions such as the court, food sovereignty advocates are re-affirming the belief that the state should be held responsible for overseeing the agricultural sector. This is a lofty demand under late capitalism and the neoliberal project, in a time where globally states are selling off private goods, abdicating from state services (or what one Ghanaian official described as "doing business"), and moving toward creating "an enabling environment" for the private sector to carry out activities that were once under the state's purview.

FSG delivered on their promise to appeal the ruling. It took a few years of fits and starts and crowd-sourcing funding for lawyer fees, but finally, in 2017, they filed their appeal. At the time of writing (February 2021), the case is still ongoing. The case is stuck in a second stage of appeals. The Ghana National Association of Farmers and Fishermen (GNAFF), who decided to join the case as a co-defendant, argued that the Human Rights High Court, where the appeal was sitting, was an unnecessary adjudicator of the matter, as the Biosafety Act stipulated that matters regarding biotechnology and biosafety ought to be heard by a tribunal established by the NBA. Upon hearing GNAFF's argument, the High Court kicked the case up to the Supreme Court, who, in July 2019, ruled that the High Court did indeed have jurisdiction over the case.

While GNAFF tried to move the case out of the national courts, they instead, and likely unintentionally, thrust the authority of the NBA and the Biosafety Act into the legal spotlight. While GNAFF and the NBA argued that the NBA should be the sole arbitrator of issues related to biotechnology, GNAFF's appeal—and the Supreme Court's ruling—may very well actually undermine the NBA's authority. In other words, in ruling that issues related to genetically modified food crops were human rights issues and remained within the jurisdiction of the national courts, the Supreme Court established that the courts also had authority over matters related to biotechnology. Singling out food crops—cowpea and rice—was a strategic move by FSG. Food is symbolic, food is powerful, and it strikes the heart of people. GMO proponents understand this too; recall in the earlier discussion about why GMO brokers decided to commercialize cotton, rather than rice or cowpea first: to ease in a wary public. Thus, though the outcome of their appeal remains unknown, FSG's court case has successfully kept GM crops in the national spotlight.

Conclusion

One day in the GAFP office, I told Nii about my conversation with John ("Does Bill Gates love Africa more than me?"). Nii smiled in agreement and said, "When you go to a funeral house, and you see a sympathizer cry more than the bereaved, then you must investigate the person's interest." In this chapter, I have shown how Ghanaian food sovereignty activists investigate and evaluate sympathizers' interests and destabilize global ideas of agricultural development. In doing so, I demonstrated how Ghanaian food sovereignty activists conceive of sovereignty, and how they mediate between their goals and state and donor policy and discourse. This is not to say that issues of hunger and food availability are not important—they are.

Instead, these vignettes indicate that food and seed in Ghana ought to be characterized beyond caloric considerations: as historical biographies; familial and cultural vessels; sites of socialization; a corporeal understanding of oneself; as a platform to discuss the past, the present, and the future. In declaring that "our stomachs are being colonized," activists use seeds (and food) as a springboard for discussing issues of sovereignty, nationhood, and citizenship to push back against teleological development models that suggest there is one way to develop and that development is desired (Davidson 2012; Escobar 1995). These models—bolstered by discourse, literature, and rock stars in the field—often place Africa versus modernity, as if the continent cannot claim modern-ness without the adoption of certain economic systems, attitudes, and governance models, and/or a victim of institutions that would like to impose modern-ness. Within this modeling, actors, ideas, and technologies that do not claim specific constructions of modernity as wholesale desirable are marked as anti-modern and anti-progress. However, in the case of Ghanaian food sovereignty activism, activists do not critique modernity in general, but rather flex to shape their version of the state, modernity, and progress (Ferguson 2006). In other words, the state apparatus is not the enemy, but rather the pinnacle, something that ought to be nurtured and defended.

Thus, while some have characterized conversations, interviews, and protests around GMOs as "debates" (Braimah et al. 2017; Ignatova 2015), discussions around GMOs are about something much larger: the nation-state, sovereignty, and Ghana's (and Africa's) position in the world. As I will show, questions about the state (and its reliance on donors) were not just important for anti-GM activists, but for the Ghanaian scientists and bureaucrats working on GM seeds as well. Conditions of coloniality violently shape everyday subjectivities, regardless of where one fell on the GMO spectrum.

CHAPTER 4

The Patents Are Out There

"From your faces, I believe you are prepared to help Ghana understand the issues." Kojo smiled, scanning the crowd from his position at the front of a hotel conference room. Kojo, an official within Ghana's National Biosafety Authority (NBA), the government body tasked with overseeing all issues related to biotechnology, was hosting a workshop on agricultural biotechnology and risk management for journalists and civil servants in Accra. I had been invited to observe, and took a seat at one of the half dozen round tables placed throughout the room.

By the time this workshop was taking place in 2016, Kojo was a veteran in Ghana's small biotechnology scene. He and his team were charged with building a regulatory regime from scratch, a task they had been working on since the early 2000s. Addressing the crowd, he continued: "You guys have been telling us and the public that [genetically modified organisms (GMOs)] cause superweeds, poverty, and monsters." An image of a corncob with the face of Frankenstein was featured on Kojo's accompanying slide. "The whole thing is that no one has become a monster yet." He continued for another twenty minutes or so, explaining current laws pertaining to GMOs and the role of the NBA.

Kojo and his colleagues present from the NBA were in a tricky position. On one hand, as authority representatives stressed throughout the workshop, the authority was technically meant to be a neutral body, advocating neither for nor against genetic modification, but rather, simply providing "facts." And for them and for other pro-GMO groups operating on the African continent, the "facts" are this: that genetic modification is a scientifically proven technology; that genetic modification poses no health risks; that any environmental or social risks will be adjudicated by government authorities; and that genetic modification results in superior and higher yielding seeds when compared to other breeding techniques. Throughout the day, authority members and other invited speakers urged attendees to share these "facts," and provided tips on how to do so.

On the other hand, the rise of the Food Sovereignty Platform, their argument that the Plant Breeders Bill (PBB) and GMOs were inextricably related, and their savvy media campaigns were dominating many stories on GMOs in Ghana. The Platform's relative success at driving the narrative had created a public relations problem for Ghana's biotech boosters—the scientists, government officials, and organizations tasked with building public support for biotech and brokering agreements between multinationals, donors, and the Ghanaian scientific community—a group that the NBA belonged to. Indeed, the rise of the Platform required boosters to craft their messaging around why both GMOs *and* the PBB were in Ghana's best interest. This is a key tension that underlines Ghana's relatively small biotechnology community: those tasked with advocating for and implementing laws related to biotechnology were often the same who advocating for the adoption of GMOs.[1]

Ghana's biotech boosters occupy complex spaces and are often tasked with playing tricky roles. In this chapter, I explore how and why some Ghanaian scientists view GMOs as "the secret" to high returns. Whereas global narratives construct GMOs as life-saving technology for African farmers (Lynas 2018; Paarlberg 2008), Ghanaian scientists did not necessarily view GM crops as technologically superior (nor even life-saving). Instead, Ghanaian scientists—and other boosters—believed the potential to claim intellectual property rights (IPRs) with genetically modified (GM) crops, via the PBB, was what made the technology appealing. As I will show through vignettes and interviews, Ghanaian officials recognized the limitations posed by IPRs and collaborations with multinational seed companies, but also envisioned IPRs as an important way to collect financial benefit from GMOs. Thus, rather than describe GMOs as a humanitarian technology, as donors sought to do, Ghanaian officials and scientists went out of their way to stress that, when coupled with IPRs, GM seeds were "the secret" to obtaining profit, revenue that was sorely needed in the post-structural adjustment era of gutted state infrastructure.

Building a Case for Biotech (and the Plant Breeders Bill)

The Accra journalist workshop was a full-day event chock-full of speakers from institutions integral to Ghana's experiments with GMOs. In addition to Kojo and colleagues from the NBA, presentations were given by scientists and officials from the Council for Scientific and Industrial Research (CSIR), the Biotechnology and Nuclear Agriculture Research Institute (BNARI), the Program for Biosafety Systems (PBS) Ghana chapter, and the International Service for the Acquisition of Agri-biotech Applications (ISAAA). Of the presenters that day, only a representative from ISAAA had come in from out of the country; the rest belonged to Ghana's small biotech booster community.

The ISAAA self-describes as a "not-for-profit international organization" with a stated mission to "[share] the benefits of crop biotechnology to various stakeholders, particularly resource-poor farmers in developing countries, through knowledge sharing initiatives and the transfer and delivery of proprietary biotechnology applications" (ISAAA 2021b). They are funded in part by pro-biotechnology organizations such as the African Agricultural Technology Foundation (AATF), the US Agency for International Development (USAID), and the US Department of Agriculture (USDA), and also private firms, such as Corteva Agriscience and Bayer. Similar to the Cornell Alliance for Science and other boosters introduced earlier, the ISAAA works to build consensus around biotech. One way they attempt to do so is by training journalists.

And at the workshop in question, the ISAAA representative did not share her organization's affiliations with biotech firms, nor did she disclose that those who fund ISAAA stand to gain immensely should Ghanaian journalists help usher in public acceptance of GMOs. Instead, she described the ISAAA as a "pro-choice" organization that "respect[s] the rights of others to make their own decisions." She began her presentation by stating that it can be difficult to communicate about a technology that some describe as a "miracle" but that others say is a "monster." The rep continued, offering suggestions on how journalists could craft stories about GMOs in a way that moved away from monster-scenarios. She described, for instance, "genetic engineering" as a "scary term," and instead instructed journalists to use the phrase "modern biotechnology." She also suggested journalists avoid using the term "contamination" in stories regarding GM crops. "Contamination" is often used to refer to when a genetically modified plant interacts (and potentially shares germplasm) with nearby non-GM plants, a serious concern for farmers globally (Stone 2010). But that concern was not addressed by the ISAAA rep, who told the audience that "contamination" gives off the idea that GM crops are an unsafe product, and thus journalists should instead use the term "co-existence."

At events such as the journalist workshop, Ghanaian boosters attempted to build a case that GMOs were for the good for the country and that they were homegrown. One presenter who attempted to do so was a program officer from PBS. Standing in front of the room, he assured the crowd he had no product to sell, nor was he there to convince the journalists to be GMO advocates. Like others speaking that day, he said, he was there to provide facts and answer questions. For, he told the crowd, Ghana has a "vibrant" media, "as high as American and British media." The problem was, he told journalists sitting just feet from him, the Ghanaian media tends to have little understanding of biotech and therefore "has the potential to perpetuate misinformation." To build his case, he said he believed that "several groups [had] increasingly confused" the PBB with the Biosafety Act, despite the two being distinct and separate.

As I discussed earlier, Ghanaian activists made sure that public discussion of GMOs was inextricable from the PBB. The bill was a key point of contention for the Platform, but also for boosters who tried for years to get the public and journalists to separate the two topics. In public, proponents of the PBB argued that the bill had nothing to do with GMOs. The Biosafety Act, they reminded reporters, established a governmental regime to handle matters related to biotechnology. "The Plant Breeders' Bill," Dr. Margaret Atikpo, director of the Open Forum on Agricultural Biotechnology in Africa (OFAB) Ghana chapter, told a reporter, "is simply to provide royalties and serves to motivate the breeders, protect our seeds, and fetch the much needed foreign exchange revenues for Ghana" (Gakpo 2014).[2] Rarely did boosters engage with the Platform's concerns regarding the PBB's definition of a "plant breeder" (Clause 9) and the proposed conditions needed for a plant to be patentable (Clause 3).

While boosters attempted to convince the public that the PBB was not related to GMOs, they also engaged in conflicting messaging. First, the same proponents of GMOs were proponents of the PBB, and crafted their messaging around the bill as being good for both plant breeders and the state. Second, the same boosters described GMOs as advantageous because they could be patented. Though this two-pronged messaging was ultimately unconvincing that the PBB and GMOs were separate, it provides insight into how and why boosters loudly advocated for the adoption of both the bill and the seeds.

As described earlier, plant breeding in Ghana is mostly housed within public research institutions. Though some donor programs, like USAID's West Africa Seed Alliance, sought to chip away at this (Amanor 1999), by and large the field of plant breeding remains one populated by public breeders. This allows for proponents of the PBB to build a narrative that IPRs are good for the state (despite the fact that there are ongoing efforts to move breeding *out of* public institutions). It's no surprise then that this argument would be baked into the bill itself. In November 2013, the parliamentary committee charged with overseeing the PBB, the Committee on Constitutional, Legal, and Parliamentary Affairs, published a report on the PBB's contents, objectives, and potential benefits. The report's authors, Alban S. K. Bagbin (member of Parliament) and Eric Owusu-Mensah (clerk of the committee), concluded that "it will be in the national interest to pass this Bill" and "without hesitation [recommended the bill] to the House for consideration and passage" (2013: 9). Their reasoning was based in part on the belief that the PBB would bolster the state's work in biotechnology. The authors wrote:

> The Committee discovered that almost all countries, including its neighbours, such as Burkina Faso and Côte d'Ivoire, are making efforts to provide plant variety protection. Ghana and Ghanaian plant breeders are at a disadvantage without any legal protection, particularly in the advent of genetic engineering. Whiles it takes up to ten (10) years or more to develop a plant variety of most plant species by conventional plant breeding, genetic engineering offers the prospect of the creation of species and varieties in a much shorter time using transfer of genes into genomes, for instance. Attached is a list of member countries of UPOV, OAPI and other countries *making frantic efforts* to be members of UPOV. (Bagbin and Owusu-Mensah 2013: 6–7; emphasis added)

At the time the PBB was introduced to Parliament, Burkina Faso was six years into its experiment with Bt cotton, and by all public reports, things were going well (Luna and Dowd-Uribe 2020). Côte d'Ivoire on the other hand was not—and still is not—pursuing research into GMOs. Nevertheless, the parliamentary memo had a competitive, dire, and explicitly anti-Pan-Africanist tone: should Ghana continue with conventional breeding, the report argued, the state would have to wait up to a decade for new varieties to reach the market, putting Ghana at a supposed disadvantage while their neighbors make "frantic efforts" to codify IPRs (through joining UPOV). The text here, echoed by Ghanaian scientists and international donors, coupled conventional breeding with a supposedly weakened state, and genetic engineering with a flourishing, modern state. Though conventional breeding can result in high-yielding varieties, this point was obscured by certain interlocutors who positioned conventional breeding as weak and ineffective for modern needs. Instead, Ghanaian boosters sought to convince the public that GMOs were "the secret" to a more prosperous state.

The Secret

In July 2014, the Ghana Academy of Arts and Sciences (GAAS) held their annual public forum at the British Council in the heart of Accra. That year, the conference was dedicated solely to the topic of GMOs, the third public forum that summer to do so.[3] Over three nights, audiences packed the Council's 250-seat auditorium hear Ghanaian academics, lawyers, and scientists discuss GMOs. All but one speaker—lawyer Yaw Opoku from Food Sovereignty Ghana—presented papers in support of Ghana adopting the technology. Dr. Ibrahim Dzido Kwasi Atokple, a scientist from the Savannah Agricultural Research Institute (a branch of the Council for Scientific and Industrial Research [CSIR], a public research institute) and former principal investigator on Ghana's Bt cowpea project, was one such speaker. As the first presenter of the forum, Dr. Atokple was to set the mood for the days ahead, and he did so by making a case against conventional breeding. Dr. Atokple argued that conventional breeding—which he (and others) marked as *everything but genetic modification*—was ill-equipped for contemporary, modern needs: "Almost [all of] the improved varieties in Ghana [are from] conventional breeding, and we cannot continue to do this. We need to adopt modern plant breeding strategies." To bolster his argument, he projected a graph onto a large screen on the side of the stage. The graph showed maize yields in the American state of Iowa, where the average farm is 359 acres and where nearly 90 percent of all maize grown is genetically modified (USDA 2020a, 2020b). "Yes," he said, a smile appearing across his face, "safe for them. That is GM, they are making billions. So that is the secret. Can we do the same in Ghana?"

GAAS Public Forum 2014. Promotional banner advertising GAAS's 2014 public forum on GMOs hangs outside the British Council in Accra.

Over the course of the forum, Dr. Atokple and colleagues presented charts and graphs to build a case for a supposedly "unproductive" Africa compared to the rest of the world: low yields, low fertilizer use, and a (supposedly) aging farmer population.[4] They pointed to these and similar charts from countries that grew GM crops to argue that GM could be harnessed to feed the future in a way that conventional breeding could supposedly never achieve. Very few historical or structural analyses were included in their presentations—the statistics stood on their own and established a static image of a geographic region fraught with avoidable issues, evidenced by "progress" elsewhere.

Dr. Marian Quain, a scientist at the Crops Research Institute in Kumasi (another branch of the CSIR), spoke after Dr. Atokple. Compared to her predecessor, Dr. Quain was seemingly dedicated to translating scientific details about genetic modification to a generalist crowd. Rather than discuss the scientific methods and specifications of GMOs as Dr. Atokple did, Dr. Quain described biotechnology as an everyday technology. She used fermentation as an example, referencing the preparation of two popular items: *pito*, a fermented millet beer, and *kenkey*, a fermented corn dish. As she described these processes, audience members smiled and nodded along: "We come home—pito preparation, kenkey . . . when you mash it, . . . you are employing micro-organisms, and its biotechnology our ancestors were doing during those times, and we're still doing it."

By positioning biotechnology as an everyday phenomenon, Dr. Quain was able to leverage her expertise to argue that biotechnology—and, by extension, GMOs—is a natural part of Ghanaian life, passed on through the generations. Notably, she utilized examples from both the southern (kenkey) and northern (pito) parts of the country, making a claim that genetic modification belonged to *all* of Ghana. The following night, Dr. Hans Adu-Dapaah reiterated the claim that genetic modification was inherently indigenous to Ghana, describing GMOs as a technology that had built on "centuries of science." These historic and cultural claims established a temporal link from past to present that created a sense of urgency to adopt genetically modified seeds. At times, attempts by scientists to establish GMOs as "homegrown" were paired with visions of a teleological path for "progress" and "development." Halfway through her presentation, Dr. Quain paused and appealed to the audience that improvements in plant breeding were no different than improvements in communication:

> And I must say, just as communication has progressed, there are times that we [used] smoke to communicate with your nearby neighbor, ... telegraphs have been used ... Now we are Skyping, now there's cellphone, WhatsApp.... That's how far communication has progressed. I think breeding should also progress. I mean, *we've been wandering around the bush for too long.* (emphasis added)

Over the course of the forum, Dr. Quain was joined by other speakers in attributing biotech as something that was natural, homegrown, and a technology that Ghanaians had possessed for a long time. Scientists also described "conventional breeding" as homegrown, yet unmodern and undesirable, keeping Ghanaians in the "bush." Thus, the transition from conventional to modern breeding was marked as a matter of evolution (Luna 2017), from the bush to WhatsApp, evidenced by remarks by Dr. Quain and Dr. Adu-Dapaah, who concluded his talk with an image and quote from Charles Darwin.

Such language of productivity was often coded in racialized benchmarks of desirability and "good farming," relegating Africa as an exceptional place of exceptional suffering and exceptionally bad farming. Meanwhile, Dr. Atokple argued that Americans, presumably Iowan and white, were ideal farmers who possessed the "secret" to "mak[ing] billions": genetically modified crops. "We are basically interested in making every Ghanaian appreciate that the world is moving on and it is time we embraced technology in all its forms," said one proponent (Gakpo 2016a). Linguistic claims that the world is "moving on" are not far from "wandering around the bush," and indeed, these arguments are rooted in racialized notions of progress (Pierre 2020). Yet, at the same time, these markers were held in tension with another oft-cited argument: speakers frequently expressed the desire for an independent state vis-à-vis *these same markers* of progress, including GMOs.

After Dr. Quain finished her presentation, someone in the audience asked why rice, cotton, and cowpea had been chosen for genetic modification. Dr. Quain explained that they were initiatives of AATF (though this is not in fact true for cotton, which was a direct partnership between CSIR and Monsanto). She continued, suggesting that maize would be a good candidate for genetic modification, but warning that "we have to generate our *own* resource commitment to GM maize," elongating "own" to emphasize her point. And this is where things got interesting.

"And that is the problem I'm personally having now," Dr. Quain said, "I also have GM sweet potato.... And because no organization is supporting it, I don't have funding to do it. I'm doing it with [Tuskegee University] and we've run out of funds, so the project has stalled. It's actually the first project which received the permits to do a confined field trial [in Ghana] and we now don't have funds to do it.... So that is for *us now*. We must commit funds to *our* research to solve *our* problems and not wait for someone to come and impose activities on us."

While Dr. Quain's initial framing of biotechnology as homegrown and an age-old technique allowed her to bypass a discussion of the multiple actors and their (conflicting) interests involved in Ghana's biotech projects (Mueller and Flachs 2021), this comment was different. Instead, in lamenting that she was unable to continue research on GM sweet potato because of lack of funding, Dr. Quain pointed out the barriers to donor-funded and managed projects, including having research priorities "imposed" on "us," presumably from the outside. This comment is reflective of the fatigue of being a recipient of development aid rather than a funded, autonomous scientist.

IPRs, some argued, were a way to reach the autonomy—as scientists, as a state—that so many desired. While Dr. Atokple wasn't explicit about IPRs in his presentation, they were lurking in the background. Remember his description of GM maize yields in Iowa: "That is GM, they are making billions. So that is the secret." Though his use of "they" is vague, when we consider the associated referent ("making billions") and his audience at the forum (scientists, academics, and policymakers), one might extrapolate that "they" was not in reference to farmers but rather to those developing and selling GM maize seeds. And it is IPRs that enable firms to commodify seeds, gain exclusive rights to them, and "mak[e] billions" (Kloppenburg 2004).

But while Dr. Atokple and others viewed IPRs as a way for the state—and state scientists—to profit financially, they also created very real barriers to the research, use, and potential development of GMOs in Ghana, as Dr. Quain pointed out. The AATF model—wherein donors control both the funding of projects and the use of genetic material—puts Ghanaian and other African scientists in an awkward position: they neither control the financial nor genetic resources essential to the project's success. Such a reality complicates arguments of GMOs being "homegrown," evidenced by Dr. Quain's plea, and, a few years later, the collapse of both the Bt cotton and NEWEST rice projects. At the heart of these failed projects are questions of IPRs, project financing, and infrastructure.

Patented Promises

Patents and IPRs are what give the agricultural biotech industry life; they are the financial and legal tool that fueled competition between early biotech and agricultural companies in the 1980s and 1990s and the tools that allowed for eventual financial domination (Kloppenburg 2004). The Rockefeller Foundation knew this and knew that IPRs would be a major hurdle in the quest to convince multinational firms to work in Africa (Schurman 2016). When the Rockefeller Foundation originally approached industry heads in 2001, they first proposed creating a "pool of intellectual property [IP]" that would be overseen by a "humanitarian organization" (which one official described to sociologist Rachel Schurman as "a pool of global public good technologies that anyone in the public sector could tap into"; Schurman 2016: 7). However, the biotech industry had little interest in sharing their IP, and instead presented the Rockefeller Foundation with "guiding principles" that stipulated their involvement (Schurman 2016: 8): the program would be limited to the African continent only, "the technology's governance would remain in the hands of the companies," and all technologies would be "licensed . . . royalty free for five years" (Schurman 2016: 7–8). "Their lawyers are smart," someone close to the negotiations told Schurman, "they are thinking, 'Between now and five years we may not see any commercial use for it.' But after five years, ergo something might happen, and we say 'this thing will do well in that place and we can make a killing. So, we are not going to give away the rights, forever'" (2016: 8).

And why would they? The leading biotech firms at the time—Monsanto, DuPont Pioneer, and Syngenta—had fought tooth and nail to dominate the market. The advent of agricultural biotechnology completely changed the landscape of seed patents in the United States—in 1980 the Supreme Court ruled that plant traits not found in nature, but rather the result of human "handiwork," were patentable (Boyd 2003: 36). Combined with the Bayh-Dole Act (1980), which "allowed for the commercialization of federally funded research," the Supreme Court's ruling generated an open-season for research, discovery, and patenting (Boyd 2003: 41–42). Companies already dominating the agribusiness and pharmaceutical industries moved swiftly, acquiring smaller companies, seeking wide patents, and suing competitors. The broadening of patenting laws in the United States in the 1980s and 1990s was at the heart of this growth: "as leading firms such as Monsanto, Novartis, and DuPont . . . sought to develop and amass patent portfolios that [were] broad enough to bar entry by new players and deep enough in terms of their control over basic technologies to give them substantial economic power in key markets, litigation over the nature and scope of these patent claims has proliferated" (Boyd 2003: 44). Adding to the frenzy was the fact that patents have limited lifespans, and once expired were fair game. Monsanto, for instance, prepared for close to a decade "for the day when Roundup [herbicide] would no longer be protected under US patent law" (Schurman and Munro 2010: 43). The company's strategizing paid off: today, Monsanto (now Bayer) holds a substantial share of the global herbicide market.

In a mere decade, patents helped spur the global consolidation of the seed industry (Howard 2015). "As breeding values were transformed into property rights, they became key vehicles for capital accumulation and, more broadly, for the industrialization of the agricultural system" (Boyd 2003: 24). This leads us back to Ghana and the question of the Plant Breeders Bill. What would a patenting regime look like for a country with only public breeders and small seed companies? Should large firms enter a country like Ghana, at best small seed companies may be bought for their access to farmers and knowledge of local contexts. At worst they would simply be edged out of the marketplace.

This history, and political economy, is obfuscated by GMO proponents who describe IPRs ("plant breeders rights") as a way to protect African breeders and crops, such as Dr. Atikpo characterizing the PBB as a way "simply to provide royalties and . . . motivate the breeders." Additionally, some proponents of the PBB describe

IPRs as gifts or donations. In an op-ed published on ModernGhana.com, a research scientist and self-described IPR advocate described seed patents and the royalties they generate "[as] just a token to say, 'thank you' for giving us higher yields and income" (Bortey 2016). And the Cornell Alliance for Science and other donor-driven GMO boosters never discuss the institutional history of AATF, instead describing it as an African institution that negotiates with "patent holders to donate certain genes royalty-free for humanitarian purposes" (Bendana 2019). Utilizing the term "patent holders" rather than naming multinational seed companies is a discursive mechanism used to blur the reality of the relationship between seed companies, AATF, and African scientists and farmers. In doing so, speakers are able to portray seed companies as humanitarians rather than as hyper-competitive oligopolies who control over half the world's seed and agricultural chemical supply. Moreover, the use of the term "donate" overlooks the actual agreements, which, as Rachel Schurman (2016: 7–8) notes, are clearly defined as licensing or leasing agreements.

But even if, we can consider for a moment, the leased genes *were* somehow donated, there are always expectations attached to gift giving (Mauss 1990). As comments from Jesus Madrazo in the Introduction demonstrated, in exchange for Monsanto partnering with CSIR to commercialize Bt cotton, they expected Ghana to reciprocate with the passage of legal reforms, such as the PBB. Additionally, gifts are not neutral nor static; they also reflect the values and worldview of the giver. Maurice Godelier writes, "The giving of gifts has become an act that creates a bond between abstract subjects: a donor who loves humankind and a recipient who, for a few months, the duration of a charity drive, embodies the world in distress" (1999: 5). Following Godelier, what would this mean, then, for those on the receiving end of the supposed "gift" of a genetic patent? And if Godelier (1999: 5) is right, if receiving a humanitarian gift comes with a sort of heaviness, an acknowledgment that you are receiving this gift because the giver thinks you, the recipient, "embod[y] the world in distress," might that help explain the recipient fatigue that runs through the countryside, civil society offices, and scientific labs?

If the genes were indeed a gift, there might be less emphasis, and less confusion, around IPRs and who actually gets to oversee the rollout of the final project. This is an important yet highly mystifying aspect of GMO projects run under AATF. These projects, as evidenced in earlier discussion about NEWEST rice, have so many layers that even some of the African scientists involved are unclear as to what would happen with licensing agreements and patent rights should a GM product they worked on go to market. Writing on the GM cowpea project—a multi-country initiative in Ghana, Burkina Faso, Malawi, and Nigeria—Jacqueline Ignatova found:

> The Bt cowpea project is an international collaboration, so it is unclear who exactly would be the direct beneficiaries of the commercial sale of Bt cowpea seed. The question of patents, that is who would hold the patented technology upon commercialization, was an issue that many of the agricultural scientists and biosafety experts either preferred to stay out of or preferred to consider later. The AATF has explained to me, "The Bt Cowpea plant variety will be owned by AATF in trust for the local partners." The lead scientist of the Bt cowpea project understood that Monsanto would hold the patent. During an interview when I asked about the Plant Breeders' Bill and patents on plants, the Program for Biosafety Systems' Country Coordinator stated, "I stay out of this" and referred me to the PBS Senior Advisor to Ghana, Dr. Walter Alhassan . . . He had an unclear answer regarding who would hold the patent in the case of the commercialization of Bt cowpea, though he recognized it as an important question. (2015: 129)

The fact that there is significant confusion around who would get to hold patents of seeds developed under an AATF partnership is important. First, it challenges the idea of industry "donating" their genetic material, as it is clear there is contestation over who will have rights over the production developed out of it. And similarly, the question of who holds future patents of AATF-sponsored GM crops—and the possibility of them *not* being owned by Ghanaian plant breeders—challenges the "homegrown" narratives that GMO advocates so often utilize.

Since Jacqueline Ignatova's interviews with biotech boosters in Ghana, Bt cowpea has been commercialized in Nigeria. This advancement offers some insight for other countries working on multinational GM projects. Similar to Ghana, the Bt cowpea project was hosted in Nigeria by a public institution—the Institute of Agricultural Research at Ahmadu Bello University—and overseen by a Nigerian PI, who ultimately filed for approval for commercial release. The technical name for the new variety is "AAT 709A," presumably in reference to AATF, who is listed as the official "developer" in the ISAAA's GM Approval Database (ISAAA 2020). While at the time of this writing it remains to be seen if and how patenting rights will play out in Nigeria, one might expect that AATF will hold full or partial patents (or rights in the case of a country without a patent law) of any GMO that is commercialized under their sponsorship. AATF was always meant to serve as a mediator between multinational companies and African scientists, entrusted to hold company secrets and represent company interests, evidenced in part by the broad indemnification clauses included in AATF contracts.

I spend time here focusing on the linguistic designation of a gift or donation because it is a powerful discursive mechanism. It elicits age-old tropes of poor Africans in need of urgent intervention and constructs those behind the supposed gift—private foundations, multinational corporations, government aid agencies—as benevolent saviors. And importantly, it obscures power relations, historical context, and capital flows. In other words, the linguistic notion of a gift allows oligopolistic multinationals to avoid blame for their role in the wildly concentrated and inequitable global food system. Instead, they are painted as humanitarian heroes.

NEWEST, a Global Rice

Dr. Quain's warning at the GAAS forum was prophetic: just a few years later, four of the six original GMO projects would be on permanent hold—effectively terminating their lifespan—in Ghana. The GM sweet potato, which was meant to be nutrient enhanced and was funded by USAID, ended soon after the project began due to funding constraints. Work on Bt and GM cotton, as discussed in the Introduction, stopped after Monsanto withdrew from its end of the agreement due to lack of legal infrastructure (e.g., the Plant Breeders Bill). And in 2017, soon after Donald J. Trump assumed presidential office in the United States, USAID partially cut funding to AATF's rice project in Ghana, Uganda, and Nigeria, where scientists were conducting field trials of genetically modified rice.

Rice—genetically modified or otherwise—receives much attention from both donor and government officials. Once reserved for the elite and special occasions, rice has more recently become a staple food across both country and class. But the rise in popularity came with its own challenges. Like many agricultural sectors, the rice sector enjoyed protections and subsidies until the 1980s when structural adjustment programs required de-regulation and liberalization. As a result, rice importations, particularly of jasmine rice varietals, from countries like Thailand and the United States, spiked (Abdulai and Huffman 2000). Today, Ghana imports around 60 percent of all rice consumed (Andam et al. 2019). Narrowing this gap has been a key goal of the Ghanaian state (Ragasa and Chapoto 2017). Accordingly, GMO rice proponents believed GM rice had the potential to increase yields and in turn decrease both rice imports and incidents of hunger.

In this section, I trace the establishment, lifespan, and ultimate suspension of the NEWEST rice project. I pay particular attention to the Ghanaians working on the project—scientists, assistants, security guards—and how decisions made in Washington, DC, and Nairobi, Kenya, impact their livelihoods. I do this to demonstrate how patents, and patent-holders, shape AATF-led GMO projects, and to analyze the stark power disparities between those funding GMO projects, those leasing *their* genetic material, and those in charge of in-country research.

The NEWEST rice project began in 2008 with a goal to develop rice that would be nitrogen use efficient and therefore would require less fertilizer. The project selected a variety of rice named NERICA, a cross between Asian and African varieties that was developed by scientists at the Africa Rice Center (Borenstein 2015: 8). The first step of the project was to produce a nitrogen use efficient rice (NUE), with the hope it would allow farmers to use less fertilizer in weak soils. The second step was to develop a triple-stacked rice with nitrogen use efficiency, water use efficiency, and salt tolerance, referred to mainly by its acronym, NEWEST (CIAT 2014). The undertaking was a worldwide affair:

> California-based Arcadia Biosciences donated the intellectual property . . . The biotechnology firm then transferred these initial lines to International Center for Tropical Agriculture (CIAT) in Cali, Colombia, which worked with Arcadia to conduct preliminary field evaluations and generate seed stocks of the most promising varieties. Arcadia and CIAT then shipped the seed to research partners in Ghana and Uganda's Agricultural Research Systems . . . Throughout this process, the African Agricultural Technology Foundation coordinated activities across the partnership, helping to navigate intellectual property and biosafety regulations in the two countries and ensuring that the confined field trials adhered to legal and environmental standards. (Powell 2013)

This text, which comes from a blog post by USAID, one of the main funders of the project, illustrates the myriad of actors—and number of places—involved in developing NEWEST rice. Though GMO proponents (in Ghana and elsewhere) argue that biotechnology projects like NEWEST are "homegrown," the reality is much more complex. In the case of the NEWEST project, for instance, rice was literally being sent around the world—from West Africa to California to Colombia to West Africa again—to be modified, tested, and revised. Though the program began in 2008, it wasn't until 2013, after two years of field trials at CIAT, that Ghanaian scientists obtained genetically modified rice strains (Arcadia Biosciences 2013). And those strains came not from Ghanaian labs, but rather were shipped from Colombia to Kumasi via DHL.

By the time I was able to first visit the project's headquarters at CSIR's Kumasi office in April 2016, there was little to see. The team had finished field trials of NUE rice and project staff were scouting and preparing new field trial locations for the NEWEST variety. I spent the afternoon with a scientist named Sam who described the project's origins:

> AATF had the funding and they selected the countries that they wanted to work in. So, they contacted us. They had their own criteria of the people they thought they wanted to work with. So, it was not really a competitive something.... I honestly don't know why we were selected. Because we were here and then we had the information that AATF wants to do this kind of thing, and they think we'll be good partners, [so] we said, "Why not?"

Low on internal funds for administrative and research purposes, and with a desire to "serve ordinary farmers," CSIR accepted the project. The project fell to a small group of researchers, one of whom told me he had never been interested in genetic modification—it was too controversial, which created even more challenges. Nevertheless, the project went on.

At the time of our conversation, the team was working exclusively with jasmine varieties. "We'll cross it into AGRA rice, we'll cross it into Jasmine 85, and many of the very good aromatic varieties we have around," Sam explained. He added that jasmine varieties were preferred by "those who really want to do rice on the big scale and have a lot of income out of it." Under the broader program of the "new" Green Revolution for Africa, and its auspice of making "agriculture as a business," it makes sense that NEWEST rice was being bred for mass commercial production. But this commercialized stance was seemingly at odds with something Sam said later in the interview: "The source we are getting the funding from is USAID, who is sponsoring this project, through the AATF in Kenya. And AATF is set up to get these technologies to improve the lives of ordinary people. So, it's basically *not for commercial benefit.*

We are supposed to do it *for the good of the ordinary people*" (emphasis added). However, the funder's desire for NEWEST rice to be for the people, Sam explained, clashed with the priorities of the government of Ghana and CSIR. He continued:

> These days, the government wants us to generate income. So, we have a policy in the institute that we'll be able to license some varieties to some companies who can pay for it. But even in that case we don't [license] it exclusively, for instance. And because rice is self-pollinated, you can grow the seed again and you have good yield. So, ... it wouldn't even be feasible if you want to license it exclusively to somebody.

The framing of GM rice as "pro-poor"—or "for the good of the ordinary people"—has been both the discourse and the supposed stated mission of the agricultural biotechnology industry for decades (Glover 2010). And certainly, advocates of GMOs for African farmers imagine, and discuss, the technology as something that will benefit even the smallest of small farmers (Paarlberg 2008). But this romanticized image of African farmers is at odds with local realities, from crop preference to government policies. What does "pro-poor" technology development look like in a country attempting to transition away from "agriculture as a way of life" to "agriculture as a business"?

Indeed, the tension between creating a commercial crop that is "not for commercial benefit" but also one that benefits people who "want to do rice on the big scale and have a lot of income out of it" is at the heart of discussions about GMOs in Ghana. In the case of Ghana, the choice of jasmine rice is further complicated by contested gastro-geographies: jasmine varieties—particularly *imported* jasmine varieties—are popular within the southern half of the country, while African varietals of rice are largely consumed in the rice-producing northern regions (Ragasa and Chapoto 2017: 319). Friends shared stories of competing rice palates causing strife and division among families. For instance, Suraj, my friend from chapter 1, told me a story about visiting his grandmother who lives in Tamale, in the north of the country. Coming from the capital of Accra, Suraj carried many gifts for his grandmother, including what he described as a bag of oburoni rice: an imported white jasmine varietal. Unfortunately for Suraj, his grandmother did not like oburoni rice. In fact, she disliked the rice so much that she kept it in her house and gave it to Suraj's wife on a later visit. The impolite gesture of re-gifting indicates how strong of an aversion his grandmother—and others—had to jasmine rice. Francis, my friend and research assistant, described constant quarrels with his wife, who, born and raised in northern Ghana, refuses to eat anything but "local" rice, while he, raised in the south, prefers jasmine varieties. What's more, a recent study by Catherine Ragasa and Antony Chapoto found that though jasmine varieties like the one Sam mentioned—Jasmine 85—might have a taste that consumers in "urban areas" prefer, they "do not have a yield advantage over local varieties" (2017: 313).

When I asked Sam about these northern tastes, he referred to them as "niche markets." Yet these "niche markets" encapsulate the five northern regions of Ghana, where food and nutritional deficits are the highest nationally (Ham 2017: 242). I left our interview wondering whom the coordinators of the NEWEST rice project envisioned becoming consumers of the genetically modified rice. Even if northern markets were niche and therefore ought not be considered in tackling rice importation, assuming that southern consumers will embrace Ghanaian-grown jasmine rice also overlooks taste preferences in southern Ghana. Many Ghanaians in southern, urban, jasmine-consuming centers prefer *imported* varieties (Andam et al. 2019). Throughout my time eating and talking about rice in Ghana, I have heard Ghanaians express many reasons for this preference: it tastes better and/ or is packaged better than its local equivalent; it is cleaner than locally produced rice which sometimes contains stones used in the milling process; and it is quicker to prepare. With these considerations in mind, it becomes clear that the issue of importation is not just a material or economic matter; it is a social one as well.

The field trials that Sam and colleagues were preparing for never took place. When I visited the project again in 2018, Sam informed me the NEWEST project was on indefinite hold (USDA FAS 2020a). He wasn't sure what happened, but he knew that USAID had cut funding to the project, and the decision was made, either at the level of USAID or AATF, to focus the remaining funds on the NUE line. The Ghanaian team were not consulted in this decision, and Sam was visibly frustrated as he relayed the information to me. As a scientist, he was disappointed; he wanted to test his hypothesis and see his experiment through to the end. Moreover, the lack of funds meant CSIR was unable to pay certain team members, including security guards mandated by law to protect the field trials. What's more, the team had just completed building a rain-out shelter to mimic drought that, though ironically destroyed in a massive storm, the team wished to rebuild for future experiments. But the money was not there, and Sam said CSIR could not "go behind their backs," meaning AATF, to seek funding from elsewhere. Arcadia Biosciences had leased the NUE and NEWEST technology through AATF, and thus Sam and his team were bound to AATF's decision-making.

And so, with little choice, the team continued with the NUE project. The next step would be regulatory trials, which Sam said are usually just one season, but that "consultants in the US," meaning those contracted by donor USAID, might want more. After the regulatory trials are complete, the team would send rice samples to the United States for toxicity reports. Finally, if the reports come back clean, the team will take the entirety of the findings and documentation to submit to the NBA for approval for commercial release. In this description alone, I was struck by how many times the rice was traveling seemingly across the globe: first from West Africa to California, where the initial genetic modification took place; then from California to Colombia, where two years of field trials took place; then to Ghana for more field trials; then to California for toxicity reports; and perhaps back again. What's more, the NEWEST rice project is being undertaken in Uganda and Nigeria as well, increasing the amount of travel this transnational rice takes.

In late 2018, IFPRI released a sixty-eight-page report on GM crops in Ghana that suggested perhaps the most "niche market" of them all was the NERICA rice variety project planners had selected for modification: the report found that the "NERICA adoption rate [in Ghana is] about 2.3 percent . . . because [it] is an upland variety of rice and . . . only 12 percent of total rice cultivated area in Ghana is upland rice" (Dzanku et al. 2018: 23). The authors continued, warning that should NERICA4 be the only rice varietal genetically modified and commercialized, they predicted only a 5 percent adoption rate for NUE rice (2018: 23). However, the authors suggested that adoption rates of NUE rice could reach as high as 60 percent should the traits be bred with more popular varieties of rice (2018: 23). (The report predicted a 15 percent adoption rate of Bt cowpea [2018: 24].)

Why was an upland variety of rice chosen for modification when so few Ghanaian farmers grow such a variety? The report stated that "a reason for the NUE variety being introgressed into an upland variety, although lowland rice is more popular, is that nitrogen deficiency is more acute in upland areas" (2018: 23). However, this explanation is unsatisfactory, and the report's findings presented an opportunity for advocates and critics alike to ask tough questions. Who decided to focus on a trait (nitrogen efficiency) that is of concern for only 12 percent of total cultivated rice? Who decided that NERICA4 be chosen for modification? And why was so much time, funding, and effort going into a crop expected to see a less than 3 percent adoption rate?

Though the report was clear that a NUE NERICA variety is likely to perform poorly on the Ghanaian market, media coverage of the report suggested otherwise.

The sole Ghanaian reporter to cover IFPRI's report—a bright, dedicated journalist who works for one of the largest media houses in Ghana, and a former fellow of the Cornell Alliance for Science—described the report as projecting "high expectations for GMO rice research in Ghana" and described NERICA as a "popular rice variety in Africa" (Gakpo 2019). Though the reporter largely avoided the report's more sobering content, he did note that Ghanaian scientists were waiting for the gene to be "de-regulated," at which time they would plan to "backcross it into most of the popular jasmine types that we have locally" (Gakpo 2019).

The NEWEST rice project speaks to the power and limitation that genetic patents play in public-private partnerships for the development of GMOs for African farmers. As scientists interviewed by myself and the journalist suggest, the Ghanaian team's hands are tied when it comes to genetically modifying other, more popular rice varieties. They must wait until Arcadia Biosciences releases their genetic material entirely to the Ghanaian team (an unlikely scenario) or their patent runs out. In either scenario, the Ghanaian team would still need ample funding and tools to carry out genetic modification in a Ghanaian lab, both difficult to come by at the time.

Another question, of course, is whether genetically modified rice, at least nitrogen use efficient rice, would be a superior product to rice bred in other ways for the same trait. Sitting in his office, Sam remarked that in the same amount of time he had been working on the NEWEST rice project—much of which had been spent waiting for funding, for approval, for *rice*, for materials—his lab had commercialized six conventionally bred varieties of rice. Though these too were donor-funded, they were bred using methods Sam and his colleagues could do from their labs in Kumasi; they did not have to wait for project partners across the globe to send materials. He told me, "We are able to feed ourselves, I believe, even though on and off we import a few things. But generally and especially with rice, I think that even if that [genetically modified] rice doesn't come in, we will still be able to find alternatives to feed ourselves. But we can do better." Sam's comment speaks to the tension of supposed humanitarian crops in a semi-food-secure country, and suggests why patents—as commercial tools—and the income they hypothetically produce are so appealing to so many.

Desire for income, especially for state scientific councils and scientists, is understandable in an era of massive disinvestment from the state, where scientists must go to donors (or wait for donors to come to them) to finance their work (Luna and Dowd-Uribe 2020). And it also makes sense in the context of the "new" Green Revolution, where humanitarian discourses underline commercial pursuits. NERICA rice and Bt cotton reveal this. As I have shown in this chapter, jasmine rice is intended for the southern half of the country, and not consumers in the more marginalized northern regions that are home to the highest rates of malnutrition and hunger. Likewise, Bt cotton was thought to be useful not to improve an already existing sector, but rather to establish a new market. These choices reveal a trickle-down economic logic that challenges altruistic discourses of hunger and malnutrition. In other words, the reasoning behind these projects is not necessarily to grow more rice to feed people, but to create export opportunities for northern farmers to grow rice for southern consumption, and to grow cotton for global distribution. Such an opportunity, planners argue, would provide northern farmers increased income and purchasing power to use to *buy* food at the market.

This scenario is reflective of what planners mean when they say they want to make agriculture "a business." Whether or not such a scenario might actually be feasible is beyond the scope of my inquiry. Instead, in this chapter I drew attention to the complexities of these particular scenarios. The complexities of public-private partnerships and global plant breeding collaborations, which are latent with competing priorities and contributions (e.g., financials, proprietary technologies, etc.) and are thus sites of power and struggle. The complexities of developing a multimillion-dollar technology that, on its own, is likely to have little impact, whether because farmers don't grow it or there is no market for it, and thus requires building external markets and convincing resource-poor farmers to make a big bet and take on enormous risk. Such complexities—comments from Dr. Quain and Sam remind us—are by design and choice. They are also not new, as policymakers have sought to transform the Ghanaian countryside for centuries. GMOs simply brought the complexities of global aid and agricultural technologies into public debate.

Conclusion

In this chapter, I have explored how and why GMOs hold an allure for certain Ghanaian biotech boosters. It is clear that for many Ghanaian scientists and bureaucrats, GMOs hypothetically offer an opportunity to increase food stock and financial return. These goals are complicated by messier aspects of the projects. The first relates to project composition. Corporate sponsors—Arcadia Biosciences and Monsanto—are an integral aspect of the rice (Arcadia), cowpea, and cotton

(Monsanto) projects, respectively. While these companies joined AATF's mission to bring genetic modification to Africa as a supposed act of goodwill (or perhaps "corporate social responsibility"; Schurman 2016: 9), their commercial interests are always centered in project design.

The complexity of corporate partnerships takes on another complicated realm with IPRs. Without IPR laws in place, and without transparent and public details of the GM projects, it is also unclear how profit and money will flow if and when GM crops are commercialized. But what *is* clear is that African scientists are often the last to be consulted and hold little power within project design. "You know," Kojo told me,

> the GM crops that are being tried in the country, the patents are with other experts [and companies] out there. They are not Ghanaian.... One day, as development goes on and experiences increase, a Ghanaian scientist may be brilliant enough to [genetically] modify a particular crop, a local variety from his own original... approach.

While the brilliance of Ghanaian scientists is not in question (and I don't believe Kojo meant to suggest so), resources and equipment are. While drafters of the PBB imagined that "the bill will encourage foreign breeders and local breeders" to work together, "resulting in technology transfer" (Plant Breeders Bill 2013: iii), so far GMO projects in Ghana—a grand example of global plant breeding partnerships—have kept genetic modification outside the country, happening elsewhere in the world. Genetically modified rice was shipped via DHL from Colombia to Kumasi, and GM cowpea made the lengthy journey to Ghana from Australia. As long as project managers continue designing projects as such, and as long as Ghanaian scientists are not supported in equipping their labs with the equipment needed to undertake genetic modification, Ghanaian GM projects are likely to continue requiring international partnerships, likely both technically and financially. This raises questions about the sustainability of the projects and the likelihood of IPRs being established in favor of local breeders.

It goes without saying that scientists and bureaucrats have much to gain entering into international agreements, projects, and communities. But the imaginaries of scientists, bureaucrats, and development practitioners—those put in charge of carrying out the GM projects—matter. These imaginaries reveal a deep anxiety about the nation-state and its ability to compete and exist in a hyper-competitive world, and the exhaustion of being on the recipient end of development projects, unable to fund the work they truly care about. Such feelings embody the concept of recipient fatigue. Throughout fieldwork, interlocutors spoke of a world system that denigrates Africa, and therefore Ghana, and scientists and bureaucrats considered plant breeding and agricultural production one avenue to pursue political freedom and food, national and seed sovereignty. For some, this meant GMOs and their associated patents.

But (how) could a system that already or always marginalizes Ghana, Ghanaian farmers, and knowledge within global racial, economic, and political hierarchies truly offer a way out vis-à-vis the same economic system (i.e., IPRs) (Pierre 2012: 8, 38–39, 74)? This is the paradox of postcolonial Ghana, wherein two (opposing) goals are always present: that of development, which is saturated in denigration of African epistemologies as "other" and "inferior," and that of political and economic freedom vis-à-vis global capitalist markets. Certainly, Ghanaian plant breeders are in a tough spot, seeking funds needed to do research while aware of the limitations—as well as possibilities—that global patent regimes offer. Indeed, for some, such as Sam, genetic modification was not an exceptional technology, nor was it necessary to feed the future. In this way, both Ghanaian boosters and food sovereignty advocates sought to disrupt global discourses of Africa (and therefore Ghana) as starving and in need of intervention.

CHAPTER 5

(Im)Possibilities

Constance and I sat facing each other over a mountain of papers, folders, and shiny NGO publications. The office fan was working overtime, as was the single AC unit that provided cool air for the four of us that shared the office. Chickens squawked below the window outside, and a soft light came in through the window curtains. Days like this at GAFP were some of my favorite fieldwork moments, cracking jokes with colleagues, walking down to the nearby canteen for lunch, and trying to complete as much work as possible while we had electricity.

Admittedly, Constance and I had sat down that day for a formal interview, by which I mean I had a list of questions and had requested to record our conversation. I dreaded these moments; the brandishing of a recorder often caused folks to grow tense and conversation would often shift from an interpersonal flow to a formalized interaction. Constance was especially resistant to these moments—she would emphasize that I had all the data I needed from a year of sharing this office, meals, and trips together. She wasn't wrong, and to ask for even more felt awkward at best, ungrateful at worst. Constance understood my mission, though, and she understood the bureaucratic red tape of grant reporting, having had to report on dozens of grants over the years working in the development sector.

So, on this day she agreed to be recorded, and I did my best to steer our conversation into the more informal route we often took. I asked if she had seen a recent interview of Bill and Melinda Gates on the sidelines of the World Economic Forum in Davos).[1] She had, and she was furious.

> I was reading Melinda, Bill Gates during the ... World Economic Forum ... and [they said] the answer to African hunger is [genetically modified organisms (GMOs)]. I'm like, 'How do you know that? ... How do you know that? How do you know that is the answer to our hunger? And even who said we are hungry?' We are not starving. Eh? We are not starving.

I nodded and thought about similar sentiments I had heard before. John, a volunteer at GAFP, had asked, "Does Bill Gates love my children more than me?" Edwin, the communications lead for Food Sovereignty Ghana, told a group of reporters that "there are no hungry people in this land." At the time I had chalked up John's and Edwin's comments to being those of skilled communicators. But it was not until I heard them again from Constance that I began to think about what they could mean aside from blanket statements about who is and who is not hungry.

In this chapter I use interviews and data gleaned from participation with Ghanaian activists as well as Ghanaian scientists and officials to argue that they share concern over donor-driven development, making them unlikely bedfellows (at least in the context of GMOs). The Ghanaians closest to the GMO projects that I spoke with—either as an oppositional force or as bureaucrats and scientists entrusted with moving GMOs from field trials into the market and onto farmers' fields—consistently, though often subtly, used language that questioned donors' commitments to Ghana and challenged donor discourse that characterized as Africa, *and therefore Ghana*, as a starving, devoid place. Interlocutors frequently said things like, "We are not starving," but in doing so, they were not denying real challenges of food and nutritional access; one would be hard-pressed to find anywhere in the world where "there are no hungry people." Instead, Ghanaians continually critiqued global discourses and development industry standards wherein philanthropists and professionals in the Global North set boundaries for conversations about hunger, collapse Africa into a homogenized, starving entity, and then prescribe solutions based on these racialized myths. These critiques are reflective of recipient fatigue and are often held in tension with discourse emanating from the same donors that sponsor the work of GMO advocates, who rely on images and texts that depict Africa as languishing and starving. To demonstrate this tension, I use a vignette from a workshop that I attended with Ghanaian members of Parliament that turned into a back-room lobbying event; a petition that was sent to Parliament soon after; and interviews with Ghanaian scientists and officials to show their precarious positions within global GMO projects, and how they work within and against these larger structures.

In doing so, I add to the growing collection of literature that approaches development as a social process (rather than a predefined outcome; Benton 2015) and challenge recent literature that characterizes anti-GMO activists as "anti-science" (Lynas 2018; Paarlberg 2008). I emphasize this point with a discussion about an ambitious project GAFP initiated; the creation of a farm and training center based on the principles of *agroecology*. GAFP sought funding from a US-based donor to explore how agroecology—an agricultural model and practice that is premised on small, biodiverse farms that use "local" resources to sustain yield and help replenish soil nutrients (Ayres and Bosia 2011; Lee 2013)—could not only be useful for Ghanaian farmers, but also be used to demonstrate alternatives to high-chemical and high-input agriculture. Agroecology was particularly appealing as it was an agricultural model that GAFP deemed modern and scientific, and thought might allow them to gather "data" to back up their claims that development could be achieved by combining existing knowledge and new science. In calling upon the Akan philosophy of sankofa, looking back to move forward, activists both reified the idea of development as good and needed, while also setting their own boundaries for defining and achieving such a goal.

Across the examples that anchor this chapter, the theoretical framing of *disidentification* is paramount. Rather than wholly submit to, or rage against, dominant discourses and ideologies, disidentification refers to how individuals work on and against them (Muñoz 1999; Pêcheux 1982). Disidentification is not synonymous with resistance, but it does signify a recognition of conditions on the part of the disidentifier. As this chapter will illustrate, disidentification is a useful theoretical lens for considering the various stances Ghanaians take on GMOs, intellectual property rights (IPRs), and the "new" Green Revolution for Africa. For just as GAFP works on and against dominant funding schemes and development discourses, Ghanaian scientists and bureaucrats also work on and against global GMO assemblages. Understanding this is essential for acknowledging and appreciating how Ghanaians are shaping the future of technology, food, and scientific research.

Lobbying for the Plant Breeders Bill

"You know it's been three years?" a USAID contractor asked me as we sat in his office sipping coffee. He was referring to the Plant Breeders Bill, which had indeed just hit its three-year anniversary of being in Parliament without a vote and with minimal debate. I had met the contractor at a conference where, after discussing over a lunch the possibility of Donald J. Trump being elected president, he invited me to his office to talk more USAID's work in Ghana's agricultural sector. The contractor was incredibly frustrated, as his office had a mandate to see that the Plant Breeders Bill was passed, a tricky diplomatic game to play. On one hand, proponents of the bill had described it as a tool for development, a seemingly apolitical, technical agreement. On the other hand, while employed by the US government, the contractor could not be seen as trying to interfere in the sovereign affairs of Ghana.

The contractor had recently sent a Ghanaian colleague to Parliament to check on the status of the bill. His colleague was received by parliamentary officials and was apparently told that members of Parliament (MPs) would be happy to resume discussions, but first required a "sitting fee." The contractor was visibly furious while relaying this story to me; he emphasized that USAID could not pay MPs to "do their job." What they could fund, he said, were workshops and trainings regarding the bill for MPs to attend. A week later, the Open Forum on Agricultural Biotechnology in Africa (OFAB) hosted one such event.

As described earlier, OFAB is the media arm of the African Agricultural Technology Foundation (AATF), whose mission in part was to help build support for biotechnology and related industry-friendly laws across the African continent. OFAB is a key part of the vast constellation of boosters and brokers across the continent working toward such a goal. They work closely with these groups and others worldwide, with whom they trade ideas and strategies, and occasionally co-organize events. In March 2016, OFAB—along with co-sponsors AATF, the Program for Biosafety Systems (PBS), and the Ghana chapter of the Cornell Alliance for

Science (CAS)—invited a group of Ghanaian MPs to gather and discuss matters related to biotechnology. In an interview, one of the organizers explained to me they were inspired to organize the event after spending time at the CAS: "Some months ago, I was in the US, in Cornell, to participate in food security programs, and advocacy and grassroots mobilization. It was a good course, and that led me to organize program for parliamentarians . . . in Koforidua. We've written to some select committees of Parliament, and they will be there, in their numbers."

And so they were. On a foggy March morning, approximately forty Ghanaian MPs gathered at a hotel in Koforidua, a town that sits in the hills an hour outside of Accra. The hotel itself was a sprawling complex, complete with a pool, tennis court, and rooms going for $100 per night. When I arrived, a receptionist at the front desk directed me to a conference room on the bottom level of the hotel. Immediately upon entering the room, I checked in with a meeting attendant and recorded my name, affiliation, phone number, and email address on a sign-in sheet. In return, I was handed a laptop case, a polo shirt, and a notepad and pen, all marked with OFAB's insignia. It was common to receive some sort of swag at events like these—notepads, folders, perhaps a T-shirt—but a laptop case was decadent.

With swag in hand, I scanned the room for a familiar face and quickly spotted Thomas, one of the more adamant biotech brokers I had encountered during fieldwork. He greeted me warmly and took me around the room, introducing me to other attendees, including a prominent Ghanaian scientist who he described as an expert on the Plant Breeders Bill. Perhaps realizing his gaffe—Ghanaian officials were adamant that the Plant Breeders Bill was unrelated to GMOs—Thomas quickly walked back on his statement, only to be interrupted by the prominent scientist, who candidly explained that if the Plant Breeders Bill was not passed, genetically modified (GM) seeds could not be commercialized.

From the date of its introduction to Parliament, scientists, MPs, and bureaucrats had continually argued that the Plant Breeders Bill and GM seeds were separate issues not to be conflated. Chatting with the prominent scientist at Koforidua was the first time I had heard a proponent make an explicit connection between the bill and GM seeds. And this moment stood out in particular because the prominent scientist made the same connection that anti-GM advocates used to build their opposition to the bill; that is, that without the Plant Breeders Bill, GMOs would likely not be commercialized. I sat down excited about the interaction, but not realizing the conversation was foreshadowing what was to come.

The room slowly filled up as the MPs arrived. Eventually, the conference room was packed. The MPs were a jovial bunch and greeted one another like old friends as they took seats at tables organized in the shape of a rectangle. At the front of the room hung a banner adorned with the logos of the event's sponsors and welcoming attendees to the meeting, titled "Awareness Creation in Biotechnology and Biosafety for Members of Parliament in Ghana." Below the banner was the *high table*, a long table at the front of the room equipped with microphones and glasses of water where honorary guests and speakers sat.

When it was time for the workshop to begin, Thomas moved to the front of the room to welcome the group. He invited the prominent scientist to join him at the front, whom he introduced as an expert in the Plant Breeders Bill. Perhaps (again) realizing his gaffe, Thomas quickly followed up with "which isn't about GMOs anyways." Laughter broke out, imaginably at the impossible tightrope GMO boosters had been attempting to walk in their effort to delink GMOs and the Plant Breeders Bill. After the brief introduction, Thomas asked the prominent scientist to lead the group in a prayer to open the meeting. He lowered his head and asked God for "awareness creation" of biotechnology and the role it would play in the socio-economic development in Ghana. "Amen," the group responded.

At the completion of the prayer, the meeting had officially begun. One by one, the master of ceremonies introduced members of the high table. Like most events I attended, the table of six contained a single woman. One member of the high table, a MP from the Parliamentary Environment Committee, welcomed his colleagues, calling the day's topic near to his heart and informing them that he received training on biotechnology in South Africa. He was certain, he told the room, that by the end of the workshop, MPs would be ready to "deal with the Plant Breeders Bill when we get back [to Parliament]." The facade between the bill and GMOs was crumbling.

After the high table was introduced, it was time for the first of three rounds of presentations to begin. The agenda was packed, with remarks from state officials, scientists, and GMO boosters. The first two presentations were more or less introductory remarks that provided broad overviews regarding agricultural biotechnology, where it's grown, and why some Ghanaian scientists were excited about it. "GM is a powerful tool that helps resolve challenges that cannot be normally resolved through conventional approaches," described one of the first speakers. Such descriptions of the technology—as scientifically sound and effective—were routine at events like this. But this was no ordinary event: the audience were MPs, representatives tasked with passing laws and establishing political precedent. The same speaker acknowledged this and expressed his excitement about interacting with MPs. Every time we meet, he said, there is a positive outcome, and explained that in 2011 similar organizers met with MPs in the same hotel, and afterwards, the Biosafety Act was passed.

After each round of presentations, there was time for Q&A. It was here that the bulk of the discussion, and conflict, occurred. In the first round of questions, MPs took turns firing inquiry after inquiry:

> There is so much misconception... Why has [the Ghanaian Council for Scientific and Industrial Research (CSIR)] left this task to Parliament to explain this to the public? We are being attacked from the left, right, and center.
>
> Why the choice of cotton, cowpea, and rice?
>
> The West has all the technology and [infrastructure] to be able to get patents; how will Ghana compete?... What measures are there to make sure that those genetically modified materials... will not be restricted to one particular person or institution?
>
> The entire continent of Europe is not [growing GMOs]... Why are the American scientists not bringing it there?
>
> To what extent is the absence of the bill inhibiting research?

During the rapid-fire exchange, one man in the back of the room waved his hand wildly. He was one of three farmers invited to the meeting, and it was clear he was eager to contribute. One of the event organizers nodded his way in recognition, but asked him to wait. Meanwhile, the same organizer called on MPs, who were allowed to freely ask questions and make comments.

After a round of questions, it was time for organizers and presenters to respond. They tried to quell concerns and assured the MPs that genetic modification *was* used in some European countries. As the organizers spoke, one MP said aloud, "But we are the guinea pigs, why? Why?" Another MP, in response to an organizer who had said that Spain and Portugal grew GM crops, retorted, "But they are poor!" The organizer, seemingly surprised, replied, "Yes, they are poor," to which the MP responded, "So it [GMOs] is for poor people!"

There was tension in the air. Tension around why only "poor" European countries grew GM crops. Tension around why American scientists focused on Africa, not Europe. Tension around whether Ghana could compete within a highly patented industry. Tension around whether Ghana was a "guinea pig" for experimentation. And in part, the questions that the MPs posed indicated an interest in discussing GMOs as a technology, as a patented commodity, and as a science that was suspended within multiple political-economic webs.

The prominent scientist—who gave the opening prayer and who was introduced as an expert on the Plant Breeders Bill—stepped in. He brought up Obaatanpa, the improved maize variety developed by Ghanaian breeders in the 1980s and spread around the continent by the Sasakawa Global 2000 initiative. Obaatanpa, he said, is used across Africa without any benefit or credit to its Ghanaian originators because there is no law in place to protect the original breeders. "The Plant Breeders Bill is in the interest of Ghanaians," he reasoned, arguing that its passage would prevent a similar situation from occurring again. By using the example of Obaatanpa, the prominent scientist was able to draw attention away from MP's questions regarding GMOs and patented seeds coming from foreign firms, and instead focus the conversation firmly on Ghana and Ghanaian plant breeders. He continued and pleaded with the MPs, telling them that he had met with MPs "about five times" over the years in the same hotel to discuss the Plant Breeders Bill. "We have never left you in the dark," he said, in reference to the bill, its contents, and supposed benefits. He warned that if the Plant Breeders Bill wasn't passed, "people will continue to take our things."

After a tense Q&A, the schedule called for a (sorely needed) coffee break. As the organizers explained where to find the beverages and snacks, one casually said to the group, "I'm sure after hearing this that when you get back [to Parliament], the Plant Breeders Bill will be passed." Before the organizer could end their sentence, they were interrupted by the MP who had asked a question about patents and competition; "Deal with my fears, deal with my concerns!"

"Honorable, don't worry," another organizer interjected. "We have a very good program today; all issues will be addressed. . . . Nothing will be swept under the rug," they assured.

With tensions still high, it was time for a coffee break. As we all got up from our seats, a MP approached the farmers sitting in the back of the room. Without introduction, the MP looked at them and said, "We are servants. Some people say we are thieves. No, we are servants!" He laughed and walked away. The farmers, looking bewildered, did not say a word.

This sort of awkward tension lasted throughout the day. Though the event's official agenda promised presentations on GMOs, one by one speakers steered their comments toward an item that was not actually on the agenda: the Plant Breeders Bill. By the time we broke for coffee, I had connected the dots: the glamour of leaving Accra and staying the weekend at a lavish hotel, the goodie bags, and the finger cakes. The purpose of this event was not necessarily what was slated on the flier—awareness creation of biotech and biosafety—but rather to persuade the MPs to return to Parliament and pass the Plant Breeders Bill, like they had accomplished five years prior with the Biosafety Act.

And I wasn't the only one who understood what appeared to be the real purpose of gathering that day. After the coffee break it was time for another round of presentations and discussion. Once again, a number of MPs focused their questions on patents and the Plant Breeders Bill (and once again, the same farmer kept his hand raised, and once again, organizers passed over him).

> You say we shouldn't interchange the Plant Breeders Bill and GMOs. So, what is the difference?
>
> How are you going to compete with the West when you do not have the technology and machines to compete? And when someone has a patent, how will you ensure that others can "enjoy" [as well as] avoid monopolies?
>
> I am getting the feeling that we are *all* confused. [Around him others said loudly, "I'm also confused!"] What interest is driving the Plant Breeders Bill? . . . What all of you scientists and professors have failed to do is convince MPs that this is where the country needs to be and provided us with costs and benefits.

Workshop organizers and presenters attempted to answer each MP's question. In an endeavor to walk away from a more monopolistic understanding of patents, one presenter described the Plant Breeders Bill as "not a patent per se, it's a *recognition*" and argued that "[the Plant Breeders Bill] is important to strengthen our CSIR and be empowered to promote technology" (emphasis added). "The US has no interest in cowpea," a presenter stated, referring to the ongoing Bt cowpea project. "It is for us here in Africa," he said, pointing at himself. He did not mention that the actual genetic modification process of seed production happened outside of Ghana, or that the Bt trait used to develop Bt cowpea was on lease from Monsanto. Instead, speakers argued that the Plant Breeders Bill would protect materials and innovations crucial to Ghanaian statecraft and development. Speakers imagined that the revenue from CSIR-developed GM seeds would flow back to CSIR, lessening their need to rely on donors and thus strengthening the state.

As MPs and organizers sparred, a scientist in attendance quietly made his way to where the farmers were seated in the back of the room and asked if they wanted to speak. They did, and the scientist went to get the attention of the organizers. Finally, an organizer allowed the eager farmer who had raised his hand earlier to address the room. "Anything 'natural' is from god, and anything 'artificial' is from man. Anything man-made needs to be researched." The farmer's comment was far from an endorsement, and the organizers quickly ushered us off to lunch.

Lunch was served poolside and the spread was impressive: banku, fufu, rice, boiled plantain, fish, chicken, and *aprapransa* (Rock 2018c). Plenty of choice and plenty of food to go around. After just an hour of break, it was time once again to return to the conference room and end the day with a series of presentations from the principal investigators (PIs) on the three GM projects that were ongoing at the time in Ghana: cotton, cowpea, and rice. One by one the scientists walked us through exactly what crop they were working on, why genetic modification was chosen, and how their research was going. It was interesting, I thought, to save these presentations for the very end. If there was a time to assuage MPs' fears about foreign monopolies or foreign interference and demonstrate that Ghanaian experts were working on GMOs, this seemed to be it. But the MPs appeared restless, perhaps from lunch, their travel from Accra, and/or the previous many hours we had all spent sitting in the conference room.

In between presentations from the PIs, one of the event organizers again called upon the prominent scientist. The organizer explained that the prominent scientist was left off the program as to not confuse the stated focus of the day—"Awareness Creation in Biotechnology and Biosafety"—with the Plant Breeders Bill. But seeing as the prominent scientist happened to be at the event, the organizer said, they thought it would be good for him to share some brief comments on the Plant Breeders Bill anyway. Why organizers continued to try to create distance between the Plant Breeders Bill and GMOs after a day of discussing the two in tandem was unclear to me. The fact that they asked the prominent scientist to speak on the bill in the middle of presentations from GMO PIs certainly didn't seem to help their attempts to convince us that the two were unrelated. Perhaps organizers thought the prominent scientist might be seen as a non-biased expert, as he was, at the time, not formally employed in any GMO research, booster, or broker activities. While the PIs were more or less contained to discussing GMOs, the prominent scientist was seemingly able to span multiple spaces, speaking to both science and policy.

Whatever the case, the prominent scientist chose his words carefully. Breeding is expensive, he told the MPs, and while state scientist salaries are paid by the government, funds for research are hard to come by. He added that "most of our projects are donor-funded, [and so] if a donor is not interested, they won't go there." Therefore, he said, the Plant Breeders Bill would allow scientists to obtain funds for the work they've done (ideally enough to circumvent donors), "promote competition and innovation," and encourage the private sector to invest in research and plant breeding.

To be sure, there was no disagreement that state institutions needed help. Similar to other public research institutions in West African nations (Dowd-Uribe 2016: 7) and increasingly the United States, the Ghanaian institute that currently oversees all GMO field trials, CSIR, is severely underfunded and relies on private projects and funding. The NEWEST rice project, as I discussed previously, is an example of this. But many scientists were not satisfied with private funding flows; they require high levels of oversight, funding is uncertain and often project-based, and project scopes were often determined by outside actors. In other words, private funding meant that Ghanaian scientists were limited in the experiments they were able to undertake, limited in the crops they were able to research and the traits they could experiment with. In the final Q&A section of the Koforidua workshop, one of the GMO PIs pleaded, "We want to develop. For heaven's sake! We must focus a little more money on science and technology. You can't just leave our scientists to look for money all over the world!" MPs shifted uncomfortably in their seats, and some yelled out, "You're right, you're right!" and "You win!"

One MP followed up with a similarly impassioned appeal:

> We have been brought here to be educated about biotechnology, but they are also asking us to pass the Plant Breeders Bill.... The relationship between Plant Breeders Bill and GMO is that a plant breeder is like any musician, anyone who produces works that is worth paying for. The person has invested knowledge [and] time.... There are many things that are being taken from Ghana for free, but this one, because it concerns our stomachs, needs to be taken very seriously.... Otherwise we are becoming anti-scientific, anti-research, [anti-] anything that is modernizing and encouraging our scientists.

The PI who had just spoken ("We want to develop") stood up, threw his arms over his head, and clapped loudly.

Food (Security) Politics

The Koforidua workshop is an example of the incredible finances and resources GMO proponents have at their disposal. While the Food Sovereignty Platform struggled to gather funds to rent space to hold events and provide bottled water to attendees (let alone invite MPs to their events), GMO and Plant Breeders Bill advocates had the financial advantage of being backed by major development agencies and organizations, like the contractor I spoke with in Accra. In Koforidua and at other workshops, GMO boosters held meetings at high-end hotels, transporting participants and, in some cases, offering per diems.[2] In other words, compared with the Platform, GMO boosters appeared to be relatively well-endowed.

However, at Koforidua and throughout the life of the Plant Breeders Bill, it was unclear whether the legislation had any champions, let alone lay support, within Parliament. As I have argued throughout the book, international actors and donors seemingly created the demand for GM seeds in Ghana by establishing research projects, introducing legislation to Parliament, and creating organizations to carry out these mandates. Building something out of (nearly) nothing proved to be an uphill battle for boosters, brokers, and scientists involved in GMO projects.[3] But they continued on, utilizing a common script at Koforidua and elsewhere: sparking a green revolution in Ghana required "an enabling environment" to "commercialize farming," and building this revolution with genetically modified seeds would spark economic development and allow Ghanaians to focus on solving "local problems" without the intercession of donors. When pressed with skepticism or questions—like those from the Platform or MPs regarding seed patents, monopolies, and industry concentration—rarely did boosters engage.

But, as the MPs in Koforidua made evident, glamorous events and tight scripts do not necessarily guarantee the outcome organizers hoped for. While Thomas, the prominent scientist, and others made pleas throughout the day for MPs to return to Parliament to pass the Plant Breeders Bill, a number of MPs used the opportunity to not only ask questions of organizers, but also to push back on the argument that

GMOs and IPRs were needed. And indeed, upon returning to work the following week, MPs did not vote on the Plant Breeders Bill.

A few months after the Koforidua workshop, a different group of GMO boosters presented a petition in support of the Plant Breeders Bill to Parliament. The petition's sponsors—CAS, CSIR, the West African Centre for Crop Improvement (WACCI), the Ghana National Association of Farmers and Fishermen, and the Biotechnology and Nuclear Agriculture Research Institute (BNARI)—had been collecting signatures online for nearly a year.[4] The petition was hosted on a website called Non-Profit Soapbox with an account belonging to CAS. Located at Cornell University, CAS is a Gates Foundation–funded initiative that aims to increase the availability and use of biotech crops globally, but mainly in the Global South. With a rallying cry of "Let Africa speak for herself!," CAS has focused much of its efforts in Ghana, providing training for Ghanaians through its fellowship program at Cornell and sending surrogates like Mark Lynas to meet with state officials.[5] In addition to supporting the country's GMO experiments, CAS had also taken up supporting the Plant Breeders Bill, further obfuscating the line Ghanaian advocates had tried so diligently to draw between GMOs and intellectual property rights. CAS threw their weight behind the Plant Breeders Bill, offering their Non-Profit Soapbox account to host the online petition, providing sponsorship for the MP workshop in Koforidua, and tweeting out support for the bill. Mark Lynas, who at the time was a visiting fellow at the Cornell Alliance for Science, tweeted, "Scientists and farmers in Ghana need your support—help push for Plant Breeders Bill to support innovation" along with a link to the online petition (Lynas 2015).

The petition began with a letter asking supporters—"those who support agricultural improvement in Ghana"—to sign the petition to "make their voices heard to policymakers!" The letter argued that an IPR regime would establish financial incentives for plant breeders to continue breeding, and that the law would protect new varieties *in general*. The bill, the letter said, *was not* related to GMOs:

> Some far-Left political groups and NGOs are promoting scare stories and conspiracy theories about the Plant Breeders Bill, asserting that the proposed legislation is an attempt to introduce GMOs and a cover for multinational corporations to take over Ghana's seed. These extreme groups, who are seemingly uninterested in development or poverty reduction, have an agenda that sees our farmers permanently trapped in a subsistence cycle with no prospect of improvement through improved seeds. ("Ghanaians Want" 2015)

A press release that was published along with the petition took their accusations a step further, and described, though not by name, food sovereignty activists as "anti-development NGOs" who "spread conspiracy theories and misinformation" and "prefer to promote the continuation of subsistence agriculture and associated rural poverty" (CitiFM 2016). The petition warned: "If the development of new varieties in Ghana is not underpinned by science and technology, the country will not attain food and nutrition security in our lifetime."

Marking activists who oppose the Plant Breeders Bill and GMOs as "extreme" conjures images of anti-GMO activists elsewhere in the world who burn fields or deface McDonald's (Heller 2013). Yet activism in Ghana has been mainly comprised of public forums, press releases and articles, street demonstrations, and dialogue with lawmakers and bureaucrats. These tactics, in other words, are standard forms of democratic engagement that are often touted by development planners to bring about "more democratic and more efficient" systems of governance (Ferguson 2005: 379; Schurman and Munro 2010: 151; Heller 2013). But instead, the petition marked activists as "far-Left" and "seemingly uninterested in development or poverty reduction," all the while denying that the bill had anything to do with GMOs, which even its own proponents knew was not true.

The petition is worth considering as a tool used by proponents to place pressure on Parliament to pass a particular law. But it's also worth considering as a *text* and therefore an artifact imbued with ideology and power. And when examined carefully, both the petition and press release supporting it contained numerous discursive irregularities that left me wondering whether the text of the documents was in fact authored by a non-Ghanaian. For first of all, the term and notion of "far-left" is not common in Ghanaian vernacular. Secondly, while at Koforidua a MP suggested that opposing GMOs and the Plant Breeders Bill was "anti-research," rarely have I heard anyone suggest that activists are anti-development or anti-poverty reduction, as the petition suggested. Marking activists as such is a powerful accusation in a country where development (as ideology and subjectivity) is a part of everyday life. In addition to being inflammatory language, the accusation of the Platform being "anti-development" was antithetical to reputations many members of the Platform—such as the Centre for Indigenous Knowledge and Organizational Development (CIKOD), the Peasant Farmers Association of Ghana (PFAG), and the General Agricultural Workers' Union of Ghana (GAWU)—have in the more general agricultural development spheres; the latter are well known for their development work, and regularly partner with public institutions to carry out programs and initiatives.

Third, and relatedly, the argument that activists are "anti-development," and that GMOs would foster much-needed food security, stood at odds with what many Ghanaian officials said behind the scenes. While development is an ever-present paradox in Ghana, rarely did interlocutors invoke or suggest that Ghana was *un*developed (let alone call activists pro-poverty, anti-development, or far-left); remember the tense interaction in Koforidua when a MP described GMOs as "for poor people!" Indeed, it is unsurprising that Ghanaian officials wouldn't dare paint themselves, or their work, as in need of aid or outside help.

In 2017, two former CAS fellows—John Dziwornu, a commercial farmer, and Rufai Ahmed Braimah, a program assistant at OFAB, published an open letter to Ghana's newly elected president Nana Akufo-Addo. "Obviously Ghana is not a hungry country," they wrote. "As far back as 2013, it became evident that we had managed to meet the Millennium Development Goal on hunger reduction, ... and we reduced the absolute number of undernourished people by half between 1990 and 2012. This is something the world rightly acknowledged us for achieving" (Dziwornu and Braimah 2017; FAO 2015: 1).[6] They continued, urging the president-elect to embrace GMOs to ensure *continued* food security.

In a country where development rules life and governance, as both an ever-unachievable standard as well as an embodied subjectivity, statistics such as the latter are significant, and even prideful. The arguments made in Dziwornu and Braimah's letter—that Ghana is not hungry—stand out considerably to the argument made in the petition ("the country will not obtain food security in our lifetime"). Thus, while global donors and institutions utilized discourses of "hunger" and "poverty reduction" when discussing GMOs, when left to their own devices Ghanaian speakers avoided such discourses all together, and/or linked back to food security indicators that labeled Ghana as food secure. Thus, the claims laid out in the petition and its accompanying letter—that activists were anti-development and that Ghana was struggling to achieve food security—were not only statistically dubious but also linguistically at odds with how Ghanaians generally discussed the Plant Breeders Bill.

In May 2016, organizers reached their goal of two hundred signatories and sent the petition, along with a press release, to Parliament and media houses. A few days after the petition was published, I visited Parliament hoping to speak to someone about the bill. I was introduced to a clerk who worked for the Legal Committee, where the bill was currently sitting. With a printed version of the petition in hand, the clerk told me they had recently received a petition from the "scientific community" in support of the bill. The clerk revealed that the attorney general planned to meet with the speaker to get the bill passed soon, but that the "noise" surrounding the bill was causing delay.

The petition, the back-end negotiations, and the lobbying events were all in response to food sovereignty advocacy efforts, indicating that the "noise" they were making had some impact. But with the petition and press release circulating in the public sphere, I wondered how members of the Platform thought about being described as "anti-development." I asked Constance one day, who hadn't seen the press release and was surprised to hear it described the Platform in such a way:

> The Plant Breeders Bill, *why* is it "development"? No, they should explain how we are anti-development! What is in the Plant Breeders Bill which says that they are going to build infrastructure? What is in the Plant Breeders Bill which says that they are going to build more schools, more health facilities, potable water? Storage facilities? Markets? . . .
>
> The Plant Breeders Bill basically is to support, or even to protect, the breeder. We actually don't have a problem if [it's for] our scientists; they are working so hard to improve seed and other things, and they need to be protected. [But] we are talking about intellectual property rights, just like what Monsanto would like to protect: their GMOs. If our scientists are going to be protected, we don't have a problem.

In asking, "Why is it 'development'?," Constance challenged the idea that IPRs—as economic and legal tools—were somehow essential to "developing" Ghana. But while she disagreed with the idea that the PBB could spur development, she did hold an important belief in common with advocates of the bill: that Ghanaian scientists should be "protected" and recognized for their work.

Biotechnology and Disidentification

The Plant Breeders Bill and GMOs are both global projects in Ghana. They have global sponsors, global developers, and global supporters. These actors work beside, as well as separate from, their Ghanaian counterparts. On the global scale, actors such as Bill Gates and CAS suggest that GMOs are needed to fight hunger in Africa (and therefore Ghana), and that the Plant Breeders Bill would encourage breeders to develop new crop varietals. But as comments made in both public and private attest, these are not necessarily the discourses used by Ghanaian GMO proponents. This is evident in the letter from Dziwornu and Braimah quoted earlier, two GMO campaigners in Ghana deeply embedded in global GMO networks. Writing that "obviously Ghana is not a hungry country" and that Ghana should embrace GMOs as an *additional* strategy for further strengthening food systems stands at great odds against arguments used by their colleagues in the Global North, for whom GMOs are a tool for fighting "malnutrition and starvation" (Wall Street Journal 2016). In fact, it is exactly this type of discourse—GMOs as a mechanism to fight poverty—that was central to a heated debate at the workshop at Koforidua, where numerous MPs stated that GMOs were "for poor people."

Similarly, as the lengthy example from the MP workshop at Koforidua demonstrates, many Ghanaian advocates viewed the Plant Breeders Bill not as a way to spark innovation—as proponents like Mark Lynas suggest—but rather as a way to explicitly raise funds for research efforts that in turn would allow scientists to fund their own research, rather than join donor-funded projects. In other words, an embrace of IPRs by some was a direct response to the gutting of the state research system in the post–structural adjustment, neoliberal era.

By pointing out the discursive differences between global and Ghanaian GMO boosters, I seek to draw attention to the ways in which seemingly global technologies, like GMOs, land in particular places and are articulated within very specific contexts. In Ghana, while many of the scientists, regulators, and boosters embedded within GMO networks are supportive of the technology and wish to see it used in country, they differ in their reasons why. For some, like Dziwornu and Braimah, GMOs are considered a way to continue to strengthen food security and Ghana's standing on the global stage. For others, like Sam the rice scientist in chapter 4, GMOs may be useful for solving breeding issues related to rice, but they also may not be. And as the Koforidua example demonstrates, some viewed GMOs—and the related Plant Breeders Bill—as both technical and financial tools to gain independence from donors and to further build state research scientific councils. In other words, Ghanaian GMO proponents held very different visions for the technology's end use than the global donors with whom they worked.

But for scholars of Ghana, this is perhaps not surprising. Kwame Nkrumah, after all, held a vision of science as an anti-colonial tool, one that could be catalyzed to build a strong and sovereign nation, one free from aid and outside assistance, both of which he considered tools of the neocolonial apparatus (Nkrumah [1965]; Osseo-Asare 2014: 141). Nkrumah's vision lives on not only with Platform members—who emphasized building and protecting local institutions—but also with many of the scientists and regulators working with GMOs in Ghana.

For instance, at a conference on food security I attended at the University of Ghana, Professor Eric Danquah, the founding director of WACCI, told the crowd, "Africa has dreamt of a world without hunger for years." As he delivered these hopeful words, he projected an image of Kwame Nkrumah on a screen, and pride washed over his face. Nkrumah is a powerful nationalist image, as well as an anti-imperialist one. Moreover, Danquah's emphasis on a *world*, rather than a continent, without hunger, marked Africa as a part of, rather than apart from, the global community. Such imagery stands at odds with the Plant Breeders Bill petition—of which WACCI was a co-sponsor—which described food security as unattainable for Ghana without intellectual property rights. Danquah's presentation presented an opposite view: that Africa, and Ghana, had *already* been working toward "a *world* without hunger *for years*," long before the Plant Breeders Bill (emphasis added).

"That man was one hundred years ahead of his countrymen," Thomas said to me over juice one day. "When you talk about Nkrumah, I get excited because the man, he has done a lot for Ghana. And it is unfortunate that we haven't followed up on certain things to increase our productivity." It was also unfortunate, he noted, that "his children are the opposite." For many, GMOs were seen as one of the "things" Ghana could adopt to continue Nkrumah's vision in the twenty-first century, and so it was disconcerting to some that his daughter, Samia Nkrumah, was publicly opposing both GMOs and the Plant Breeders Bill. "[Kwame] Nkrumah built all this, and you want to destroy it?" balked one National Biosafety Authority board member in reference to Samia.

Accordingly, similar to when activists called upon the historic and political symbolism of Nkrumah, the invocation of Nkrumah by researchers and bureaucrats was a similarly historically situated reflection and critique on the nation and what it meant to be a part of it. Whether or not speakers were actually espousing Nkrumahist theory is beyond the point. Rather, the issue here is that they used Nkrumah to imagine GMOs as a vehicle for strengthening state institutions. In doing so, scientists and officials challenge the neoliberal architecture of the "new" Green Revolution for Africa, which meant to put power in the hands of the private, rather than state, sector. A leading GMO proponent told me he imagined agreements between agribusiness companies and state breeders would make "public institutions vibrant once again!" The use of "once again" is an important temporal marker, invoking the Ghanaian state immediately post-independence, and thus indicating that the future the speaker wants is not only known, but possible. Rather than imagine a "new" Green Revolution driven by the private sector, as global donors did, many Ghanaians saw it, and GMOs, as an opportunity to build a stronger state.

The examples I've surveyed here of Ghanaian GMO proponents demonstrate the ways in which the latter regularly engage in *disidentification*. Disidentification, as articulated by Michel Pêcheux (1982) and later José Esteban Muñoz (1999), serves as an intervention for thinking about ideology and subjects operating within it. While Louis Althusser (1971) theorized that ideology rendered subjects either as "good"—those who assimilate with the dominant ideology—or "bad"—those who oppose it—Pêcheux considered such a binary unrealistic, arguing that it did not capture those who operate somewhere in between, or perhaps outside, this dyad. Thus, Pêcheux proposed a "third modality," that of disidentification (1982: 158). Disidentification pertains to a situation wherein ideology "operates . . . *on and against itself*, through the 'overthrown-rearrangement' of the complex of ideological formations" (1982: 159; emphasis in the original). To be clear, Pêcheux argues that ideology and "the process of interpellation of individuals as subjects" are "eternal" and "[do] not disappear" (1982: 159). Instead, as Muñoz clarifies, to disidentify is to recognize the ideological constraints one is in, but also to use this recognition as a strategy to "[work] on and against" said ideology:

> Disidentification is the third mode of dealing with dominant ideology, one that neither opts to assimilate within such a structure nor strictly opposes it; rather, disidentification is a strategy that works on and against dominant ideology. Instead of buckling under the pressures of dominant ideology (identification, assimilation) or attempting to break free of its inescapable sphere (counteridentification, utopianism), this "working on and against" is a strategy that tries to transform a cultural logic from within, always laboring to enact permanent structural change while at the same time valuing the importance of local or everyday struggles of resistance. (1999: 12)

Using disidentification as a theoretical lens helps illuminate the ways in which Ghanaian scientists, officials, farmers, and activists within and against the "(im)possibility that dominant culture," in this case the development apparatus, "generates" (Muñoz 1999: 6). This is especially true with efforts to build a "new" Green Revolution and introduce GMOs in Ghana, both of which are discursively (i.e., ideologically) heavy with attempts to render farmers and citizens as either good or bad subjects. Consider the examples spread throughout this manuscript: pro- vs. anti-GMO, good vs. bad farming, commercial vs. subsistence farming, biotechnology vs. conventional breeding, development vs. anti-development. These discursive landscapes generate (im)possibilities, in that they narrow language use, policy orientation, and funding directives. At the same time, actors—whether scientists, GMO boosters, activists, farmers, or otherwise—find possibilities for appearing as "good subjects" while at the same time working "on and against" the structure (Muñoz 1999: 6, 12). The rice scientist who is dedicated to the GM rice project but also believes that he and his colleagues can improve rice without it. The boosters who want to see GMOs adopted in Ghana not for their technological superiority, but for the potential patents that come with it. John Dziwornu and Rufai Ahmed Braimah, who write, "obviously Ghana is not a hungry country" while using the benchmarks that would otherwise denigrate it—food security indicators—as a point of pride.

These are all examples of disidentification, of Ghanaians recognizing the (im)possibilities of being suspended within global plant breeding programs, funded by donors with their own motives, and of partnering with industry. Ghanaian GMO proponents recognized these limitations while also maintaining a goal of not having to rely on "our development partners for support" (Gakpo 2016b). For many, freedom from donors was the pinnacle of state sovereignty. I discussed this point with Appiah, who at the time served as the director of a GMO booster organization:

> Rock: Hypothetically, GMOs come, the Plant Breeders Bill is passed, [...an] initial victory for your side.... What happens if the things that the Food Sovereignty people are saying—that Monsanto, Bayer, DuPont [will] put CSIR out of business—what happens if that's true? What happens if GMOs are here, you can access them, the farmers can go for them if they want, they have the choice, but they are not buying from CSIR—they're buying from DuPont, Bayer, Syngenta, one of these big non-Ghanaian multinationals?

Appiah: When I sit back in my room, maybe I will cry having disappointed my farmers, or my colleagues, who hope it never happens. Because for now, I don't see how that will happen. The reason is that, for example if you take the cowpea ... we got the gene and we will put it in the local variety, which is *ours*. So, and then I believe and I know that before all these things started ... there was a negotiation and an agreement, so how is one going to renege on that agreement or negotiation? I don't see that happening. It will only happen when the public disallow the local scientists to do the development of the crop, using our local varieties. If there's a crop, let's say cowpea, and we have a variety from the US, the crop is developed there and then the seedlings are sent to us, then we assure that we are going to meet that situation. But where we have it in our local varieties, from where I sit now, I don't see it happening. And should it—that would be sad.

Rock: Because for you the passion is that it should be local, it should be Ghanaian?

Appiah: It should be *Ghanaian*.

In this section, I have shown how the Ghanaian scientists and officials working on GMO projects envision the technology to be useful for building a strong, independent state. Similar to the desires of food sovereignty activists explored earlier, I note here how this vision is explicitly tied within demands for a lessened reliance on donors. That does not mean that Ghanaian officials and scientists wish to decline offers to work on international projects. Instead, Ghanaian GMO proponents work "on and against" global GMO projects, (dis)identifying and weighing the potential gains alongside potential losses. As Appiah and others expressed, many hold an ardent hope that the Plant Breeders Bill will genuinely benefit Ghanaian breeders. At the end of the day, though this group is diverse, they too are bonded by a vision, as Samia Nkrumah said earlier, for freedom and self-sufficiency.

Data, Funding, and the Search for Alternatives

As I have argued, the context of the "new" Green Revolution is essential for understanding the story of GMOs in Ghana. At the center of efforts to build a Green

Revolution was the phrase "making agriculture a business." Part of building any business is the process of identifying risks. Risks to your profits, to your operations, to your brand. Identifying risk is also an integral part to the work of biosafety officials, who must determine the biological, environmental, and, sometimes, socio-economic risks that a genetically modified organism poses upon release. At an internal meeting I attended of the National Biosafety Authority, I learned that Ghanaian officials identified potential risks to the general acceptance of GMOs in Ghana. Board members spent the day conducting a "stakeholder mapping" exercise, identifying different groups in Ghanaian society that may be interested in GMOs, and then measuring whether they were a risk to the project, an ally, or uninterested. High on the risk list was the Platform, who were labeled as "Anti's" on the map. A few months later I visited the National Biosafety Authority, and when I arrived at their office I noticed a number of three-ring binders lining the shelves, each with a name of a member group of the Platform. The Authority was clearly keeping track of who they referred to as the "Anti's."

I asked an official about why the Authority viewed the Platform as a "risk." They responded:

> I think it was regarded that way because the Anti group in the developed countries are different in approach than the Anti group in developing countries like Ghana. In developed countries, their level of knowledge is so high.... They know what they want, and they push for it in an objective manner as much as possible.
>
> But what we are seeing here in Africa, in the emerging countries, is that, for them [activists], whether you are making sense or not, it is "no." You see? Whether you are making sense or not, . . . "we don't want it." Whether the product is good or not, it is "no." No matter how well you introduce the product, no matter how well you explain the role of biosafety. Even if a toddler, excuse me to say, will understand and say, "Okay for this one, it is okay," in the developed countries, they will appreciate it . . . [and] where they have doubts, they will also insist.
>
> But here, no matter how well you explain, for them, the "no" is the going. I think that is the reason why [the Platform was] tagged as risk. Apart from that I don't think there is any reason why one should tag them as risk, because they are expressing their position. But again, let me emphasize that *where* they adopt that position that no matter what—even if it's good for *us*, our position is no—they become a risk to society. They become a risk to the system.

In this short response, the official created two categories of activists: those in "the developed countries" (presumably Europe and the United States), whom they described more or less as professionalized and "objective," and those in the developing countries (presumably Ghana), whom they infantilized. The official suggested that conversations around risk and safety related to GMOs were so simple even a toddler "in the developed countries" could understand it, but that for activists in developing countries, "the 'no' is the going." In doing so, the official reinforced racialized hierarchies of knowledge and progress in a similar manner that I've discussed throughout the book.

I spend time on this example—and others like it—to emphasize that, in many ways, the idea of "making agriculture a business," at least that which circulates at global and local levels, was shrouded in the denigration of African expertise. To be sure, "making agriculture a business" as a discourse and a project predates the current "new" Green Revolution moment. But that is precisely my point: the origins of this phrase, at least in Ghana, are rooted in and contributed to colonial rule, and maintain similar linguistic characteristics today.

At the risk of sounding redundant, I am re-emphasizing this point to stress the incredible challenge that such a discursive landscape—one that denigrated anyone who raised questions about the efficacy of GMOs, and one that centered foreign expertise—presented for food sovereignty advocates, whose platform was predicated, at least on part, on the knowledge and labor of Ghanaian farmers. Though the Platform tried in various ways to come to the table with Ghanaian scientists, regulators, and officials, and though they were quite consistent in their political-economic critiques of GMOs, the country's biosafety regulator deemed them a risk to the system. By simply labeling the Platform as "Anti," those tasked with building biosafety systems in Ghana foreclosed opportunities to bring in Platform members as valued contributors, representatives of farming communities, or even (much-needed) constructive critics.

Food sovereignty advocates not only had to navigate a discursive environment that marked small-scale farmers as inadequate and a threat to food security, and activists as unreasonable, but they also had to compete within a climate of "data-driven" development. Data are an important aspect of the neoliberal, entrepreneurial, tech-centered moment. And indeed, this is yet another way global funders attempt to make the African countryside, and its inhabitants (whose behavior continued to elude donors), legible with charts and graphs (Scott 1998).

Data are also a logical extension for those promoting agribusiness, a sector that relies on statistics, record-keeping, and technology.

Osman, a union representative and member of the Platform, explained how the emphasis on agribusiness was changing the development scene:

> Those on the other side have a lot of money and they are pushing for research, sponsoring research work, sponsoring training programs, sponsoring key government officials, sponsoring government trips ... But we do not have the money to push for some research work[,] trainings ... [and] generate strong data, ... the so-called "evidenced-based" kind of data, and push.

Despite tongue-in-cheek remarks about "so-called 'evidenced-based' kind of data" (which I heard often), many activists conceded that they would need to produce similar data to compete for funders, legitimacy, and hearts and minds. However, for food sovereignty activists, many of whom belonged to organizations that were reliant on unstable funding sources such as donors, this became a challenge. GAFP's agroecology project is one such example.

Faced with pressure to supply data and evidence, GAFP turned to a donor in the Global North to pitch a project on agroecology. Worldwide, food sovereignty organizations contend that agroecology—and the small farmers who practice it—can feed the future, without need for large tracts of land, high-tech tools and inputs, or an orientation toward international markets (Holt-Giménez and Altieri 2013). The Alliance for Food Sovereignty in Africa (AFSA) describes agroecology as the "bold future for Africa," and "knowledge intensive, building on traditional agricultural practices with modern research and technology, strengthening the sovereignty of small-scale family farmers" (AFSA 2015).

The aim of the project was to create a working agroecological farm that would be 1) a way to produce data to show that good yields can be achieved with safe, scientifically proven environmental practices; 2) a training center on agroecological farming; and 3) a self-funding enterprise. The latter was especially crucial to keep the farm running without the assistance of donors. "The issue of sustainability is something we've been thinking all the while," Nii from GAFP explained. "How do you sustain a project like this, especially if you get initial funding and . . . [then] the funding dries up?"

I will share a few ethnographic vignettes from the beginning stages of the project to show how GAFP and partners envisioned agroecology working in Ghana. To clarify, at the time of writing, the project is ongoing, and so I will not be using this space to discuss outcomes, assess whether goals were met, or muse on whether the project should be "scaled." Instead, I dig deep here into understanding the social processes around the development and life of this project (Benton 2015), and to argue that there are lessons to be learned from the mundane meetings and project planning that often constitute much of any NGO's time. And chiefly, as I'll show here, recipient fatigue is not just something experienced and expressed by unwilling recipients of development aid; it is part and parcel of the development experience, even when an NGO seeks funding from another seemingly allied in ideological and political leanings.

In early February 2016, project partners met in Accra to hash out the details of the project. In her opening address, Constance explained why GAFP was pursuing such an ambitious project:

> [One] reason is the Plant Breeders Bill . . . as for GMOs, no matter what the scientists say . . . no matter what label they put on it, we are not going to accept GMOs, at least from the GAFP perspective, and we stand by that. We may do other things, but GMO, no. So, we're going into agroecology to refute the idea that GMO is the best to eradicate hunger.

In other words, GAFP wanted data, graphs, and charts to project onto screens in conference rooms, print in laminated reports, and circulate via viral social media posts. It was hard to blame organizational leadership for this desire; after all, not only were they and their farmer base not taken seriously at meetings, but they were also facing constant attacks from GMO advocates and occasionally government officials.

And in particular, Constance and GAFP considered agroecology to be a reflection of sankofa and therefore relevant both for the Ghanaian context and for the neoliberal, "new" Green Revolution moment. With its emphasis on its scientific components, Constance and GAFP considered agroecology a model that could compete with the scientific discourses of modern agriculture. Constance told the audience:

> Agroecology is... traditional, but it is now an innovation. Why do I say this? When I was growing up, I never knew fertilizer, I never saw chemical fertilizer. My uncles were just farming. Even my mother was farming.... We used to go out and pick cow dung early in the morning.... But then at a certain point, it looked like this whole thing was put to sleep because of technology and the quick pace at which the world is running.
>
> We can't wait, we don't have time, chemical fertilizer is... handy to get quick yields,... [but] now the idea of using chemical fertilizer is passing off due to so many reasons that you and I know: health, living, the cost of chemical fertilizer, the environmental effect... climate change, and all that. Now we are going back to agroecology and it is, as far as the past is concerned, it is a new way of going into agriculture.

Constance described agroecology at once as "traditional" but "an innovation," as something that Ghanaians would go "back to" but also "a new way of going into agriculture." This is sankofa. Read in the context of the "new" Green Revolution, Constance's use of the term "innovation" was not neutral; it was a nod to the tech-centric, agribusiness discourse circulating at the time. Urgency underlined the text as well—"We can't wait, we don't have time"—a critical need to produce food differently due to climate change, the detrimental effect of chemical fertilizer (on health, income, and land), and "all that."

"Look, our people are endowed with knowledge," Nii said, as he projected an illustration on to the screen. In the middle of the graphic was AGROECOLOGY in all caps, surrounded by a box. Flowing into it were arrows connecting academic disciplines—ecology, anthropology, sociology, ethnoecology, economics, agricultural sciences—and "traditional farmers' knowledge" to agroecology, "creating a dialogue of wisdoms" (Third World Network 2015: 6). But even the graphic seemingly established hierarchical categories, with farmers' knowledge standing on its own on the right, and the academic sciences grouped together on the left. A less cynical read, perhaps, would interpret "farmers' knowledge" as standing on its own and unique from, academic inquiry. To be fair, I don't know the graphic artist's intentions. However, the image was certainly up for interpretation, raising questions about how such "wisdoms" were in "dialogue."

The combination of academic sciences and farmers' knowledge was one of the aspects of agroecology that made the model appealing to organizations like GAFP. "Sometimes we conclude our people are backwards, but these things are not helping us," Nii said. Nii walked us through the different schools of thought that are integrated in the agroecological model, as well as the different activities GAFP planned to undertake to achieve their objectives of an agroecological future, including the design and dissemination of a baseline survey (data, of course, was needed) and establishing opportunities for "policy dialogues" at local and national levels on agroecology, climate change, and the Plant Breeders Bill.

Both Constance and Nii explicitly marked agroecology as originating from the outside, which was both a hindrance and an advantage. Juxtaposed against the mantra of agriculture as a business, GAFP's vision of an agroecological Ghana is an idea of how Ghanaian agriculture can proceed in a commercialized, yet "traditional" and sustainable, manner. Throughout the various stages of the project that I witnessed, tension between agroecology as an outside, scientific tool versus something that is already known reared its head in a number of ways. At the inception meeting, I spent a coffee break in the courtyard with Kwesi and a professor of crop sciences. "You know Bill Gates wouldn't fund my research," she said with a smirk, half joking but half frustrated, and explained that she and her colleagues had incredible difficulty securing funding to research indigenous crops.

"Sometimes I don't know about this 'research,'" Kwesi replied, "because research told us that our crops aren't good, [and then] brought hybrids, [but] now research is telling us we should go back," in reference to agroecology. Indeed, the context of recipient fatigue shaped how some members of GAFP and the larger platform viewed agroecology. While donors in the Global North emphasized that the agroecological model differs according to context, on the ground in Ghana there was disagreement over whether agroecological principles were set in stone or flexible. In other words, was agroecology yet another donor-driven development plan, or something that was truly collaborative with farmers, practitioners, and donors?

Back at the meeting, participants discussed the idea of seed banking. One young farmer in attendance had recently returned from India, where he had spent time at Navdanya, a farm and training center run by an organization headed by Vandana Shiva. He told the group about how he and other program participants learned of seed banking, the labeling and storing of seeds for community use. The young farmer was eager to integrate what he had learned. "One farmer at a time, one community at a time," he said to a captivated room, "we will restore dignity to nature."

A tense exchange followed between the presenter and Mark, who was concerned that depositing seed supply in a single place left the seeds vulnerable to fire and other means of destruction. Mark urged the group to not simply replicate what was being done elsewhere, and he told the group about a seed festival his organization had held in northern Ghana. On the day of the festival, Mark said, community members, mostly women, displayed their seeds in a public setting so everyone could see who had what, and take record. "That's how they do it *traditionally*," he said, emphasizing "traditionally" to create a clear linguistic and ideological line between seed banks and seed festivals. He suggested that the young farmer "go to local people, learn from them, they have their own strategies."

A few months later, Nii and I made our way north to visit the farmer who had trained at Navdanya. In talking with him and other farmers, there was tension around the idea of "local" and "indigenous" foods and staple crops. Though adherents of agroecology tout the model as one of many tools people can use to "go back" to re-claim "traditional" ways of farming, eating, and cooking, in travels with the agroecology project as well as my own field research, people described substantial changes in growing and eating patterns within the last generation. Many linked these changes to the introduction of NGOs and new agricultural technologies (such as fertilizer). The young farmer who had trained at Navdanya expressed concern that children don't find "consumption of indigenous food ... attractive." Indeed, when we visited this farmer's community and held a town meeting, women told us that their husbands insisted on growing maize. The women, however, were tired of doing so, as maize did not grow well without required inputs (water and fertilizer). Instead, they advocated that their families should return to growing millet, which matured (grew) early (fast), stored well, and was nutritious. The men fumbled and told us that maize received support from companies and NGOs, but millet did not. This interaction clearly shows tension between, and challenges, linguistic designations between crops considered "staple" (maize) and "traditional" (millet). It also raises the question of how a crop becomes a staple, or how a crop that was once a staple becomes designated instead as traditional.

The agroecology farm serves as an example of how GAFP and other Ghanaian food sovereignty activists regularly engage in disidentification. Rather than either completely capitulate and adopt agriculture as a business, or completely reject it, GAFP and other organizations on the Platform work on and against hegemonic structures to eke out alternatives. At the same time, seeking these alternatives is not simple. While GAFP and others approached agroecology as reflective of sankofa, there was also disagreement over just how agroecological methods should be carried out. This is not to disparage GAFP's efforts. Instead, I do so to show how even models thought to be alternatives to hegemonic systems—like agroecology—are contested and reshaped on the ground.

Conclusion

In this chapter, I have explored how Ghanaian scientists, officials, and anti-GM activists navigate the (im)possibilities of global development. For scientists, a sovereign future requires research funding, a mythical thing long abdicated by the state in the era of structural adjustment. Funding from development agencies, however well intended, comes with an incredible amount of red tape and global bureaucracy, aspects of funding that can slow down a project for years and that can funnel effort toward crops not well suited for a particular context. These are but some of the reasons why Ghanaian scientists and officials supported the Plant Breeders Bill, for the lure of plant patents offers the hope of steady financial return. And it is for similar, though different, reasons that GAFP and others are turning toward agroecology. At once a tradition and innovation, the capital-S scientific underpinnings of agroecology offer legitimacy in a world dominated by proponents of the "new" Green Revolution and biotechnology who so often over-rely on simplified discourses of "science." And more to the point, GAFP hopes their agroecology farm will one day produce enough income through crop sale and training services to be self-sustaining, no longer in need of grants from allied NGOs in the Global North.

I have shown how Ghanaian actors work on and against dominant ideologies, discourses, and policies that circulate within the development sphere. Disidentification is one of the creative and strategic ways Ghanaian scientists, activists, farmers, and others work within the reality of recipient fatigue; solidly suspended within global webs of funders, markets, politics, and more, while working for different futures. By asking, "Why is it 'development'?" in regard to the Plant Breeders Bill, Constance draws our attention to the ways in which the stuff of life for any country—infrastructure, social services, potable water—is sidelined in the era of neoliberal development. And by listing that very stuff when confronted with an accusation of being "anti-development," Constance flips the gaze, challenging the potential of IPRs to secure basic needs for Ghanaians.

Across the spectrum of actors, Ghanaian scientists, officials, and activists often place their arguments and experiments within the context of colonial rule, its ugly remnants, and a desire to squash it once and for all. As the ethnographic vignettes I explored here demonstrate, utterances of anti-colonialism by speakers are not simply discursive tactics; they are reflective of both contemporary life and imagined futures in postcolonial Ghana (Fanon 1952; Nkrumah 1965; Pierre 2012). In resisting international discourses of Africa as a singular, starving place, Ghanaians insist that assumptions of food deficiency are not the best place to start conversations regarding food and agriculture (Reese 2019a; Rock 2019). Instead, Ghanaian scientists and activists alike call our attention to what is abundant—knowledge, determination, food—and that which many desire: freedom from donors. If this in fact is the pinnacle of state sovereignty, then both GMO boosters and the Platform share a similar goal and, within it, a similar version for the struggle for food sovereignty in Ghana.

Epilogue

It is July 2019 and I'm sitting in GAFP's Accra office. I've come for a short visit this time, just a month, and I'm trying to catch up with folks as much as I can. Constance and I are chatting about something when Kwesi interrupts us, holding a turquoise booklet in-hand entitled *Report on Stakeholders Forum on Genetically Modified Organisms in Ghana: The Benefits, Threats and Policy Implications* (Frempong 2007). The report, published by the Science and Technology Policy Research Institute (a wing of the Council for Scientific and Industrial Research), is early material culture from the beginning of the biotech conversation in Ghana. Laughing, Kwesi asks me to read the report's "conclusions and recommendations." My eyes hurriedly scan the section to find the text that has sent my friend into giggles: "Ghana must invest in its own *homegrown* GM technology but with capacity building *obtained from elsewhere*" (CSIR 2005: 58; emphasis added).

"Homegrown" but "obtained from elsewhere." This tension that sparked deep laughter from Kwesi is also that which animates the topic of GMOs in Ghana. It is the crux of activists' opposition to GMOs, who question the sustainability of a technology directed and "obtained from elsewhere." The tension also fuels scientists' skepticism of their role in, and eventual success of, projects over which they have little control. And finally, the reality of trying to build a homegrown technology that relies almost completely on funding and expertise from elsewhere, like fitting a square peg into a circular hole, is the explanation for why a majority of GMO projects in Ghana have yet to come to fruition. This complexity, or what my colleague Rachel Schurman and I describe (2020) as "complex choreographies," is key to understanding why biotech has had little success in Ghana and elsewhere on the continent. It is this point that I will spend much of the concluding chapter exploring, as is it this tension which has the most potential for broad applicable lessons.

Starting in 2013, Ghana, along with international partners, set out to assess six genetically modified crop varieties: Bt cotton, Bt cowpea, GM cotton, NEWEST rice, NUE rice, and nutrient-enhanced sweet potato. Of these, only two remain in the pipeline—NUE rice and Bt cowpea—the rest were suspended indefinitely (see table 3). But the projects have not been without effort. GMO proponents and donors have created a multitude of organizations to help usher in an era of GMOs in Africa: the African Agricultural Technology Foundation (AATF), created by the Rockefeller Foundation, which brokers agreements between donors, multinational companies, and African scientific councils; the African Biosafety Network of Expertise, which sits at the level of the African Union and assists African officials to pass biosafety laws and review applications for GMOs; Program for Biosafety Systems, which, at the mandate of the US government, assists African governments to draft and pass biosafety laws and train officials; the Open Forum on Agricultural Biotechnology in Africa (OFAB), which does the same, but at the mandate of AATF; and the Cornell Alliance for Science, which trains African journalists, farmers, and officials to be "science communicators," and which operates from the bottom line of "Africa needs GMOs" (AATF and OFAB 2018). The same set of donors—the Rockefeller Foundation, the Bill & Melinda Gates Foundation (BMGF), and the US Agency for International Development—fund and/or have created all of these scientific, regulatory, booster, and managerial organizations. The decks, in other words, are seemingly stacked toward acceptance and approval (Rock and Schurman 2020). But approval is not happening, at least not yet, and this conclusion is not limited solely to Ghana.

In Burkina Faso, a country which donors, biotech supporters, and industry heads alike touted for so long as a new dawn of biotech for Africa, the failed legacy of Bt cotton lingers (Luna and Dowd-Uribe 2020). There has been talk of, but so far no action, toward reintroducing genetically modified varieties for the country's cotton sector. Elsewhere, Tanzania abruptly cancelled its participation in genetically

TABLE 3. Status of GM Crops in Ghana (2021)

CROP (VARIETY IF KNOWN)	FACILITATOR	TECHNOLOGY PARTNER	STATUS
GM sweet potato	Tuskegee University	n/a	Suspended
Bt cotton	Monsanto	Monsanto	Suspended
GM cotton	Monsanto	Monsanto	Suspended
Bt cowpea (Songotra)	AATF	Monsanto	Ongoing
NUE rice (NERICA)	AATF	Arcadia Biosciences	Ongoing
NEWEST rice (NERICA)	AATF	Arcadia Biosciences	Suspended

Note: Adapted from Rock and Schurman (2020: 14).

modified (GM) maize and cassava research programs in January 2021, citing concern over relying on foreign companies. In announcing the news, Tanzania's Minister of Agriculture said, "We have a big task to protect our seed sovereignty and so far we are not doing well" (Kitabu 2021). Similarly, in Uganda, President Yoweri Museveni has refused to sign two drafts of a biosafety bill which he says favors large corporations rather than small farmers (Afedraru 2019). The country continues to house a number of GMO projects despite the fact that it does not have a biosafety law in place (Schnurr and Gore 2015).

Uganda is not alone in operating in this sort of legal gray area. In Kenya, which AATF, the Alliance for a Green Revolution in Africa (AGRA), and International Service for the Acquisition of Agri-biotech Applications (ISAAA) all call home, scientists, officials, and industry work toward commercializing GM crops despite the fact that the country has upheld a ban on GMOs since 2012. Weary of this bureaucratic hurdle, in 2019 the BMGF, one of the largest funders of GMO research in Kenya as elsewhere, threatened to pull project funding if Kenya didn't reverse the ban (Andae 2019). While the ban technically remains in place as of the time of this writing, Kenya's national biosafety authority has forged ahead with considering biotech applications, approving cultivation of Bt cotton in 2019 (Obi 2020) and national performance trials of GM cassava in 2021 (Ngotho 2021).

Biotech proponents have had some more seemingly decisive victories in Nigeria, where regulators have approved nearly thirty GM varietals for importation and/or cultivation in a relatively short span of time (ISAAA 2021a). Though most of these approvals are for maize and soybean, in June 2021 Nigeria released the AATF-developed Bt cowpea for commercial sale (Emejor 2021). It is unclear when the other countries involved in the Bt cowpea project, Ghana and Burkina Faso, will apply for commercial approval.

Finally, in the years that have passed between conducting fieldwork and finalizing this manuscript, there have been some major movements in Ghana as well. In 2019, officials passed updated biosafety legislation, effectively operationalizing the original 2011 Biosafety Act (Ibrahim 2019). Moreover, after almost eight years of debate and struggle, on November 5, 2020, the Plant Breeders Bill was passed. Earlier in the year, the bill had been reintroduced to Parliament and renamed the "Plant Variety Protection Bill," but the content was the same. On the day of the parliamentary vote, there was little debate on a somewhat empty Parliament floor, and the bill that had caused so much strife was passed rather unceremoniously. Speaking to reporters after the bill's passage, Dr. Owusu Afriyie Akoto, the Ghanaian Minister of Food and Agriculture, told reporters, "It has nothing to do with multinationals ... that is the kind of propaganda that goes out to scare people" (Gakpo 2020). Who will ultimately benefit from the bill remains to be seen. At the time of writing, the bill has not yet been implemented, and the Food Sovereignty Platform continues to rally against it.

By and large, biotech proponents have little to show for a decade and a half of efforts in plant breeding, institutional development, and international collaboration (Schnurr 2019). Indeed, it is the complexity of these massive global projects, perhaps more than the actual scientific outcome of any breeding effort or field trial results, that helps explain why in Ghana and elsewhere GM crops are still not on the market (Rock and Schurman 2020). There are broad lessons here in project design, the efficacy (or lack thereof) of giant global projects, and the reality of trying to transform patented, protected material into a humanitarian technology.

And yet, people continue to try. In an op-ed in the *Washington Post*, Purdue University president Mitch Daniels wrote: "[Denying] Africans ... the benefits of modern technology is not merely anti-scientific. It's cruel, it's heartless, it's inhumane" (2017). It should perhaps not be surprising that proponents use the same humanitarian discourse to support GMOs as they do celebrity-infused charity campaigns in Africa. And yet this discourse—cloaked in supposedly moral arguments—goes hand-in-hand with another insidious set of ideas and images: that of darkness. The "new" Green Revolution for Africa is premised on the idea that capital inputs, markets, and financial freedom will green a "Dark Continent." Proponents of this massive project conjure images of darkness and light in interviews with journalists, in videos uploaded to YouTube, in speeches, and in organizational discourse. These racialized, colonial-era images are familiar to Western audiences, and are used to conjure classic humanitarian responses. Yet, Green Revolution proponents don't seek humanitarian support from the common consumer—they seek the attention of investors, ready to dedicate massive amounts of cash toward "Africa's lucrative markets" (Introduction, AGRA News 2015: 5). This task, we are told, "is both an economic and moral imperative" (AGRA News 2015: 5). Here, the dialectic of darkness and morality is used to mobilize and circulate capital.

To be sure, supporters of GMOs and the "new" Green Revolution are not unique in the deployment of this dyad. As Walter Rodney (1972) and others have emphasized, there is an extensive history of Europeans moving to the continent in the name of morality and bringing Africans out of darkness, only to make room for capital interests to spread and local populations to be plundered. European missionaries, US- and European-backed coups, international development projects. The list is long. And it is this particular history—these five hundred years of imperial and colonial rule, of structural adjustment, of expert advice, of the upending of agricultural lands, of millions lost to slaving, of a drying climate—that underlines the fatigue of so-called recipients of international development aid. For farmers in the Ghanaian countryside, deadened soil acts as a moral geography, linking lands to far-away fertilizer companies and development agencies. For Ghanaian scientists, the reality of government abdication of funding is a daily reality, one which is pierced by international funding agencies and private companies with whom they engage in public-private partnerships.

And it is these realities that Constance, Kwesi, and others call attention to when they mock a CSIR recommendation, take to the streets with placards, petition Parliament, and sue the National Biosafety Authority. For GMOs have animated a much larger discussion in Ghana, one that has to do with the country's place in the world. GMOs are not an exceptional technology, nor are they even perhaps an exceptional threat, for a place that has endured, and resisted, so much. Instead, GMOs in Ghana, given their backing of the world's most powerful development funders and agribusiness companies, have provided the Ghanaian food-sovereignty movement with a global platform to air their larger grievances and to demand the African continent be a more central focus of discussions of food, taste, and power.

"We are not starving" is not a denial of hunger. It is a challenge to those in the development industry, to outside observers, and to people in power to question their analytical frameworks, personal worldviews, and political renderings. To strip and lay bare the assumption that discussions of food and agriculture in Africa must begin with hunger and end with the insertion of outside expertise. And Constance's words are also this—an affirmation of agency, a demand to be taken and viewed seriously, an ode to those who came before, and a guide for those who will come after.

"We are not starving, eh? We are not starving."

Notes

Introduction

1. In Ghana, a majority of farmers are considered smallholders, which means they operate on approximately five acres of land or fewer (CDD 2011: 15; Sungbaahee and Kpieta 2020).
2. Regulations regarding GMOs are often referred to as "biosafety" laws, and the regulatory bodies are often referred to as national biosafety authorities.
3. In 2018, Monsanto was acquired by German pharmaceutical giant Bayer. However, given that a majority of my research took place before the acquisition, I will refer to the company as Monsanto throughout the manuscript.
4. Bobo-Dioulasso is a city in southwestern Burkina Faso.
5. In this instance, "stacks" refers to crops that are stacked with multiple inserted traits, including those featured in MON15985. For instance, Monsanto's Roundup Ready Bollgard II Cotton is a stacked variety that contains two traits: MON15985—for pest resistance—and MON1445, for herbicide tolerance.
6. Following Adam Moe Fejerskov, I utilize the term "private" rather than "philanthropic" foundation, as "the abstract altruism affiliated with philanthropy is not . . . guaranteed in

the endeavors of private foundations" (2018: 48).

7. Imbued with a sense of racial ("civilized") superiority, colonizing forces across the globe marked indigenous populations as poor stewards of land. This was one mechanism by which colonizers sought to enclose land and its inhabitants for capital exploitation and gain. Across North America and Africa, for example, national parks served as important projects of white nationalism, where "indigenous populations . . . were viewed as both a part of and a threat to pristine nature" (Gosine 2010: 152).

8. See Scoones and Glover (2009) for a thorough and critical review of *Starved for Science*.

9. In 2018, Mark Lynas published a biotech manifesto entitled *Seeds of Science: Why We Got It So Wrong on GMOs*. It is worth noting that the book was funded in part by the African Agricultural Technology Foundation, a BMGF- and USAID-funded biotech broker that oversees a number of GMO projects on the African continent.

10. Lynas and others use the undifferentiated term "Anti" to refer broadly to those who oppose GMOs.

11. The conversation between Kevin Folta and Mark Lynas occurred on an episode of *Talking Biotech*, a podcast hosted by Kevin Folta, professor of horticultural science at the University of Florida.

12. In 2019, DowDuPont, the parent company of DuPont Pioneer, announced that the company would split into three companies: Dow, DuPont, and Corteva Agriscience. Corteva handles the agricultural and seed work previously undertaken by DuPont Pioneer.

13. After the ABNE project ended in 2014, the BMGF awarded MSU an additional $12 million grant to "to help African governments build functional regulatory systems for biotech crops," but it is unclear whether this money went to ABNE or elsewhere. https://www.gatesfoundation.org/about/committed-grants/2014/08/oppgd1406.

14. As per official project documents obtained from MSU through public records requests and publicly available information: https://www.canr.msu.edu/cgc/projects/african_biosafety_network_of_expertise.

15. Documents obtained via Michigan Freedom of Information Act.

16. The prevalence of GM maize, soy, and cotton in Africa tracks with global GMO trends. As Glenn Davis Stone writes, "by 2018, GM seed accounted for 78 percent of all soybean, 30 percent of all maize, and 76 percent of all cotton planted worldwide" (2021: 5).

17. The Nyéléni Forum Steering Committee was comprised of representatives from CNOP, LVC, ROPPA, the World Women's March, the World Forum of Fish Harvesters and Fish Workers, the World Forum of Fisher Peoples, Friends of the Earth International, the International Planning Committee for Food Sovereignty Rome, and the Food Sovereignty

Network (list compiled from Nyéléni Steering Committee 2008: 3).

18. Self-described as "the international peasants' voice," LVC is a global network of "peasants, small and medium size farmers, landless people, rural women and youth, indigenous people, migrants and agricultural workers" ("International Peasants' Voice," n.d.) with a mission "to halt neoliberalism and construct alternative food systems based on food sovereignty" (Holt-Giménez 2009). Though LVC is largely credited with sparking the global food sovereignty movement, peasant collectives in Mexico, Panama, and Costa Rica had already been using, and debating, the term since the 1980s (Edelman 2014).

19. Though AFSA formally launched in 2011, according to their website, the alliance was "first conceived in 2008" (AFSA 2019).

20. I received clearance from American University's Institutional Review Board to carry out research (Protocol #15005).

21. These categories are not static. For instance, many food sovereignty activists are also farmers. And so, while these categories allow me to organize my methodology, they are not reflective of a more fluid reality.

Chapter 1. Agricultural Development and So-Called NGOs

1. I tried to pump the borehole and, likely to no one's surprise, was unsuccessful in producing a single drop of water.
2. Hereafter, any mention of "smallholder" farmers designates *non*-cocoa farmers.
3. This artificial division of crop production would later be essentialized by the development industry as "gender roles," obfuscating the historical and intentional reconfiguration of the Ghanaian farm.
4. I thank Brandi Simpson Miller for sharing these sources with me.
5. For a fascinating examination of how *Kofi the Good Farmer* changed over time in both print and film, see Blaylock 2020.
6. Sasakawa is a controversial figure. Prior to Japan's defeat in World War II, Sasakawa was an active figure in far-right politics, going so far as to "[form] his own private air force" to "support Japan's expansion into China and the rest of Asia" (Associated Press 1995; Rafferty 1995). Sasakawa was also famously known for flying "one of his 20 bombers to Rome to pose for pictures with Mussolini" (Associated Press 1995).
7. SG 2000 officials were so pleased with maize yields in Ghana that they "commissioned a British filmmaker ... to prepare a documentary about the project ... [titled] *Feeding the Future—A Green Revolution for Ghana*" (Sasakawa Africa Association 2015: 31).

8. See examples from Anyane 1963 and Amanor 1999.
9. Conversations with both Amina and Ama were in Twi and were double-translated—first by Francis, and then by QuickScribe GH.
10. In Hanson Nyantakyi-Frimpong and Rachel Bezner Kerr's (2015) study of attitudes toward and use of hybrid maize in northern Ghana, some farmers referred to hybrid seeds as "agric."

Chapter 2. From Peasantry to Prosperity

1. Gold Star Beach Hotel is a pseudonym.
2. In coverage of President Obama's trip to Ethiopia, the *New York Times* published an article entitled "Obama, on China's Turf, Presents U.S. as a Better Partner for Africa" (Baker 2015).
3. The ECOWAS agreement harmonized seed standards and legislations across member countries and allowed "seed of any variety registered in one country [to] be produced and commercialized in all," and "seed produced, controlled and certified in one country [to] be commercialized in all" (FAO 2008).
4. DuPont also partnered with the US youth agricultural club, 4-H, using 4-H school programs throughout Ghana to distribute hybrid maize seeds. There, school gardens effectively acted as demonstration plots, and DuPont officials hoped students would tell their parents of the good news (Butler 2014).
5. This was in reference to *Adikanfo*.
6. Under Article 19 of the Cartagena Protocol, signatories needed to "designate one national focal point . . . responsible for performing the administrative functions required by [the] Protocol" (Secretariat of the Convention on Biological Diversity 2000: 15). For many countries, this required building new authorities, like Ghana's National Biosafety Council/Authority.
7. The scientific teams initially focused on single-trait enhancement (insect resistance, nitrogen resistance, for example), but, as time went on, applied for—and received—approval to introduce stacked (multiple) traits into cotton and rice, respectively.
8. In August 2021, the Cornell Alliance for Science moved institutional homes, and it is now housed at the Boyce Thompson Institute. Given that the alliance was housed at Cornell University for most of the time I researched this book, I've decided to continue to include "Cornell" when referring to the alliance.

9. A video of the full event is viewable on YouTube: "Cornell Alliance for Science Event at United Nations 25 Stories," https://www.youtube.com/watch?v=ieHvu2KUwPc. The event was held on November 17, 2015.

Chapter 3. Our Stomachs Are Being Colonized

1. The similarity in name of these two groups can be confusing. I refer to the network as the Platform and to the organization as FSG.
2. Years later I had the chance to have dinner with Dr. Shiva after she gave a talk in the Department of Nutrition and Food Studies at New York University where I was a postdoctoral fellow. I shared that I had seen her speak in Accra and she told me that the Ghanaian food sovereignty movement was one of the most impressive and inspiring groups she had met.

Chapter 4. The Patents Are Out There

1. And as described earlier, the phenomena of biosafety officials advocating *for* biotechnology is not unique to Ghana; it is true elsewhere in the continent as well (Harsh 2014; Luna and Dowd-Uribe 2020; Schnurr 2019; Schnurr and Gore 2015).
2. Such argumentation has a long history in Ghana. In 1964, Ghanaian researchers similarly "drew the economic gains for plant research along broad, nationalized lines" (Osseo-Asare 2014: 149).
3. In addition to the Vandana Shiva and GAAS events, the Africa Nutrition Society, UK Nutrition Society, and University of Chester held a "public debate" on "biotechnology and GM foods" in Accra in July 2014.
4. While a supposedly aging farmer population is often used in narratives about African farming to justify intensive interventions, there is actually little data to back up this claim. The International Fund for Agricultural Development describes this "commonly repeated finding" as one from a "bygone era" (Arslan 2019). A recent study by Felix Kwame Yeboah and Thomas S. Jayne suggests that the average age of African farmers is more likely somewhere between forty-one and forty-eight years old (2018: 826). In fact, they find that "farming remains the single largest source of employment among young people" (2018: 826). In Ghana, approximately 40 percent of farmers are between the ages

of fifteen to thirty-four (2018: 815), and the agricultural labor force has grown consistently over the past few decades (Hazell et al. 2019: 105). For a point of comparison, the average American farmer is 57.5 years old (USDA 2019).

Chapter 5. (Im)Possibilities

1. Constance was replying to Bill Gates's remarks: "The Europeans have decided they don't want to use it ... which is fine, they're not facing malnutrition and starvation.... [But] the Africans, I think, will choose to let their people have enough to eat" (Wall Street Journal 2016).
2. Per diems are standard offerings at conferences, meetings, and workshops in Ghana, often to cover travel expenses.
3. To be sure, there have been ardent Ghanaian agricultural biotech supporters working to integrate GM crops into Ghanaian farming systems for quite some time. But taken as a sum, boosters have had to build infrastructure and public interest from nearly the ground up.
4. The petition listed the Cornell Alliance for Science, *not* its Ghana chapter, as a petition sponsor.
5. At the time of writing, seven Ghanaians had completed CAS-sponsored training at Cornell University in the United States, including journalists, officials from OFAB's and PBS's Ghana chapters (respectively), and commercial farmers. In 2016, two former fellows established an Alliance for Science Ghana chapter (OFAB Ghana 2016).
6. Ghana received an award from the FAO for being "the first African country to meet the Millennium Development Goal (MDG) 1 of halving poverty and hunger" (Steiner-Asiedu et al. 2017: xiii), and hunger levels have fallen consistently between 2000 and 2020 (Global Hunger Index 2020). However, there are massive regional disparities between northern and southern Ghana when it comes to hunger levels and food access (Ham 2017: 242).

Bibliography

Abdulai, Awudu, and Wallace Huffman. 2000. "Structural Adjustment and Economic Efficiency of Rice Farmers in Northern Ghana." *Economic Development and Cultural Change* 48(3): 503–20.

ACDI/VOCA. 2015. "ADVANCE III Quarterly Report." Report on USAID Cooperative Agreement No. AID-641-A-14-00001.

Adams, Vincanne. 2012. "The Road to Serfdom: Recovery by the Market and the Affect Economy in New Orleans." *Public Culture* 24(1): 185–216.

Adesina, Akinwumi. 2014. "Agriculture in Africa: Revival Strategies." *The African Executive*, no. 499. Http://www.africanexecutive.com.

———. 2016. "Agriculture as a Business." *African Development Bank* website, February 16. Http://www.afdb.org/en/news-and-events/article/agriculture-as-a-business-approaching-agriculture-as-an-investment-opportunity-15398/.

Adjei, Prince Osei-Wusu, Peter Ohene Kyei, and Kwadwo Afriyie. 2014. "Global Economic Crisis and Socio-Economic Vulnerability: Historical Experience and Lessons from the 'Lost Decade' for Africa in the 1980s." *Ghana Studies* 17: 39–61.

Advisory Committee on Imperial Questions. 1944a "Nutrition in the Colonies." Report, April, no. 369.

———. 1944b. "Recommendations with Regard to Nutrition in the Colonial Territories." Report, March, no. 266.

Afedraru, Lominda. 2019. "Plans to Introduce GMO Crops in Disarray, Legislators Angry after

Uganda's President Rejects GMO Cultivation Law for Second Time." *Genetic Literacy Project* website, September 9. Https://geneticliteracyproject.org/2019/09/09/plans-to-introduce-gmo-crops-in-disarray-legislators-angry-after-ugandas-president-rejects-gmo-cultivation-law-for-second-time/.

African Agricultural Technology Foundation and Open Forum for Agricultural Biotechnology (AATF and OFAB). 2018. "GMO Myths in Africa." *Cornell Alliance for Science* website. Https://allianceforscience.cornell.edu/gmo-myths-in-africa/.

Al-Hassan, Ramatu, and Colin Poulton. 2009. "Agriculture and Social Protection in Ghana." *Future Agriculture Consortium* Working Paper No. SP04.

Alliance for a Green Revolution in Africa (AGRA). 2013. *Program Performance Scorecard*. Nairobi: Alliance for a Green Revolution in Africa.

———. 2017a. "AGRA's Tribute to Dr. Rajiv Shah, President of Rockefeller Foundation." Video, May 22, https://www.youtube.com/watch?v=R6g29IkCO2U.

———. 2017b. *Strategy Overview for 2017–2021: Inclusive Agricultural Transformation in Africa*. Nairobi: Alliance for a Green Revolution in Africa.

Alliance for a Green Revolution in Africa (AGRA) News. 2015. *A New Dawn for Inclusive African Agriculture*, no. 7.

Alliance for Food Sovereignty in Africa (AFSA). 2015. "Agroecology—the Bold Future for Africa." African Civil Society Statement: FAO Regional Symposium on Agroecology for Food Security and Nutrition in sub-Saharan Africa, Dakar, October 27.

———. 2019. "About Us." *Alliance for Food Sovereignty in Africa* website. Https://afsafrica.org/about-us/.

Althusser, Louis. 1971. *Lenin and Philosophy and Other Essays*. New York: Monthly Review Press.

Altieri, Miguel A. 2009. "Agroecology, Small Farms, and Food Sovereignty." *Monthly Review* 61(3): 102–13.

Amanor, Kojo. 1999. "Global Restructuring and Land Rights in Ghana: Forest Food Chains, Timber, and Rural Livelihoods." *Nordic Africa Institute*, no. 108.

———. 2011. "From Farmer Participation to Pro-Poor Seed Markets." *IDS Bulletin* 42(4): 48–58.

———. 2019a. "Global Value Chains and Agribusiness in Africa: Upgrading or Capturing Smallholder Production?" *Agrarian South: Journal of Political Economy* 8(1–2): 30–63.

———. 2019b. "Mechanised Agriculture and Medium-scale Farmers in Northern Ghana: A Success of Market Liberalism or a Product of a Longer History?" *Agricultural Policy Research in Africa*. Working Paper 023.

Andae, Gerald. 2019. "Kenya at Risk of Losing Funding for GMO Crops Development." *The Business Daily*, June 20. Https://www.businessdailyafrica.com/datahub/

Kenya-at-risk-of-losing-funding-for-GMO/3815418-5164456-guu3enz/index.html.

Andam, Kwaw S., et al. 2019. "Can Local Products Compete against Imports in West Africa? Supply- and Demand-side Perspectives on Chicken, Rice, and Tilapia in Accra, Ghana." *IFPRI Discussion Paper* 01821.

Annan, Kofi. 2004. "Africa's Green Revolution: A Call to Action." Speech. Addis Ababa, July 5.

Antwi-Agyei, Philip, et al. 2012. "Mapping the Vulnerability of Crop Production to Drought in Ghana Using Rainfall, Yield and Socioeconomic Data." *Applied Geography* 32: 324–34.

Anyane, S. La. 1963. *Ghana Agriculture: Its Economic Development from Early Times to the Middle of the Twentieth Century*. London: Oxford University Press.

"Application for Confined Field Trial in Ghana." 2013. Application to the National Biosafety Authority of Ghana. May 3.

Arcadia Biosciences. 2013. "Field Trials of New Nitrogen Use Efficient Rice Show Increased Productivity, Leading to Increased Food Security and Reduced Fertilizer Dependence." Press Release, September 10. Https://arcadiabio.com/field-trials-of-new-nitrogen-use-efficient-rice-show-increased-productivity-leading-to-increased-food-security-and-reduced-fertilizer-dependence/.

Arslan, Aslihan. 2019. "How Old Is the Average Farmer in Today's Developing World?" *IFAD Blogs*, July 1. Https://www.ifad.org/en/web/latest/blog/asset/41207683.

Associated Press. 1995. "Ryoichi Sasakawa, 96, Rightist and Gambling Figure in Japan." *New York Times*, July 20.

Ayres, Jeffrey, and Michael J. Bosia. 2011. "Beyond Global Summitry: Food Sovereignty as Localized Resistance to Globalization." *Globalizations* 8(1): 47–63.

Bacchi, Umberto. 2017. "Future of African Youth Lies in Agriculture, Not Europe: Food Prize Laureate." *Reuters*, June 26.

Bagbin, Alban S. K., and Eric Owusu-Mensah. 2013. "Report of the Committee on Constitutional, Legal and Parliamentary Affairs on the Plant Breeders' Bill." Parliament of Ghana.

Baker, Peter. 2015. "Obama, on China's Turf, Presents U.S. as a Better Partner for Africa." *New York Times*, July 29.

Bavier, Joe. 2017. "How Monsanto's GM Cotton Sowed Trouble in Africa." *Reuters*, December 8.

Bendana, Christopher. 2019. "Royalty-Free Genes Reduce GMO Seed Cost in Africa." *Cornell Alliance for Science* website, May 28. Https://allianceforscience.cornell.edu/blog/2019/05/royalty-free-genes-reduce-gmo-seed-costs-africa/.

Benin, Samuel. 2019. "Public Expenditure on Agriculture and Its Impact." In *Ghana's Economic and Agricultural Transformation: Past Performance and Future Prospects*, edited by Xinshen Diao et al., 170–209. Oxford: Oxford University Press.

Benton, Adia. 2015. *HIV Exceptionalism: Development through Disease in Sierra Leone.* Minneapolis: University of Minnesota Press.

Berry, Sara. 1993. *No Condition Is Permanent: The Social Dynamics of Agrarian Change in Sub-Saharan Africa.* Madison: University of Wisconsin Press.

Bezner Kerr, Rachel. 2013. "Seed Struggles and Food Sovereignty in Northern Malawi." *Journal of Peasant Studies* 40(5): 867–97.

Bigg, Matthew Mpoke, and Kwasi Kpodo. 2014. "Once a Model for Africa, Ghana's Economy Loses Its Shine." *Reuters*, June 13.

Bini, Valerio. 2018. "Food Security and Sovereignty in West Africa." *African Geographical Review* 37(1): 1–13.

Biosafety Act. 2011. Parliament of Ghana. Act 831.

Black, Robert, et al. 2011. "Case Studies on the Use of Biotechnologies and on Biosafety Provisions in Four African Countries." *Journal of Biotechnology* 156(4): 370–81.

Blaylock, Jennifer. 2020. "The Persistent Instructor: 45 Years of Kofi the Good Farmer in Ghana." *Journal of African Cinemas* 12(1): 71–86.

Boafo, James, and Kristen Lyons. 2021. "The Rhetoric and Farmers' Lived Realities of the Green Revolution in Africa: Case Study of the Brong Ahafo Region in Ghana." *Journal of Asian and African Studies*: 1–18.

Bobo Shanti. 2015. "G M O." Video, November 21, https://www.youtube.com/watch?v=n8LLeO-rJw0.

Bokpe, Seth J. 2016. "The Watermelon Glut—Good for Consumers, Bad for Farmers." *The Graphic Online*, June 13. Https://www.graphic.com.gh/features/opinion/the-watermelon-glut-good-for-consumers-bad-for-the-farmers.html.

Borenstein, Daniel. 2015. "The Social Realities of Technology Transfer: Smallholder Farmers' Encounter with a New Rice Variety." *African Geographical Review* 34(1): 8–12.

Borras, Saturnino M., Jr. 2008. "La Via Campesina and Its Global Campaign for Agrarian Reform." *Journal of Agrarian Change* 8(2–3): 258–89.

Bortey, Hillary Mireku. 2016. "Misconceptions about the Plant Breeders' Rights System." *ModernGhana*, April 27. Https://www.modernghana.com.

Bourgois, Philippe. 2009. "Recognizing Invisible Violence." In *Global Health in Times of Violence*, edited by Barbara Rylko-Bauer, Linda Whiteford, and Paul Farmer, 17–40. Santa Fe: School for Advanced Research Press.

Boyd, William. 2003. "Wonderful Potencies? Deep Structure and the Problem of Monopoly in Agricultural Biotechnology." In *Engineering Trouble: Biotechnology and Its Discontents*, edited by Rachel A. Schurman and Dennis Doyle Takahashi Kelso, 24–62. Berkeley: University of California Press.

Boyer, Jefferson. 2010. "Food Security, Food Sovereignty, and Local Challenges for Transitional

Agrarian Movements: The Honduras Case." *Journal of Peasant Studies* 37(2): 319–51.

Braimah, Joseph A., et al. 2017. "Debated Agronomy: Public Discourse and the Future of Biotechnology Policy in Ghana." *Global Bioethics* 28(1): 3–18.

Brenner, Carliene. 2004. "Telling Transgenic Technology Tales: Lessons from the Agricultural Biotechnology Support Project (ABSP) Experience." *The International Service for the Acquisition of Agri-biotech Applications (ISAAA)*. Ithaca, NY: ISAAA.

Brinkley, Douglas. 1996. "Bringing the Green Revolution to Africa: Jimmy Carter, Norman Borlaug, and the Global 2000 Campaign." *World Policy Journal* 13(1): 53–62.

British Broadcasting Company (BBC). 2015. "Ghana Suspends High Court Judges After Anas Aremeyaw Anas' Film." *BBC*, October 6.

British Film Institute. n.d. "Kofi the Good Farmer." *Collections Search Record*. Http://collections-search.bfi.org.uk/web/Details/ChoiceFilmWorks/150007957.

Burnett, Kim, and Sophia Murphy. 2014. "What Place for International Trade in Food Sovereignty?" *Journal of Peasant Studies* 41(6): 1065–84.

Butler, Kiera. 2014. "How America's Favorite Baby-Goat Club Is Helping Big Ag Take Over Farming in Africa." *Mother Jones*, November/December.

Buttel, Frederick H. 2003. "The Global Politics of GEOs: The Achilles' Heel of the Globalization Regime?" In *Engineering Trouble: Biotechnology and Its Discontents*, edited by Rachel A. Schurman and Dennis Doyle Takahashi Kelso, 152–73. Berkeley: University of California Press.

Carney, Judith A., and Richard Nicholas Rosomoff. 2009. *In the Shadow of Slavery: Africa's Botanical Legacy in the Atlantic World*. Berkeley: University of California Press.

Carruthers, Jane. 1989. "Creating a National Park, 1910–1926." *Journal of Southern African Studies* 15(2): 188–216.

Chalfin, Brenda. 2010. *Neoliberal Frontiers: An Ethnography of Sovereignty in West Africa*. Chicago: University of Chicago Press.

Centre for Indigenous Knowledge and Organizational Development (CIKOD), ActionAid, and the Peasant Farmers Association of Ghana (PFAG). 2014. "Concerns of Stakeholders on the Plant Breeders' Bill and Genetically Modified Organisms in Ghana." Accra: CIKOD, ActionAid, and PFAG.

Chicago Tribune. 2003. "Biotech Conference Begins Amid Protest." June 24.

CGTN Africa. 2014. "Ghanaians Take a Stand Against GMOs." Video, February 1, https://www.youtube.com/watch?v=zPBEpAXm0lQ.

CitiFM. 2016. "Group Petitions Parliament on Plant Breeders Bill." *CitiFM Online*, May 31.

Clapp, Jennifer, and S. Ryan Isakson. 2018. *Speculative Harvests: Financialization, Food and Agriculture*. Manitoba: Fernwood Publishing.

Cleveland, David A., and Stephen C. Murray. 1997. "The World's Crop Genetic Resources and the Rights of Indigenous Farmers." *Current Anthropology* 38(4): 477–515.

Cohen, Michael, and Eric Ombok. 2016. "African Farmers Struggle to Feed Continent's Booming Population." *Bloomberg*, February 16.

Conway, Gordon R., and Edward B. Barbier. 1990. *After the Green Revolution: Sustainable Agriculture for Development.* London: Earthscan Publications Ltd.

Cornell Alliance for Science. 2015. "Our Story." *Cornell Alliance For Science* website. Http://allianceforscience.cornell.edu/our-story.

Council for Scientific and Industrial Research (CSIR). n.d. "About Us." *CSIR* website. Http://www.csir.org.gh/index.php/about-csir.

Daley, Patricia. 2013. "Rescuing African Bodies: Celebrities, Consumerism and Neoliberal Humanitarianism." *Review of African Political Economy* 40(137): 375–93.

Daniels, Mitch. 2017. "Avoiding GMOs Isn't Just Anti-Science. It's Immoral." *Washington Post*, December 27.

Darton, John. 1994. "In Poor, Decolonized Africa, Bankers Are New Overlords." *Los Angeles Times*, June 20.

Daswani, Girish. 2020. "On Cynicism: Activist and Artistic Responses to Corruption in Ghana." *Cultural Anthropology* 35(1): 104–33.

Davidson, Joanna. 2012. "Basket Cases and Breadbaskets: Sacred Rice and Agricultural Development in Postcolonial Africa." *Culture, Agriculture, Food and Environment* 34: 15–32.

Decker, Corrie, and Elisabeth McMahon. 2021. *The Idea of Development in Africa: A History.* Cambridge: Cambridge University Press.

Dekeyser, Koen, Lise Korsten, and Lorenzo Fioramonti. 2018. "Food Sovereignty: Shifting Debates on Democratic Food Governance." *Food Security* 10: 223–33.

Democracy Now. 2003. "USDA Opens $3 Million Biotech Conference in Sacramento; Agriculture Ministers From Over 100 countries Are Attending; 1000 March in Protest." June 24. Https://www.democracynow.org/2003/6/23/usda_opens_3_million_biotech_conference.

Dizengoff Ghana. 2016. Twitter Post (May 9), https://twitter.com/Dizengoffgh/status/729656851969646592.

Dowd-Uribe, Brian. 2016. "GMOs and Poverty: Definitions, Methods and the Silver Bullet Paradox." *Canadian Journal of Development Studies* 38(1): 129–38.

Dowd-Uribe, Brian, and Matthew A. Schnurr. 2016. "Burkina Faso's Reversal on Genetically Modified Cotton and the Implications for Africa." *African Affairs* 115(458): 161–72.

Duncan, Beatrice Akua. 1997. *Women in Agriculture in Ghana.* Accra: Friedrich Ebert Foundation.

DuPont. 2013. "The Science Behind Maize Hybrids." *DuPont* website. Http://www.dupont.com/corporate-functions/our-approach/global-challenges/food/articles/science-behind-maize-hybrids.html.

Dzanku, Fred, et al. 2018. "Adoption of GM Crops in Ghana: Ex Ante Estimations for Insect-Resistant Cowpea and Nitrogen-Use Efficient Rice." *IFPRI Discussion Paper* 1775.

Dziwornu, John, and Rufi Ahmed Braimah. 2017. "Open Letter to Ghana's President: Support Biotech." *Cornell Alliance for Science* website, January 18. Http://allianceforscience.cornell.edu/node/12656.

Economist. 2015a. "Climbing Aboard the African Train." September 25.

———. 2015b. "A Sub-Saharan African Scramble." January 22.

Eddens, Aaron. 2019. "White Science and Indigenous Maize: The Racial Logics of the Green Revolution." *Journal of Peasant Studies* 46(3): 653–73.

Edelman, Marc. 2014. "Food Sovereignty: Forgotten Genealogies and Future Regulatory Challenges." *Journal of Peasant Studies* 41(6): 959–78.

Ekboir, Javier, Kofi Boa, and A. A. Dankyi. 2002. "The Impact of No-Till Technologies in Ghana." *CIMMYT Economics Program* Paper 02-01.

Emejor, Chibuzor. 2021. "AATF Launches New Variety of Cowpea in Nigeria." *The Independent*, June 28.

Emory University. 2013. Trans-Atlantic Slave Trade Database. Http://www.slavevoyages.org/.

Escobar, Arturo. 1995. *Encountering Development: The Making and Unmaking of the Third World*. Princeton, NJ: Princeton University Press.

Esipisu, Isaiah. 2016. "Agriculture Investment Yields Growth and Nutrition Gains for Africa." *Reuters*, September 5.

Ewusi, Kodwo. 1989. *The Impact of Structural Adjustment on the Agricultural Sector in Ghana*. Accra: Institute of Statistical, Social and Economic Research, University of Ghana.

Ezezika, Obidimma C., and Abdallah S. Daar. 2012. "Overcoming Barriers to Trust in Agricultural Biotechnology Projects: A Case Study of Bt Cowpea in Nigeria." *Agriculture & Food Security* 1, S5. Https://doi.org/10.1186/2048-7010-1-S1-S5.

Fairclough, Norman. 2012. "Critical Discourse Analysis." In *The Routledge Handbook of Discourse Analysis*, edited by James Paul Gee and Michael Handford, 9–20. London: Routledge.

Fairhead, James, and Melissa Leach. 2005. "Misreading Africa's Forest History." In *The Anthropology of Development and Globalization: from Classical Political Economy to Contemporary Neoliberalism*, edited by Marc Edelman and Angelique Haugerud, 282–91. Malden: Blackwell Publishing.

Fanon, Frantz. 2008[1952]. *Black Skin, White Masks*. New York: Grove Press.

Fejerskov, Adam Moe. 2018. *The Gates Foundation's Rise to Power: Private Authority in Global Politics*. Oxon, UK: Routledge.

Ferguson, James. 1994. "The Anti-Politics Machine." *The Ecologist* 24(5): 176–81.

———. 2005. "Seeing Like an Oil Company: Space, Security, and Global Capital in Neoliberal Africa." *American Anthropologist* 107(3): 377–82.

———. 2006. *Global Shadows: Africa in the Neoliberal World Order*. Durham: Duke University Press.

Flachs, Andrew. 2019. *Cultivating Knowledge: Biotechnology, Sustainability, and the Human Cost of Cotton Capitalism in South India*. Tucson: University of Arizona Press.

Folta, Kevin. 2017. "Interview with Mark Lynas." *Talking Biotech Podcast*. Audio, October 30. Https://geneticliteracyproject.org/2017/10/30/talking-biotech-former-anti-gmo-activist-mark-lynas-resistance-crop-biotechnology-hurts-small-african-farms/.

Forum for Agricultural Research in Africa (FARA). 2012. "Africa in Search of Safe and High-Quality Biotech Crops: 1st Pan-African Conference on Stewardship of Agricultural Biotechnology." Accra, Ghana. Conference Proceedings.

Forum for Food Sovereignty, Nyéléni. 2007. *Declaration of Nyéléni*. Https://nyeleni.org.

Food and Agriculture Organization of the United Nations (FAO). 2008. *Harmonized Seed Legislation in West Africa*. Leaflet.

———. 2015. *Country Fact Sheet on Food and Agriculture Policy Trends: Ghana*. Report.

Food and Water Watch. 2013. *Biotech Ambassadors: How the US State Department Promotes the Seed Industry's Global Agenda*. California: Food and Water Watch.

Food Sovereignty Ghana (FSG). 2014. "Special Announcement: FSG Removes Duke Tagoe from Post." *FSG* Website, December 8. Https://foodsovereigntyghana.org/special-announcement-fsg-removes-duke-tagoe-from-post.

Frempong, Godfred. 2007. *Report on Stakeholders Forum on Genetically Modified Organisms in Ghana: The Benefits, Threats and Policy Implications*. Accra: Science and Technology Policy Research Institute.

Gakpo, Joseph Opoku. 2014. "GM Foods Not Harmful." *MyJoyOnline*, June 12.

———. 2016a. "GMO Is Not Risk-Free But No Technology Is—Scientist." *MyJoyOnline*, January 16.

———. 2016b. "Parliament Is 'Taking Us for a Ride' over Plant Breeders' Bill—Farmers Association." *MyJoyOnline*, November 10.

———. 2017a. "Ghana GMO Debate Intensifies Ahead of First Biotech Crop Release." *Cornell Alliance for Science*, October 6.

———. 2017b. "Ghana Suspends Trials of GMO Cotton." *Cornell Alliance for Science*, May 12.

———. 2017c. "Stop Throwing Dirt at GMOs—Former Deputy Agric Minister." *MyJoyOnline*, May 7.

———. 2018a. "Africa Kicks Against Proposed Gene Drive Moratorium at UN Biodiversity Conference." *Cornell Alliance for Science* website, November 20. Https://allianceforscience.cornell.edu/blog/2018/11/africa-kicks-proposed-gene-drive- moratorium-un-biodiversity-conference.

———. 2018b. "Ghana Urged to Pass Law to Encourage Improved Seed Breeding." *Cornell Alliance for Science* website, November 15. Https://allianceforscience.cornell.edu/blog/2018/11/ghana-urged-pass-law-encourage-improved-seed-breeding/.

———. 2018c. "Why Africa Will March for Science." *Cornell Alliance for Science* website, April 12. Https://allianceforscience.cornell.edu/blog/2018/04/africa-will-march-science.

———. 2019. "High Expectations for GMO Rice Research in Ghana." *Cornell Alliance for Science* website, January 29. Https://allianceforscience.cornell.edu/blog/2019/01/high-expectations-gmo-rice-research-ghana.

———. 2020. "Government Confident Passage of Plant Variety Protection Bill Into Law Will Increase Agricultural Productivity." *MyJoyOnline*, November 22.

Gebre, Samuel. 2016. "AGRA Plans to Invest $500 Million in African Seed Companies." *Bloomberg Markets*, September 7.

Ghana Center for Democratic Development (CDD). 2011. *The Political Economy of Agriculture in Ghana: Some Contemporary Issues*. Political Economy of Change Series. Accra: Ghana CDD.

Ghana News Agency. 2013. "Breeders' Bill Has Nothing to Do with GMOs—CSIR." *Ghana News Agency*, December 20.

"Ghanaians Want the Plant Breeders Bill Passed!" 2015. Petition. Http://cas.nonprofitsoapbox.com/ghana-pbrb.

GhanaWeb. 2014. "Ga Priests Reject GMO Maize for Homowo." *GhanaWeb* website, July 18. Https://allianceforscience.cornell.edu/blog/2019/01/high-expectations-gmo-rice-research-ghana.

Gieryn, Thomas F. 1983. "Boundary-Work and the Demarcation of Science from Non-Science: Strains and Interests in Professional Ideologies of Scientists." *American Sociological Review* 48(6): 781–95.

Global Hunger Index. 2020. "Ghana." *Global Hunger Index* website. Https://www.globalhungerindex.org/ghana.html.

Glover, Dominic. 2010. "The Corporate Shaping of GM Crops as a Technology for the Poor." *Journal of Peasant Studies* 37(1): 67–90.

Gold Coast Cocoa Marketing Board. 1950. *Kofi the Good Farmer*. Accra: Gold Coast Public Relations Department.

Godelier, Maurice. 1999. *The Enigma of the Gift*. Cambridge: Polity Press.

Gombay, Nicole. 2010. "Community, Obligation, and Food: Lessons from the Moral Geography of Inuit." *Geografiska Annaler: Series B, Human Geography* 92(3): 237–50.

González, Roberto J., and Rachael Stryker. 2014. "On Studying Up, Down, and Sideways: What's at Stake?" In *Up Down, and Sideways: Anthropologists Trace the Pathways of Power*, edited by Rachael Stryker and Roberto J. González, 1–26. New York: Berghahn.

Gosine, Andil. 2010. "Non-White Reproduction and Same-Sex Eroticism: Queer Acts Against Nature." In *Queer Ecologies: Sex, Nature, Politics, Desire*, edited by Catriona Mortimor-Sandilands and Bruce Erickson, 149–72. Bloomington: University of Indiana Press.

Gupta, Akhil. 1998. *Postcolonial Developments: Agriculture and the Making of Modern India*. Durham, NC: Duke University Press.

Halberstam, Jack. 2005. *Queer Temporalities and Post-Modern Geographies*. New York: New York University Press.

Ham, Jessica. 2017. "Cooking to Be Modern but Eating to Be Healthy: The Role of Dawa-Dawa in Contemporary Ghanaian Foodways." *Food, Culture & Society* 20(2): 237–25.

Hansen, Thomas Blom, and Finn Stepputat. 2006. "Sovereignty Revisited." *Annual Review of Anthropology* 35: 295–315.

Harrison, Faye V. 2002. "Global Apartheid, Foreign Policy, and Human Rights." *Souls* 4(3): 48–68.

Harsh, Matthew. 2014. "Nongovernmental Organizations and Genetically Modified Crops in Kenya: Understanding Influence Within a Techno-Civil Society." *Geoforum* 53: 172–83.

Hausermann, Heidi. 2018. "'Ghana Must Progress, but We Are Really Suffering': Bui Dam, Antipolitics Development, and the Livelihood Implications for Rural People." *Society & Natural Resources* 6: 633–48.

Hazell, Peter, Xinshen Diao, and Eduardo Magalhaes. 2019. "Ghana's Agricultural Transformation: Past Patterns and Sources of Change." In *Ghana's Economic and Agricultural Transformation: Past Performance and Future Prospects*, edited by Xinshen Diao et al., 97–120. Oxford: Oxford University Press.

Heller, Chaia. 2013. *Food, Farms and Solidarity: French Farmers Challenge Industrial Agriculture and Genetically Modified Crops*. Durham, NC: Duke University Press.

Hodžić, Saida. 2017. *The Twilight of Cutting: African Activism and Life After NGOs*. Oakland: University of California Press.

Holsey, Bayo. 2007. *Routes of Remembrance: Refashioning the Slave Trade in Ghana*. Chicago: University of Chicago Press.

Holt-Giménez, Eric. 2009. "From Food Crisis to Food Sovereignty: The Challenge of Social Movements." *Monthly Review*, July 1.

Holt-Giménez, Eric, and Miguel A. Altieri. 2013. "Agroecology, Food Sovereignty and the New Green Revolution." *Agroecology and Sustainable Food Systems* 37(1): 90–102.

Howard, Phillip. 2015. "Intellectual Property and Consolidation in the Seed Industry." *Crop Science* 55: 2489–95.

Ibrahim, Abubakar. 2018. "We Are Still Open to Resuming GMO Work in Ghana—Monsanto." *MyJoyOnline*, February 16.

———. 2019. "Ghana's Parliament Gives GMO Crops a Boost." *Cornell Alliance for Science* website, November 18. Https://allianceforscience.cornell.edu/blog/2019/11/ghanas-parliament-gives-gmo-crops-a-boost.

Ignatova, Jacqueline. 2015. *Seeds of Contestation: Genetically Modified Crops and the Politics of Agricultural Modernization in Ghana*. PhD Dissertation, University of Maryland-College Park.

Iles, Alastair, and Maywa Montenegro de Wit. 2015. "Sovereignty at What Scale? An Inquiry into Multiple Dimensions of Food Sovereignty." *Globalizations* 12(4): 481–97.

International Center for Tropical Agriculture (CIAT). 2014. "Improved NEWEST Rice Variety to African Farmers." *CIAT* website. Http://ciatblogs.cgiar.org/agbio/improved-rice-variety-the-newest-hope-to-african-farmers/.

International Food Policy Research Institute (IFPRI). 2017. "Program for Biosafety Systems." *IFPRI Outcome Stories*, September 11.

"International Peasants' Voice: Globalizing Hope, Globalizing the Struggle!" *La Via Campesina* website. Https://viacampesina.org/en/international-peasants-voice/.

International Planning Committee (IPC) for Food Sovereignty. 2008. "Civil Society Statement on the World Food Emergency: No More 'Failures-as-Usual'!" Press Release. Http://www.ukabc.org/foodemergency/docs/22-05-2008-cso-foodemergency-en.pdf.

International Service for the Acquisition of Agri-biotech Applications (ISAAA). 2020. "GM Approval Database." *ISAAA* website. Https://www.isaaa.org/gmapprovaldatabase.

———. 2021a. "GM Crop Events Approved in Nigeria." *ISAAA* website. Https://www.isaaa.org/gmapprovaldatabase.

———. 2021b. "ISAA in Brief." *ISAAA* website. Https://www.isaaa.org/inbrief/default.asp.

International Union for the Protection of Plant Varieties (UPOV). 2013. *Guidance for the Preparation of Laws Based on the 1991 Act of the UPOV Convention*. Guidance Document.

ISSAfricaTV. 2012. "An African Green Revolution." Video, September 3, https://www.youtube.com/watch?v=AwnJubqZ4Kw.

Jafaru, Musah Yahya. 2017. "No Money to Compensate Fall Army Worms Victims—Agric

Minister Says." *The Graphic Online,* August 23.

Johnson, Michael, et al. 2019. "Agricultural Transformation in the Savannah." In *Ghana's Economic and Agricultural Transformation: Past Performance and Future Prospects,* edited by Xinshen Diao et al., 142–69. Oxford: Oxford University Press.

Juma, Calestous. 2011. "Africa—From Basket Case to Breadbasket." *New Agriculturalist,* February 2011.

Kalibata, Agnes. 2017. "In Africa, Expecting More from Agriculture Than Food Security." *AGRA Impact,* April–June 2017 issue.

Karembu, Margaret, Faith Nguthi, and Ismail Abdel-Hamid. 2009. *Biotech Crops in Africa: The Final Frontier.* Nairobi: ISAAA AfriCenter.

Kitabu, Gerald. 2021. "Ministry Cancels GMO Seed Trials." *IPPMedia,* January 14.

Kloppenburg, Jack Ralph. 2004. *First the Seed: The Political Economy of Plant Biotechnology, 1492–2000.* Madison: University of Wisconsin Press.

Komen, John, et al. 2020. "Biosafety Regulatory Reviews and Leeway to Operate: Case Studies from Sub-Sahara Africa." *Frontiers in Plant Science* 11: 1–30.

Komer, R. W. 1966. "Memorandum from the President's Acting Special Assistant for National Security Affairs (Komer) to President Johnson." Department of State: Office of the Historian. March 12.

Konadu-Agyemang, Kwadwo. 2000. "The Best of Times and the Worst of Times: Structural Adjustment Programs and Uneven Development in Africa: The Case of Ghana." *The Professional Geographer* 52(3): 469–83.

Kothari, Uma. 2006. "Critiquing 'Race' and Racism in Development Discourse and Practice." *Progress in Development Studies* 6 (1): 1–7.

Kumasi, Tyhra Carolyn, Philip Antwi-Agyei, and Kwasi Obiri-Danso. 2019. "Small-holder Farmers' Climate Change Adaptation Practices in the Upper East Region of Ghana." *Environment, Development and Sustainability* 21: 745–62.

La Fleur, J. D. 2012. *Fusion Foodways of Africa's Gold Coast in the Atlantic Era.* Boston: Brill.

La Via Campesina. 2014. "Our Members." *La Via Campesina* website. Https://viacampesina.org.

Laird, Siobhan E. 2007. "Rolling Back the African State: Implications for Social Development in Ghana." *Social Policy and Administration* 41(5): 465–86.

Leap, William L. 1999. "Introduction." In *Public Sex/Gay Space,* edited by William L. Leap, 1–22. New York: Columbia University Press.

———. 2010. "Homophobia as Moral Geography." *Gender and Language* 4(2): 187–220.

Lee, Richard Philip. 2013. "The Politics of International Agri-food Policy: Discourses of Trade-Oriented Food Security and Food Sovereignty." *Environmental Politics* 22(2): 216–34.

Li, Tania Murray. 2007. *The Will to Improve: Governmentality, Development, and the Practice of*

Politics. Durham, NC: Duke University Press.

Logan, Amanda. 2020. *The Scarcity Slot: Excavating Histories of Food Security in Ghana*. Oakland: University of California Press.

Luna, Jessie K. 2017. "Getting Out of the Dirt: Racialized Modernity and Environmental Inequality in the Cotton Sector of Burkina Faso." *Environmental Sociology* 4(2): 221–34.

Luna, Jessie K., and Brian Dowd-Uribe. 2020. "Knowledge Politics and the Bt Cotton Success Narrative in Burkina Faso." *World Development* 136. https://doi.org/10.1016/j.worlddev.2020.105127.

Lynas, Mark. 2015. Twitter Post (July 3). Https://twitter.com/mark_lynas/status/617006670590410752. Accessed September 9, 2021.

———. 2018. *Seeds of Science: Why We Got It So Wrong on GMOs*. London: Bloomsbury.

Marston, Jasmin. 2017. *Aid and Agriculture: A Constructivist Approach to a Political Economy Analysis of Sustainable Agriculture in Ghana*. PhD Dissertation, University of Freiburg.

Masset, Edoardo, Jorge García-Hombrados, and Arnab Acharya. 2020. "Aiming High and Failing Low: The SADA-Northern Ghana Millennium Village Project." *Journal of Development Economics* 143: 1–16.

Massicotte, Marie-Josée. 2014. "Feminist Political Ecology and La Vía Campesina's Struggle for Food Sovereignty through the Experience of the Escola Latino-America de Agroecologia." In *Globalization and Food Sovereignty*, edited by Peter Andrée et al., 255–87. Toronto: University of Toronto Press.

Mauss, Marcel. 1990. *The Gift: The Form and Reason for Exchange in Archaic Societies*. New York: W. W. Norton & Co.

McGranahan, Carole. 2016. "Theorizing Refusal: An Introduction." *Cultural Anthropology* 31(3): 319–25.

McMichael, Philip. 2014. "Historicizing Food Sovereignty." *Journal of Peasant Studies* 41(6): 933–57.

McMichael, Philip, and Mindi Schneider. 2011. "Food Security Politics and the Millennium Development Goals." *Third World Quarterly* 32(1): 119–39.

Mikell, Gwendolyn. 1989. *Cocoa and Chaos in Ghana*. Washington, DC: Howard University Press.

Moseley, William G. 2016. "The New Green Revolution for Africa: A Political Ecology Critique." *Brown Journal of World Affairs* 23(2): 177–90.

Moseley, William G., Matthew A. Schnurr, and Rachel Bezner Kerr, eds. 2016. *Africa's Green Revolution: Critical Perspectives on New Agricultural Technologies and Systems*. New York: Routledge.

Mueller, Natalie G., and Andrew Flachs. 2021. "Domestication, Crop Breeding, and Genetic

Modification Are Fundamentally Different Processes: Implications for Seed Sovereignty and Agrobiodiversity." *Agriculture and Human Values*. https://doi.org/10.1007/s10460-021-10265-3.

Muñoz, José Esteban. 1999. *Disidentifications: Queers of Color and the Performance of Politics*. Minneapolis: University of Minnesota Press.

Muraguri, Lois. 2010. "Unplugged! An Analysis of Agricultural Biotechnology PPPs in Kenya." *Journal of International Development* 22: 289–307.

MyJoyOnline. 2016. "DKM Fiasco: Police Inundated with More Complaints." *MyJoyOnline*, June 4.

Nkrumah, Kwame. 1957. "Independence Speech." Transcript of speech delivered in Accra, Ghana, March 6, http://www.bbc.co.uk/worldservice/focusonafrica/news/story/2007/02/070129_ghana50_independence_speech.shtml.

———. 1961. *I Speak of Freedom: A Statement of African Ideology*. New York: Frederick A. Praeger.

———. 1969 [1965]. *Neo-Colonialism, the Last Stage of Imperialism*. New York: International Publishers.

Ngotho, Agatha. 2021. "Kenyan Government Approves Genetically Modified Cassava." *The Star*, June 24.

Nyantakyi-Frimpong, Hanson, and Rachel Bezner Kerr. 2015. "A Political Ecology of High-Input Agriculture in Northern Ghana." *African Geographical Review* 34(1): 13–35.

Nyéléni Steering Committee. 2008. *Nyéléni 2007: Forum for Food Sovereignty*. Report.

Nyo, Abass K. 2016. "Inadequate Infrastructure: The Bane Behind Food Loss and Food Security in the Savannah Zone of Ghana." *Journal of Developments in Sustainable Agriculture* 11: 43–47.

Obi, Leopold. 2020. "After Bt Cotton Nod, Kenya Sets Sights on Biotech Food Crops." *The Business Daily*, July 9.

Ojanji, Wandera, and Daniel Otunge. 2018. *Media Reporting on Biotechnology in Africa: Perspectives from African Journalists*. Nairobi: African Agricultural Technology Foundation.

Open Forum on Agricultural Biotechnology in Africa (OFAB)—Ghana Chapter. 2016. "Alliance for Science (AFS) Ghana—We Have a Say." Video, September 7, https://www.youtube.com/watch?v=_iDcAR1NfyQ&feature=youtu.be.

Osei, J. K. 1973. "Farming as a Business." *The Ghana Farmer* 17(2): 71–75.

Osseo-Asare, Abena Dove. 2014. *Bitter Roots: The Search for Healing Plants in Africa*. Chicago: University of Chicago Press.

Otunge, Daniel, et al., eds. 2017. *The Open Forum on Agricultural Biotechnology: A Decade of Success, 2006–2016*. Nairobi: African Agricultural Technology Foundation.

Paarlberg, Robert. 2008. *Starved for Science: How Biotechnology Is Being Kept Out of Africa*. Cambridge, MA: Harvard University Press.

Patel, Raj. 2013. "The Long Green Revolution." *Journal of Peasant Studies* 40(1): 1–63.

Pearce, Richard. 1992. "Ghana." In *Structural Adjustment and the African Farmer*, edited by Alex Duncan and John Howell, 14–47. Portsmouth, NH: Overseas Development Institute.

Pêcheux, Michel. 1982. *Language, Semantics and Ideology*. New York: St. Martin's Press.

Perkins, John H. 1997. *Geopolitics and the Green Revolution: Wheat, Genes, and the Cold War*. New York: Oxford University Press.

Pierre, Jemima. 2012. *The Predicament of Blackness: Postcolonial Ghana and the Politics of Race*. Chicago: University of Chicago Press.

———. 2020. "The Racial Vernaculars of Development: A View from West Africa." *American Anthropologist* 122 (1): 86–98.

Pimbert, Michael. 2009. *Towards Food Sovereignty*. London: International Institute for Environment and Development.

Plant Breeders Bill. 2013. Parliament of Ghana. Legislative Bill.

Plants and Fertilizer Act. 2010. Parliament of Ghana. Act 803.

Poku, Adu-Gyamfi, Regina Birner, and Saurabh Gupta. 2018. "Why Do Maize Farmers in Ghana Have a Limited Choice in Improved Seed Varieties? An Assessment of the Governance Challenges in Seed Supply." *Food Security* 10: 27–46.

Polman, Paul, and Sunny Verghese. 2016. "Africa's Food Market Could Be Worth US$1trn in 15 Years, This Is How . . ." *CNBC Africa*, June 11.

Powell, Tracy. 2013. "NEWEST Rice Marks Latest Milestone." *US Agency for International Development* website, April 26. Https://blog.usaid.gov/2013/04/newest-rice-marks-latest-milestone/.

Rafferty, Kevin. 1995. "Tainted History of a Rich Good Guy: Obituary of Ryoichi Sasakawa." *The Guardian*, July 20.

Ragasa, Catherine, and Antony Chapoto. 2017. "Limits to Green Revolution in Rice in Africa: The Case of Ghana." *Land Use Policy* 66: 304–21.

Ragasa, Catherine, et al. 2013. "Patterns of Adoption of Improved Maize Technologies in Ghana." Working Paper 36. Washington, DC: International Food Policy Research Institute.

Reese, Ashanté. 2019a. *Black Food Geographies: Race, Self-Reliance, and Food Access in Washington, DC*. Chapel Hill: University of North Carolina Press.

———. 2019b. "Refusal as Care: Ethnography from Elsewhere." *Anthropology News*, June 4. Http://www.anthropology-news.org/index.php/2019/06/04/refusal-as-care/.

Reynolds, Edward. 1985. *Stand the Storm: A History of the Atlantic Slave Trade*. London: Allison & Busby.

Richardson, Jill. 2013. "Do Purchases Motivated by Symbolic and Social Needs Undermine Food Sovereignty?" Conference Paper presented at Food Sovereignty: A Critical Dialogue, Yale University.

Robins, Jonathan E. 2018. "'Food Comes First': The Development of Colonial Nutritional Policy in Ghana, 1900–1950." *Global Food History* 4(2): 168–88.

Rock, Joeva. 2018a. "Abject Lessons." *Popula*, August 8.

———. 2018b. "Catering Ghana's Agricultural Development." *Anthropology News*, August 12.

———. 2018c. "Complex Mediascapes, Complex Realities: Critically Engaging with Biotechnology Debates in Ghana." *Global Bioethics* 29(1): 55–64.

———. 2019. "'We Are Not Starving': Challenging Genetically Modified Seeds and Development in Ghana." *Culture, Agriculture, Food and Environment* 41(1): 15–23.

Rock, Joeva, and Jacob M. Grumbach. 2019. "Donald Trump's Africa Policy." *Africa Is a Country*, February 15. Https://africasacountry.com/2019/02/making-a-buck-under-donald-trumps-usaid.

Rock, Joeva, and Alex Park. 2019. *Mapping Financial Flows of Industrial Agriculture in Africa*. Report. San Francisco, CA: Thousand Currents.

Rock, Joeva, and Rachel Schurman. 2020. "The Complex Choreography of Agricultural Biotechnology in Africa." *African Affairs* 119(477): 499–525.

Rodney, Walter. 1972. *How Europe Underdeveloped Africa*. Washington, DC: Howard University Press.

Rutten, Martine, and Monika Verma. 2014. *The Impacts of Reducing Food Loss in Ghana: A Scenario Study Using the Global Economic Simulation Model MAGNET*. Wageningen: LEI Wageningen UR.

Sam, Samuel. 2015. "Big Deal for Cotton, Textile Industry." *B&FT Online*, November 18. Http://thebftonline.com/business/economy/16103/big-deal-for-cotton-textile-industry.html.

Sampson, Devon, and Chelsea Wills. 2013. "Culturally Appropriate Food: Researching Cultural Aspects of Food Sovereignty." Conference Paper presented at Food Sovereignty: A Critical Dialogue, Yale University.

Sasakawa Africa Association. 2015. *Take It to the Farmer: The Sasakawa Experience in Africa*. Tokyo: Sasakawa Africa Association.

Schiavoni, Christina M. 2017. "The Contested Terrain of Food Sovereignty Construction: Toward a Historical, Relational and Interactive Approach." *Journal of Peasant Studies* 44(1): 1–32.

Secretariat of the Convention on Biological Diversity. 2000. *Cartagena Protocol on Biosafety to the Convention on Biological Diversity: Text and Annexes*. Montreal: Secretariat of the Convention on Biological Diversity.

Shackford, Stacey. 2014. "New Cornell Alliance for Science Gets $5.6 Million Grant." *Cornell Chronicle*, August 21.

Schnurr, Matthew A. 2019. *Africa's Gene Revolution: Genetically Modified Crops and the Future of African Agriculture*. Montreal: McGill-Queen's University Press.

Schnurr, Matthew A., and Christopher Gore. 2015. "Getting to the 'Yes': Governing Genetically Modified Crops in Uganda." *Journal of International Development* 27: 55–72.

Schurman, Rachel. 2016. "Building an Alliance for Biotechnology in Africa." *Journal of Agrarian Change* 17(3): 441–58.

Schurman, Rachel, and William A. Munro. 2010. *Fighting for the Future of Food: Activists Versus Agribusiness in the Struggle Over Biotechnology*. Minneapolis: University of Minnesota Press.

Scoones, Ian, and Dominic Glover. 2009. "Africa's Biotechnology Battle." *Nature* 460: 797–98.

Scott, James C. 1998. *Seeing Like a State: How Certain Schemes to Improve the Human Condition Have Failed*. New Haven: Yale University Press.

Shilomboleni, Helena. 2017. The African Green Revolution and the Food Sovereignty Movement: Contributions to Food Security and Sustainability. PhD Dissertation, University of Waterloo.

———. 2018. "African Green Revolution, Food Sovereignty and Constrained Livelihood Choice in Mozambique." *Canadian Journal of African Studies / Revue Canadienne des Études Africaines* 52(2): 115–37.

Simpson, Audra. 2007. "On Ethnographic Refusal: Indigeneity, 'Voice' and Colonial Citizenship." *Junctures* 9: 67–80.

Soper, Rachel. 2020. "From Protecting Peasant Livelihoods to Essentializing Peasant Agriculture: Problematic Trends in Food Sovereignty Discourse." *Journal of Peasant Studies* 47(2): 265–85.

Sumberg, James. 2011. "'Good Farmers' in Sub-Saharan Africa: Evolving Narratives." *Outlook on Agriculture* 40(4): 293–98.

Stahl, Ann B. 2001. *Making History in Banda: Anthropological Visions of Africa's Past*. Cambridge: Cambridge University Press.

Steiner-Asiedu, Matilda, Saa Dittoh, Sam Kofi Newton, and Charity Akotia. 2017. *Addressing Sustainable Development Goal 2: The Ghana Zero Hunger Strategic Review*. Accra: World Food Program.

Stone, Glenn Davis. 2010. "The Anthropology of Genetically Modified Crops." *Annual Review of Anthropology* 39: 381–400.

———. 2021. "Genetically Modified Crops." *Oxford Research Encyclopedia of Anthropology*, March 25. Https://doi.org/10.1093/acrefore/9780190854584.013.296.

Sturgeon, Noël. 2010. "Penguin Family Values." In *Queer Ecologies: Sex, Nature, Politics, Desire*, edited by Catriona Mortimer-Sandilands and Bruce Erickson, 102–33. Bloomington: Indiana University Press.

Sungbaahee, Sylvester B., and Alfred B. Kpieta. 2020. "Smallholder Farmers' Perception of Sustainable Land Management Practices (SLMPs) in the Upper West Region, Ghana." *African Geographical Review*: 1–15.

Sutton, Inez. 1989. "Colonial Agricultural Policy: The Non-Development of the Northern Territories of the Gold Coast." *International Journal of African Historical Studies* 22(4): 637–69.

Third World Network. 2015. *Agroecology: Key Concepts, Principles and Practices*. Penang: Third World Network.

Thomas, Deborah A., and M. Kamari Clarke. 2013. "Globalization and Race: Structures of Inequality, New Sovereignties, and Citizenship in a Neoliberal Era." *Annual Review of Anthropology* 42: 305–25.

Thomas, Phillip. 2002. "The River, the Road and the Rural-Urban Divide: A Postcolonial Moral Geography from Southeast Madagascar." *American Ethnologist* 29(2): 366–91.

Thompson, Carol B. 2014. "Philanthrocapitalism: Appropriation of Africa's Genetic Wealth." *Review of African Political Economy* 41(141): 389–405.

Urdal, Henrik. 2006. "A Clash of Generations? Youth Bulges and Political Violence." *International Studies Quarterly* 50: 607–29.

United Nations (UN) Environment. 2018. *Terminal Evaluation of the Global Environmental Facility / UN Environment Project, "Implementation of the National Biosafety Framework for Ghana."* Evaluation Report.

US Department of Agriculture (USDA). 2019. *Census of Agriculture Highlights: Farm Producers*. Report ACH17–2. Washington, DC: USDA.

———. 2020a. "Adoption of Genetically Engineered Crops in the U.S. Data Set (spreadsheet)." Https://www.ers.usda.gov/data-products/adoption-of-genetically-engineered-crops-in-the-us.

———. 2020b. *Iowa Ag News—Farms and Land in Farms*. Des Moines: USDA Upper Midwest Regional Office.

US Agency for International Development (USAID). 2012. *Request for Applications: West Africa Seed Program (WASP): Program Description*. Request for Applications (RFA) Number: USAID/WA-RFA-624-12-00005. Annexure A.

———. 2015. "Subsistence to Surplus: How Gifty Went from Barely Making Ends Meet to Meeting President Obama." *USAID* website, June 28. Https://bloguat.usaid.gov/2015/07/from-subsistence-to-surplus-how-gifty-went-from-barely-making-ends-meet-to-meeting-president-obama/.

———. 2017. *Private Sector Partnerships in Agricultural Value Chains*. Washington, DC: USAID.

US Department of Agriculture Foreign Agricultural Service (USDA FAS). 2005. *Ghana: Agricultural Biotechnology Annual Report*. Accra: Office of Agricultural Affairs, American Embassy, July 15.

———. 2006. *Ghana: Agricultural Biotechnology Annual Report*. Accra: Office of Agricultural Affairs, American Embassy, July 26.

———. 2007. *Ghana: Agricultural Biotechnology Annual Report*. Accra: Office of Agricultural Affairs, American Embassy, August 31.

———. 2008. *Ghana: Agricultural Biotechnology Annual Report*. Accra: Office of Agricultural Affairs, American Embassy, June 27.

———. 2009a. *Agricultural Biotechnology Annual (Nigeria)*. Lagos: US Consulate.

———. 2009b. *Ghana: Agricultural Biotechnology Annual Report*. Accra: Office of Agricultural Affairs, American Embassy, July 16.

———. 2011a. *Agricultural Biotechnology Annual (Nigeria)*. Lagos: US Consulate.

———. 2011b. *Ghana: Agricultural Biotechnology Annual Report*. Accra: Office of Agricultural Affairs, American Embassy, August 30.

———. 2020a. *Ghana: Agricultural Biotechnology Annual Report*. Accra: Office of Agricultural Affairs, American Embassy, October 27.

———. 2020b. *Planting Seeds (Ghana)*. Accra: Office of Agricultural Affairs, American Embassy, April 8.

Van Asselt, Joanna, Federica Di Battista, Shashi Kolavalli, and Christopher Udry. 2018. *Agronomic Performance of Open Pollinated and Hybrid Maize Varieties: Results from On-Farm Trials in Northern Ghana*. Working Paper 44. Accra: IFPRI Ghana.

Vercillo, Siera. 2020. "The Complicated Gendering of Farming and Household Responsibilities in Northern Ghana." *Journal of Rural Studies* 79: 235–45.

Vitalis, Robert. 2015. *White World Order, Black Power Politics: The Birth of American International Relations*. Ithaca, NY: Cornell University Press.

Wall Street Journal. 2016. "Bill Gates: GMOs Will End Starvation in Africa." Video, January 22. http://www.wsj.com/video/bill-gates-gmos-will-end-starvation-in-africa/3085A8D1-BB58-4CAA-9394-E567033434A4.html.

Walley, Christine J. 2002. "'They Scorn Us Because We Are Uneducated': Knowledge and Power in a Tanzanian Marine Park." *Ethnography* 3(3): 265–98.

West African Civil Society Institute (WACSI). 2015. *The State of Civil Society Organisations' Sustainability in Ghana: Striving, Surviving or Thriving?* Accra: WASCI.

Welthungerhilfe, IFPRI, and Concern Worldwide. 2012. *Global Hunger Index: The Challenge of Hunger and Ensuring Sustainable Food Security Under Land, Water, and Energy Stresses*.

Report. Http://dx.doi.org/10.2499/9780896299429.

West Africa Centre for Crop Improvement (WACCI). 2014. "Success Stories." WACCI website. http://wacci.ug.edu.gh/content/success-stories.

WikiLeaks. 2002. "Developing Countries Seek Empowerment in Biotech from Intellectual Property Rights." Cable 02ROME3648_a, July 24.

———. 2005a. "Ghana Economic Highlights—June/July 2005." Cable 05ACCRA1435_a, July 21.

———. 2005b. "Request for Funds for Biotechnology." Cable 05ACCRA110, January 14.

———. 2005c. "South Africa, Biosafety Update and State Senior Biotech Advisor Visit." Cable 05PRETORIA2374_a, June 20.

———. 2010. "Proposal for U.S. Biotech Speaker to Visit Ghana in Fy." Cable 10AACRA59, January 20.

Wilson, Kalpana. 2012. *Race, Racism and Development: Interrogating History, Discourse and Practice*. New York: Zed Books.

Wodak, Ruth. 2012. "Politics as Usual: Investigating Political Discourse in Action." In *The Routledge Handbook of Discourse Analysis*, edited by James Paul Gee and Michael Handford, 525–40. New York: Routledge.

Wolfenson, Karla D. Maas. 2013. *Coping with the Food and Agriculture Challenge: Smallholders' Agenda*. Rome: Food and Agriculture Organization of the United Nations.

The World Bank. 2013. "Africa's Food Markets Could Create One Trillion Dollar Opportunity by 2030." Press Release, March 4. Http://www.worldbank.org/en/news/press-release/2013/03/04/africas-food-markets-could-create-one-trillion-dollar-opportunity-2030.

Wright, Sarah. 2014. "Food Sovereignty in Practice: A Study of Farmer-Led Sustainable Agriculture in the Philippines." In *Globalization and Food Sovereignty*, edited by Peter Andrée et al., 199–227. Toronto: University of Toronto Press.

Yankah, Kwesi. 1990. "Oral Traditions and the Physical Environment." *Geografisk Tidsskrift-Danish Journal of Geography* 90(1): 5–9.

Yarrow, Thomas. 2011. *Development Beyond Politics: Aid, Activism and NGOs in Ghana*. New York: Palgrave Macmillan.

Yeboah, Felix Kwame, and Thomas S. Jayne. 2018. "Africa's Evolving Employment Trends." *Journal of Development Studies* 54(5): 803–32.

Ziem, Joseph. 2013. "Tamale—West Africa's Fastest Growing City." *GhanaWeb*, April 14.

INDEX

A

Adesina, Akinwumi, xxiii; on farming as business, xlii, 14–15; on globalization, xxiv, xxvii
Adikanfo maize, 42
Adjei, Dennis, 85–86
Adu-Dapaah, Hans, 100
Advanced Maize Seed Adoption Program, 39
African Agricultural Technology Foundation (AATF), 95, 148, 154n9; Cornell Alliance for Science and, 104, 120–21; creation of, xxxiii, xliv; on GM crops, xxxv–xxxvi, 47–48, 62, 102–10, 149; in Kenya, 48, 107, 108, 149
African Biosafety Network of Expertise (ABNE), xxxiv–xxxvi, 59, 148, 154n13
African Development Bank, 14
African Enterprise Challenge Fund, 23
African Union (AU), 148; ABNE of, xxxiv; Forum for Agricultural Research of, 46
Agric, 21, 29–30, 156n10
Agricultural Biotechnology Support Program (ABSP), xxxii
agricultural development, 1–3; demonstration plots of, 19, 39; government programs for, 16–21
Agricultural Development and Value Chain Enhancement Project (ADVANCE), 39, 42
agricultural exit theory, xxx–xxxi
agroecology, xxxix, 79, 119, 140–45; recipient fatigue and, 143
Ahmadu Bello University, 105
Akoto, Owusu Afriyie, 150
Akufo-Addo, Nana, 131
Alhassan, Walter, 85, 105
Alliance for a Green Revolution in Africa (AGRA), 38, 57; on agricultural exit theory, xxx; BMGF and, xxi; goals of, xxiv–xxvi; Osei on, 14
Alliance for Food Sovereignty in Africa

(AFSA), xxxviii, 78, 84, 140
Alliance for Science Ghana, 57, 58
Althusser, Louis, 61, 135
Amanor, Kojo, 13–14, 23
Ameyaw, David, xxv
Angelou, Maya, 82
Annan, Kofi, xx–xxi
Anyane, S. La, 11–12
Appiah, Gifty Andoh, xvi, 136–37
Appiah-Oppong, Marietta Brew, 38, 50–51
Apullah, Patrick, xvi
Arcadia Biosciences, 107, 110, 112–14, 149
Atikpo, Margaret, 88, 96, 103
Atokple, Ibrahim Dzido Kwasi, 98–102
Australia, 47, 114
Aventis Corporation, xxxii–xxxiii

B

Bacillus thuringiensis (Bt) cotton, xvi–xix, xxxiv, 47, 48–49; difficulties of, 106, 113, 148, 149
Bacillus thuringiensis (Bt) cowpea, xxxvi, 47, 48–49, 84–85, 90, 149; adoption of, 111, 148–50; Atokple and, 98; Ignatova on, 105; leasing of, 125
Baffour, Edwin Kweku Andoh, xvi, xx, 86–87
Bagbin, Alban S. K., 97
Barbier, Edward B., xxii
Bayer Corporation, 95, 103, 136, 153n3
Bayh-Dole Act (1980), 103
Belay, Million, 79, 83
Berlin Conference (1884), xxv, 66
Bill & Melinda Gates Foundation (BMGF), xx, 65, 118, 132, 148–49; AGRA and, xxi;

agroecology and, 143; Cornell Alliance for Science and, 129; PBS and, 68–69
Biosafety (Management of Biotechnology) Regulations (2019), 37, 49
Biosafety Act (2011), 37, 43–49, 68; importance of, 44, 60, 61; Plant Breeders Bill and, 52, 60, 96
biotechnology, xix–xxii; boosters of, xliv–xlv, 37–38, 49, 53–62, 93–98, 148; Bush on, xxxi; disidentification and, 132–35; "enabling environments" for, 13, 46, 50, 53, 60, 89, 128; Frimpong-Boateng on, xix; genetic engineering versus, 95; "homegrown," 147–48; Paarlberg on, xxvii. *See also* Green Revolution
Biotechnology and Nuclear Agriculture Research Institute (BNARI), 44, 95, 129
Biotechnology Industry Organization, xxxi
Borlaug, Norman, xxi, xxvii, 18
Bosompem, Kwabena Mantey, 88
Boyce Thompson Institute, 156n8
Braimah, Rufai Ahmed, 131, 133, 136
Burkina Faso, xxxi; AATF in, 48; ABNE in, xxxiv; Bt cotton in, xvi–xviii, xxxiv, 97, 148; Bt cowpea in, 150; OFAB in, 54
Bush, George W., xxxi, 44

C

Cartagena Protocol on Biosafety, xiv–xv, xxxiv, 43–44, 60, 156n6
Carter, Jimmy, xxvii, 18, 19
cassava, 4–5, 46, 55, 149
Centre for Indigenous Knowledge and Organizational Development (CIKOD),

78, 83, 130
Chamba, Emmanuel, xix
climate change, 77; economic growth and, 36; March for Science and, 57; neoliberalism and, 29
cocoa production, 5–7, 9–10, 16, 155n2
Colombia, 107, 114
colonialism, 66–67, 76, 81; decolonization and, 37, 75–76; education system and, 75–76; neocolonialism and, 12, 64, 133–34; neoliberalism and, 3, 24, 79; postcolonialism, 11, 24, 78, 115, 146
commercialization: of farming, 6, 13–23, 36–37, 128, 139, 143; of GMOs, 43–45, 48–49, 73–74, 105, 121–22, 125, 149–50
Concerned Ghanaians for Responsible Governance, 74
confined field trials (CFTs), xviii, 48, 107
Consultative Group on International Agricultural Research (CGIAR), 31
contamination, from GM crops, 96
Convention People's Party, 73, 84
Conway, Gordon R., xxii, 46
Coordination Nationale des Organisations Paysannes (CNOP), xxxvi
Cornell Alliance for Science (CAS), 53, 95, 148; AATF and, 104, 120–21; Boyce Thompson Institute and, 156n8; *Food Evolution* film of, 58–59; Gates Foundation and, 129; Global Leadership Fellow Program of, 56–57
Corteva Agriscience, xxix–xxx, 95, 154n12
Côte d'Ivoire, 97
cotton. See *Bacillus thuringiensis* (Bt) cotton
Council for Scientific and Industrial Research (CSIR), xix, 95, 129; Bosompem on, 88; Crops Research Institute of, xii, 19, 47, 99; field trials of, 86; funding of, 127, 136; NEWEST rice and, 108–9; OFAB in, 54; Savanna Agricultural Research Institute of, xii, 47, 98; Science and Technology Policy Research Institute of, 147
cowpea. See *Bacillus thuringiensis* (Bt) cowpea
CropLife (agribusiness association), 57
Cultivating New Frontiers in Agriculture, 41

D

Daley, Patricia, xxix
Daniels, Mitch, 150
Danquah, Eric, 134
decolonization, 37, 75–76. *See also* postcolonialism
development discourses, xxvi–xxxi, 33, 130–33; agricultural exit theory and, xxx; educational system and, 75–76; farming as business and, 6, 13–14, 36–37, 128, 139, 143; modernization and, 10–11, 24, 61, 90–91, 100–101; Pierre on, xxvii; poverty and, 81, 123–24, 151; "pro-poor," 108–9; racialization of, 100–101, 118–19, 139, 150–51
DeVries, Joe, xxiv
disidentification, 31–32, 119–20; agroecology and, 144–45; Appiah on, 136–37; biotechnology and, 132–35; Muñoz on, 135–36; Pêcheux on, 135
donors, xlv–xlvi, 15, 101; Chinese, 85; GMO corporations and, 86, 88–89; NGOs and, 22. *See also particular organizations*

DowAgro, xxxii–xxxiii
DowDuPont, 154n12
Du Bois, W. E. B., 11
DuPont Pioneer, 60, 136, 154n12; 4-H Clubs and, 156n4; hybrid maize seeds of, xxix–xxx, 39–40; Rockefeller Foundation and, xxxii–xxxiii, 103; USAID and, xxix–xxx, 23, 39–43
Dziwornu, John, 131, 133, 136

E

ECOWAS agreement, 41, 42, 156n3
Electricity Company of Ghana (ECG), 74–75
"enabling environments," 13, 46, 50, 53, 60, 89, 128
environmentalism: fertilizers and, 19; indigenous peoples and, 154n7
Ethiopia, 18; AATF in, 48; DuPont Pioneer and, 39–40; OFAB in, 54
Europe, 3–7, 45, 151; GMO ban in, xxxi, 86–88, 123, 158n1; partition of Africa by, xxv, 66; slave trade and, 3–5, 66, 81, 82

F

Fairclough, Norman, xxvi, xlv
Fairhead, James, xxvii
Fanon, Frantz, 76
farmer demographics, xxx, 99, 157n4
Feed the Future program, xxiv, 23, 39
Feeding the Future (film), 155n7
Fejerskov, Adam Moe, 153n6
fertilizers, 11, 70, 142, 144; "addiction" to, 21; cost of, 29, 33, 77; nitrogen-efficient rice and, 107; SG 2000 and, 18–23. *See also* Plants and Fertilizer Act
Folta, Kevin, xxviii, 154n11
Food and Water Watch, xxxv
Food Evolution (film), 58–59
Food Price Crisis (2007–8), xxii–xxiii; Nyéléni Forum and, xxxvii–xxxviii
food security politics, 128–32
food sovereignty, xxxvii, xxxviii; seeking of, xxvi–xxxviii; studying of, xxxviii–xl
Food Sovereignty Ghana (FSG), 63–90; corruption scandal of, 78, 83–84; lawsuits of, 83–90
Food Sovereignty Platform, xlii–xliv, 63–83, 138; conflicts in, 83–84; GAFP and, 35, 65, 76; members of, 67, 131–32; successes of, 94
4-H Clubs (Ghana), 156n4
Freedom Centre, 63–64, 67–68, 74
Freire, Paolo, 75
Frimpong-Boateng, Kwabena, xix

G

Ga people, 64–65, 77
Gakpo, Joseph Opoku, xiv, xvi, 57
Gates, Bill, xiv, 65, 118, 132, 143, 158n1. *See also* Bill & Melinda Gates Foundation
General Agricultural Workers' Union of Ghana (GAWU), 130
genetically modified organisms (GMOs), xxxv, 47; boosters of, xliv–xlv, 37–38, 49, 53–62, 94, 148; commercialization of, 43–45, 48–49, 73–74, 105, 121–22, 125,

149–50; contamination from, 96; EU markets and, xxxi, 86, 87, 123; fears of, 49, 56, 93, 129–30; as foreign initiative, xx; Bill Gates on, xiv, 118; law suits against, 84–90; Mark Lynas on, xxviii–xxix, 54; Samia Nkrumah on, 80

Ghana, xvi–xix, 4–6; independence of, 11; map of, xii; oil industry of, 74; postcolonial, 11–14; rice imports of, 106–7, 110; slave trade in, 3–5, 81

Ghana Academy of Arts and Sciences (GAAS), 98–102

Ghana Agricultural and Rural Development Journalists Association (GARDJA), 57

Ghana Alliance for Science, 53

Ghana Association of Food Producers (GAFP), xiii–xiv; agroecology project of, 119, 141; annual conference of, 35–38; anti-GMO movement and, 70–73; Food Security Platform and, 35, 65, 76; on infrastructure development, 72–73; participant observation in, xlii–xliv, 25–28, 66

Ghana Grains Partnership, 23

Ghana National Association of Farmers and Fishermen (GNAFF), 89–90, 129

Ghana Seed Company, 17, 40–41

globalization. *See* neoliberalism

Godelier, Maurice, 104

Gold Coast Cocoa Marketing Board, 7–10, 13, 22

González, Roberto J., xli

Green, Mark, xxix–xxx

Green Revolution, xx–xxv, 33; "longue durée" of, xxi, xxx

Green Revolution, "new," xv, xx–xxxvi, 37, 150–51; agricultural exit theory and, xxx–xxxi; alternatives to, 137–45; Annan on, xx–xxi; food sovereignty movement against, xxxviii; Heller on, xli; neoliberalism and, 134–35, 141–42

Guinea, xxvii

Gupta, Akhil, xxii

Guri, Bernard, 78, 79, 82

H

Halberstam, Jack, xxiv

Heller, Chaia, xli

herbicides, 11; cotton tolerant of, xviii, 47, 153n5; Roundup, 19, 103

Hodžić, Saida, 24

Homowo festival, 64–65

human rights, 84

I

Ignatova, Jacqueline, 48, 105

India, xxii, 143

infrastructure development, 11, 15, 28, 132, 145; by donors, 42, 48, 53, 60, 62; GAFP on, 72–73; GMOs and, 59, 73–74, 86–87, 95

Initiative to End Hunger in Africa, 44

insecticides, 18–19; Bt cotton and, xvii; developed by local farmers, 53

intellectual property rights (IPRs), xix, 60, 127; disidentification and, 119–20; patents and, 102–6; Plant Breeders Bill and, 37–38, 68, 94–95, 103–4. *See also* patents

International Center for Tropical Agriculture (CIAT), 107
International Food Policy Research Institute (IFPRI), 21, 43–44, 68, 111–12
International Monetary Fund (IMF), xxii–xxiii, 17–18, 71
International Service for the Acquisition of Agri-biotech Applications (ISAAA), 57, 95–96, 105
International Union for the Protection of New Varieties of Plants, 50, 96
Iowa State University, xxix, 41, 61
irrigation projects, 11, 13–14, 16, 29

J

Johnson, Lyndon B., 12
Joy News media outlet, xvi, 57

K

Kalibata, Agnes, xxv–xxvi
kenkey, 99–100
Kenya, 48, 57, 107, 108, 149
Kenyan Agricultural Research Institute (KARI), xxxii
Kerr, Rachel Bezner, xxxix, 20
Kofi the Good Farmer (booklet), 7–10, 13, 22
Komer, Robert W., 12
kpokpoi, 64–65
Kyetere, Denis, 54

L

La Via Campesina (LVC), xxxvi, 154nn17–18
Logan, Amanda, 2, 5–7
Lynas, Mark, xxviii–xxix, 54, 129, 133, 154n9

M

Madrazo, Jesus, xviii–xix, 104
maize, 60, 149; fertilizers for, 20; history of, 4–5, 64–65; *Homowo* festival and, 64–65; hybrid, xxix–xxx, 39, 42, 72, 156n10; from Iowa farms, 98, 101–2; millet and, 144; Obaatanpa, 31, 51, 124; Quain on, 101; *Sika-Aburo*, 42; subsidies for, 20
Malawi, xxxix, 48
Mali, xxxi, xxxvi–xxxviii, 154n17
Malthusianism, xxi
March Against Monsanto (2015), 84
March for Science movements, 57–58
Marston, Jasmin, 42
Masara N'arziki, 23
Matlon, Peter, xxxiii
Mensah, Kofi Essel, 85
methodology, xl–xli
Mexico, xxii, xxxix, 18, 155n18
Michigan State University, xxxiv–xxxv, 154n13
Mikell, Gwendolyn, 6–7
Millennium Challenge Corporation, 74
Millennium Development Goals, 131, 158n6
Millennium Village Project, 23
millet, 4, 13, 99, 144
Ministry of Environment, Science, Technology and Innovation (MESTI), 84–85

Ministry of Food and Agriculture (MOFA), 15–16
modernization, 10–11, 24, 61, 90–91, 100–101. *See also* development discourse
Monsanto, 40–41, 47, 113–14, 136; Bayer's acquisition of, 103, 153n3; GM sweet potato of, xxxii; Rockefeller Foundation and, xxxii–xxxiii, 103; Roundup herbicide of, 19, 103; WASA and, 41. See also *Bacillus thuringiensis* (Bt) cotton
Mozambique, xxxix, 48
Muñoz, José Esteban, 135–36
Museveni, Yoweri, 149

N

Nader, Laura, xli
National Biosafety Authority (NBA), 46, 49, 84–85, 138; Cartagena Protocol and, 156n6; media workshops of, 93–95
National Biosafety Committee, 44, 84
National Biosafety Framework, xliv, xxxv
National Biotechnology Development Agency, 54
National Democratic Congress (NDC), 28
neocolonialism, 12, 64, 133–34. *See also* colonialism
neoliberalism, 61, 74; Adesina on, xxiv; agribusinesses and, 18; climate change and, 29; colonialism and, 3, 24, 79; government support of, 41, 44, 62; "new" Green Revolution and, 134–35, 141–42
NERICA rice, 47, 107, 111–13, 149
Network of Peasants and Farmers in West Africa (ROPPA), xxxvi

New Alliance for Food Security and Nutrition, xxiv
New Patriotic Party (NPP), 28
NEWEST rice, 48, 106–14, 127; AATF and, 149; CSIR and, 47; WACCI and, 54–55
Nigeria: AATF in, 48; Bt cowpea in, xxxvi, 105; cocoa production in, 6; GMOs in, 106, 111; March for Science in, 57
Nigeria Agricultural Biotechnology Project, xxxv
Nkrumah, Kwame, 11–12, 37; Convention People's Party of, 73; coup against, 12–13; on neocolonialism, 12, 133–34
Nkrumah, Samia, 73, 79–80, 137
"No More 'Failures-as-Usual'" statement, xxxviii
nongovernmental organizations (NGOs): development donors and, 22; Ghanaian headquarters of, 22; rural growth of, 22–25; as vanguards of civil society, 22
Novartis, 103
NUE rice, 47, 108, 110–12, 148, 149
Nyantakyi-Frimpong, Hanson, 20
Nyéléni Forum (Mali), xxxvi–xxxviii, 154n17

O

Obaatanpa maize, 31, 51, 124
Obama, Barack, xxiv, 23, 39
oburoni, 3, 20, 76
Open Forum on Agricultural Biotechnology in Africa (OFAB), 53–54, 59, 88; lobbying by, 120–21; mission of, 53–54, 148
Opoku, Yaw, 79–80, 98
Ormsby-Gore, William, 6, 7

Osei, J. K., 13–14
Owusu-Mensah, Eric, 97

P

Paarlberg, Robert, xxvii–xxix
palm oil, 5, 12
Pan-Africanism, 11–13, 46, 83, 97–98
Park, Alex, xxxiv
participant observation, xl–xliv, 25–28, 66
Patel, Raj, xxx
patents, 102–6, 123–25, 150–51; AATF and, 47, 62; from Ghanaian research, 51, 124, 136, 145; Plant Breeders Bill and, 50, 52, 60, 68, 80–81, 96–97. *See also* intellectual property rights
Peasant Farmers Association of Ghana (PFAG), 83, 130
Pêcheux, Michel, 135
Philippines, xxxix
Pierre, Jemima, xxvii, xxix
pito, 99–100
Plant Breeders Bill (PBB), xix, xliii, 49–52, 121–30, 141; Appiah-Oppong on, 50–51; Biosafety Act and, 52, 60, 96; Clause 3 of, 96; Clause 9 of, 68, 96; Clause 58 of, 80–81; conspiracy theories about, 129–30; government report on, 97; importance of, 61, 94, 114; IPRs and, 37–38, 68, 94–95, 103–4; Samia Nkrumah on, 80; passage of, 150; Shiva on, 79
Plants and Fertilizer Act (2010), 37, 41–43, 50, 60, 61
postcolonialism, 11, 24, 78, 115, 146; decolonization and, 37, 75–76. *See also* colonialism
Pratt, Kwesi, Jr., 79, 81, 84
Program for Biosafety Systems (PBS), xxxiv, 43–44, 59, 68, 148; as biotech booster, 95; lobbying by, 120–21; USAID and, 68–69
public-private partnerships (PPPs), xx, xliv

Q

Quain, Marian, 99–102, 106, 113

R

racialization, xxvii, 7, 82, 154n7; of development discourse, 100–101, 118–19, 139, 150–51; World Bank and, 17
Rawlings, Jerry John, 18–19
recipient fatigue, xv, 25–32, 71, 101; agroecology and, 141, 143; collective memory and, xliii, 82, 151; educational system and, 76; frames of analysis and, 82
Reese, Ashanté, 32
Réseau des Organisations Paysannes et de Producteurs de l'Afrique de l'Ouest (ROPPA), xxxvi
rice, 85, 90, 109; NERICA, 47, 107, 111–13, 149; NUE, 47, 108, 110–12, 148, 149. *See also* NEWEST rice
Robins, Jonathan, 6, 7
Rockefeller Foundation, xx, xxxii–xxxiii, 46, 148; AATF and, xxxiii; AGRA and, xxi; IPRs and, 102–3

Rodney, Walter, xxx–xxxi, 4, 151
Roundup herbicide, 19, 103

S

Sabara, Francis Adi, 27
Sampson, Devon, xxxix
sankofa, 77–78, 119, 141–42, 144
Sasakawa, Ryoichi, 18, 155n6
Sasakawa Global (SG) 2000 initiative, 18–23, 41; Carter and, 18, 19; Obaatanpa maize and, 31, 51, 124
Schiavoni, Christina M., lv
Schnurr, Matthew A., xxxv
Schurman, Rachel, xxxii–xxxiii, 102–4, 148
Shanti, Bobo, 84
Shilomboleni, Helena, xxxix
Shiva, Vandana, 66, 78–80, 143
Sika-Aburo maize, 42
slave trade, 3–5, 66, 81, 82, 151
social media, 69, 83
Socialist Forum of Ghana, 63, 67
Songotra. See *Bacillus thuringiensis* (BT) cowpea
Soper, Rachel, xxxix
sorghum, 4
South Africa, xxvi, xxxvi, 23, 47, 48
Stone, Glenn Davis, 154n16
structural adjustment programs, 3; aftermath from, 36–41, 71, 145; Electricity Company of Ghana and, 74–75; of IMF, xxii–xxiii, 17–18, 71; NGOs and, 22; rice imports and, 106–7
Stryker, Rachael, xli

sweet potatoes, xxxii, 47, 101, 106, 149
Syngenta, 103, 136

T

Tagoe, Duke, 83–84
Tanzania, xxvi, 48, 148–49
Thailand, 106
tomatoes, xxxi–xxxii, 56
Tono irrigation project, 13–14
tractors, soil depletion from, 70
Trump, Donald J., 106, 120
Tuskegee University, 47, 101, 149

U

Uganda, 149; AATF in, 48; GMOs in, xxviii–xxix, 106, 111; March for Science in, 57
United Nations: Environment Program of, 44; Food and Agricultural Organization of, xxiv, xxxiii, 131, 158n6; World Food Summit of, xxxvi–xxxviii
US Agency for International Development (USAID), xx, 59; DuPont Pioneer and, xxix–xxx, 23, 39–43; as GMO booster, 95, 148; NEWEST rice and, 108, 110; Program for Biosafety Systems and, 68–69; West Africa Seed Alliance of, 97
US Department of Agriculture (USDA), xxxi, 44–46, 59, 95

V

value chains, global, xxx, xxxvii–xxxviii, 39
Vegetarian Association of Ghana, 67, 84

W

Walley, Christine, xxvi
watermelon, 73
Wayo, George Tetteh, 86, 88–89
West Africa Centre for Crop Improvement (WACCI), 55, 134
West Africa Seed Alliance, 97
West African Biotechnology Network, xxxv
West African Seed Alliance (WASA), 41–43
Wills, Chelsea, xxxix
Wilson, Kalpana, xxvii, xxix
Wodak, Ruth, xlv
World Bank, xxii–xxiii, xxx, 17–18, 71
World Food Prize, xxiii
World Trade Organization (WTO), xxxi
Wright, Sarah, xxxix

Y

Yakubu, Ahmed Alhassan, xiv
Yara agrochemical company, 39
"youth bulge" demographic, xxiii

Rodney, Walter, xxx–xxxi, 4, 151
Roundup herbicide, 19, 103

S

Sabara, Francis Adi, 27
Sampson, Devon, xxxix
sankofa, 77–78, 119, 141–42, 144
Sasakawa, Ryoichi, 18, 155n6
Sasakawa Global (SG) 2000 initiative, 18–23, 41; Carter and, 18, 19; Obaatanpa maize and, 31, 51, 124
Schiavoni, Christina M., lv
Schnurr, Matthew A., xxxv
Schurman, Rachel, xxxii–xxxiii, 102–4, 148
Shanti, Bobo, 84
Shilomboleni, Helena, xxxix
Shiva, Vandana, 66, 78–80, 143
Sika-Aburo maize, 42
slave trade, 3–5, 66, 81, 82, 151
social media, 69, 83
Socialist Forum of Ghana, 63, 67
Songotra. See *Bacillus thuringiensis* (BT) cowpea
Soper, Rachel, xxxix
sorghum, 4
South Africa, xxvi, xxxvi, 23, 47, 48
Stone, Glenn Davis, 154n16
structural adjustment programs, 3; aftermath from, 36–41, 71, 145; Electricity Company of Ghana and, 74–75; of IMF, xxii–xxiii, 17–18, 71; NGOs and, 22; rice imports and, 106–7
Stryker, Rachael, xli

sweet potatoes, xxxii, 47, 101, 106, 149
Syngenta, 103, 136

T

Tagoe, Duke, 83–84
Tanzania, xxvi, 48, 148–49
Thailand, 106
tomatoes, xxxi–xxxii, 56
Tono irrigation project, 13–14
tractors, soil depletion from, 70
Trump, Donald J., 106, 120
Tuskegee University, 47, 101, 149

U

Uganda, 149; AATF in, 48; GMOs in, xxviii–xxix, 106, 111; March for Science in, 57
United Nations: Environment Program of, 44; Food and Agricultural Organization of, xxiv, xxxiii, 131, 158n6; World Food Summit of, xxxvi–xxxviii
US Agency for International Development (USAID), xx, 59; DuPont Pioneer and, xxix–xxx, 23, 39–43; as GMO booster, 95, 148; NEWEST rice and, 108, 110; Program for Biosafety Systems and, 68–69; West Africa Seed Alliance of, 97
US Department of Agriculture (USDA), xxxi, 44–46, 59, 95

V

value chains, global, xxx, xxxvii–xxxviii, 39
Vegetarian Association of Ghana, 67, 84

W

Walley, Christine, xxvi
watermelon, 73
Wayo, George Tetteh, 86, 88–89
West Africa Centre for Crop Improvement (WACCI), 55, 134
West Africa Seed Alliance, 97
West African Biotechnology Network, xxxv
West African Seed Alliance (WASA), 41–43
Wills, Chelsea, xxxix
Wilson, Kalpana, xxvii, xxix
Wodak, Ruth, xlv
World Bank, xxii–xxiii, xxx, 17–18, 71
World Food Prize, xxiii
World Trade Organization (WTO), xxxi
Wright, Sarah, xxxix

Y

Yakubu, Ahmed Alhassan, xiv
Yara agrochemical company, 39
"youth bulge" demographic, xxiii